Library of
Davidson College

Cambridge Studies in Social Anthropology

General Editor: Jack Goody

53

INEQUALITY AMONG BROTHERS

For other titles in this series turn to page 191.

Inequality among brothers
Class and kinship in South China

RUBIE S. WATSON

CAMBRIDGE UNIVERSITY PRESS
Cambridge
London   New York   New Rochelle
Melbourne   Sydney

Published by the Press Syndicate of the University of Cambridge
The Pitt Building, Trumpington Street, Cambridge CB2 1RP
32 East 57th Street, New York, NY 10022, USA
10 Stamford Road, Oakleigh, Melbourne 3166, Australia

© Cambridge University Press 1985

First published 1985

Printed in the United States of America

Library of Congress Cataloging in Publication Data
Watson, Rubie S. (Rubie Sharon), 1945–
Inequality among brothers.
(Cambridge studies in social anthropology; no. 53)
Rev. version of thesis (Ph.D.) – London School
of Economics, 1982.
Bibliography: p.
1. Social classes – Hong Kong – Case studies.
2. Kinship – Hong Kong – Ha Tsuen – Case studies.
3. Ha Tsuen (Hong Kong) – Rural conditions – Case
studies. 4. Hong Kong – Rural conditions – Case
studies. I. Title. II. Series: Cambridge studies
in social anthropology; no. 53.
HN755.2.C6W37   1985   305.5'0951'25   84–14991
ISBN 0 521 26770 6

To my mother and father

Contents

Preface		*page* ix
Maps		xi
1	**Introduction**	1
2	**The development of the Teng lineage:**	
	Ha Tsuen's early history	12
3	**Lineage organization and ideology**	36
4	**Economic organization: the land and the market**	55
5	**Local political organization**	83
6	**Class differences in Ha Tsuen:**	
	the social and cultural dimension	98
7	**Marriage, affinity, and class**	117
8	**Economic and political changes: 1945–1978**	137
9	**Social and cultural transformations**	156
10	**Class and kinship**	168
References		176
Glossary		185
Index		187

Preface

The fieldwork upon which this book is based was carried out in the Hong Kong village of Ha Tsuen, where I lived for 12 months in 1977–8. In 1978, Ha Tsuen had a population of approximately 2,500 people living in 11 hamlets or neighborhoods. The people of Ha Tsuen speak a subdialect of Cantonese common to Hsin-an County and are descendants of Han Chinese pioneers who first settled in this coastal region during the twelfth century.

The research for this study was made possible by grants from the Social Science Research Council (United Kingdom) and the University of London Central Research Fund; I very much appreciate their support. The present book is a revised version of my 1982 Ph.D. thesis at the London School of Economics. Professor Maurice Bloch and Dr. Jonathan Parry supervised the thesis writing, and I am indebted to them for the generous way in which they gave of both their time and their advice. Professor Jack Goody and Dr. Chris Fuller examined the thesis, and I gratefully acknowledge their comments and criticism.

Dr. Stephen Morris was my supervisor at the London School of Economics until his retirement in 1979, and I thank him for his encouragement during my research. The hours of discussion that I had with my fellow students while writing and revising this study were very important in formulating and clarifying many of the arguments that appear in this book. I owe a special debt to Frances Pine, Brian O'Neill, Alexis Gardella, and Margaret Stott for their comments and support.

Thanks are also due to the staff of the Universities Service Centre and especially its director, John Dolfin, for the use of their facilities during my research in Hong Kong. My work was made considerably easier by their assistance. I am also grateful to the librarians at Hong Kong University who helped me to locate and use their collections of genealogies and printed sources on the New Territories. The staff of the Yuen Long District Office were always most cooperative, and I especially thank the district officer, Michael Cartland, for his kind assistance. Poon Suk-ye, Amy Fan, and Ted Fung helped with many of the documentary aspects of this study.

The Asian Studies Program at the University of Pittsburgh provided a grant

Preface

that helped with the final preparation of the manuscript. Rhonda Andrews drafted the maps that appear in this book, and Chung Yuet-fong assisted in the preparation of the Glossary.

I gratefully acknowledge the hospitality and generosity of my friends in Ha Tsuen. Teng Hop-wan was instrumental in seeing me well settled in Ha Tsuen. I owe a special debt to Teng Tim-sing, Teng Ying-lan, and Steven Teng whose kindness and unflagging support were crucial to my work. What understanding I have of Ha Tsuen is due in large part to their efforts.

James L. Watson shared the fieldwork with me. During the writing of this study he has given of his time and patience most generously, and I am deeply grateful to him.

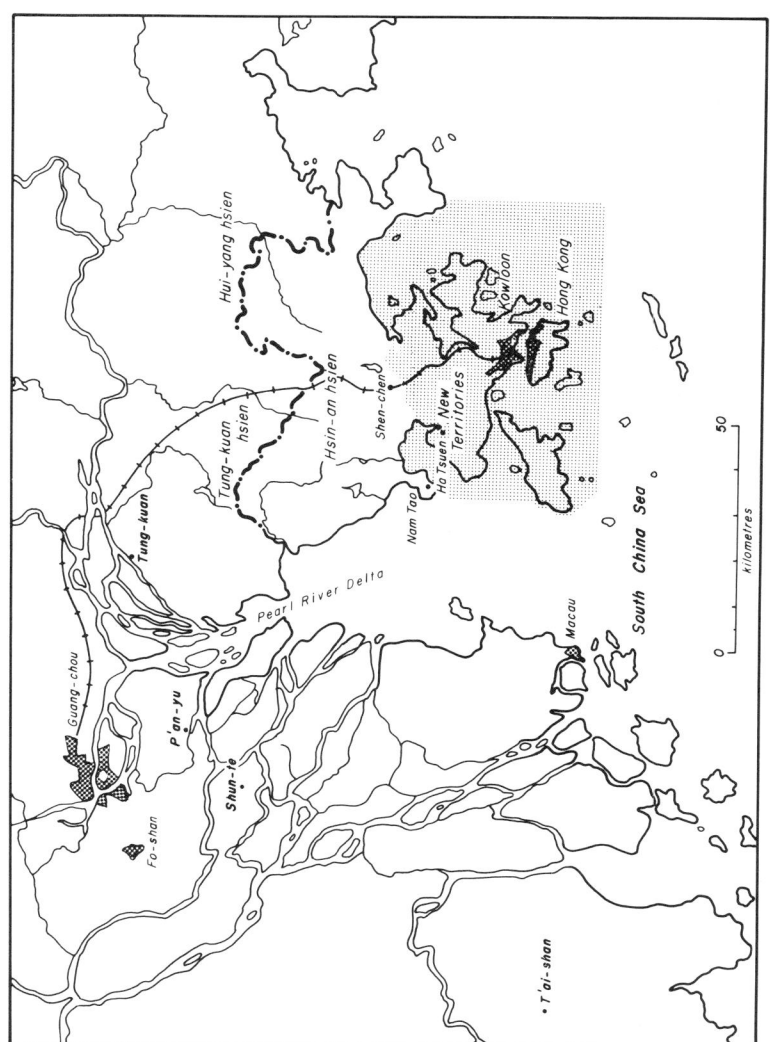

Map 1. Canton Delta region. Dotted line depicts Anglo-Chinese border.

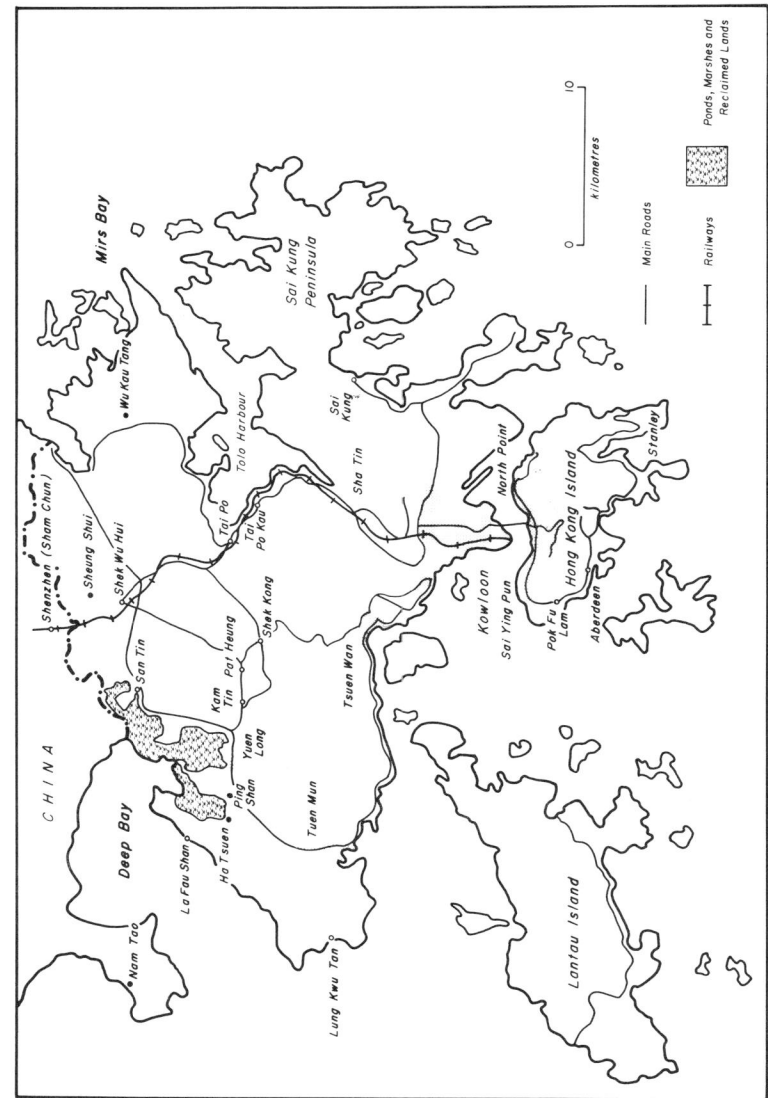

Map 2. Hong Kong New Territories.

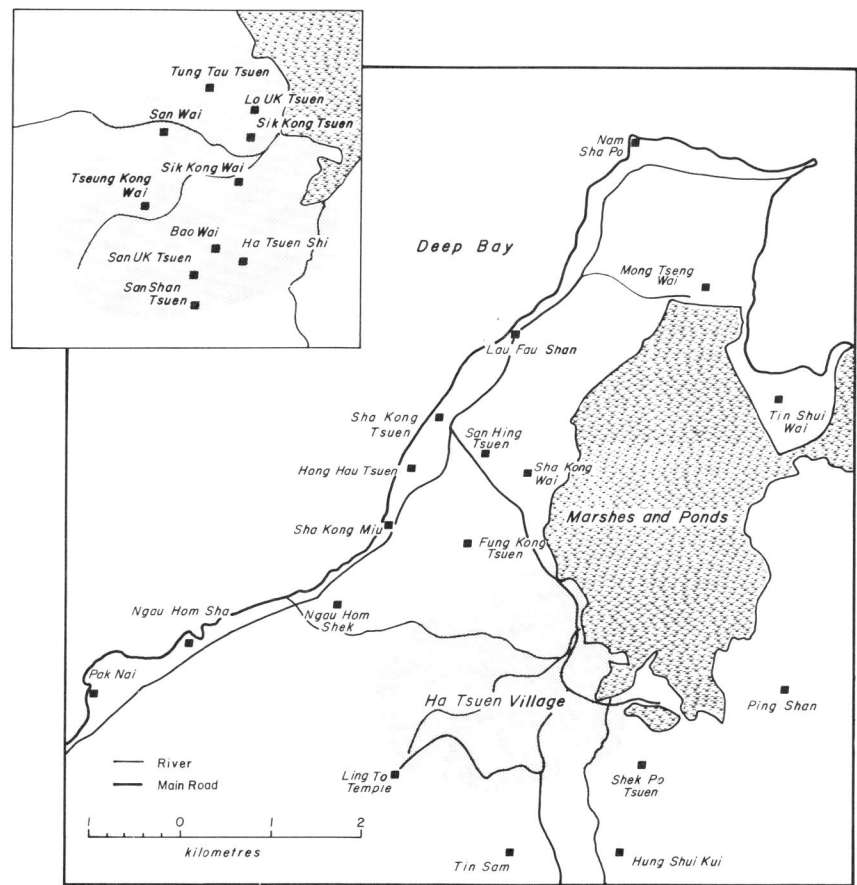

Map 3. Ha Tsuen District. Inset: Ha Tsuen hamlets.

1
Introduction

The hamlet of Sik Kong Wai is situated in the extreme northwestern section of Hong Kong's New Territories. The hamlet is centuries old, and like many rural communities in southeastern China, Sik Kong Wai is walled (*wai* in fact, means "enclosure").[1] The hamlet's stout brick walls (15 feet high and 2 feet thick) were built to withstand bandit attacks and jealous neighbors; they still serve to discourage the casual visitor. The only entrance to the hamlet is through a massive wooden gate set in the western wall. Just inside the gate is a small anteroom that houses the shrine of a local god. This "god of the gate" has the responsibility of guarding hamlet residents against dangerous outsiders, both human and supernatural. Near the shrine is a stone bench worn smooth from centuries of daily use by the hamlet's other guardians. Every afternoon Sik Kong Wai's elderly women gather at the gate to talk, smoke, and watch over grandchildren. Little happens in Sik Kong Wai that is not observed by the hamlet's temporal gatekeepers.

Once inside the hamlet walls, the visitor is confronted by row after row of small gray brick houses. The doors of these houses open directly onto narrow stone paths that link the rows of houses to a central avenue – itself only 5 feet wide. Most of the houses measure about 15 feet by 8 feet and are divided into two rooms. Each has a pitched roof that provides a loft for storage or extra sleeping space. In 1978 there were 110 houses and 2 small temples packed inside the walls of Sik Kong Wai. The temples, dedicated to the god Yang Hou and the goddess T'ien Hou, are very modest structures by local standards. They contain little more than an altar and a small image of the deity; during much of the year the temples double as storage sheds for agricultural tools. Two watchtowers, also used for storage, stand on the southeastern and southwestern corners

---

1 Concerning Chinese terms and place names: Chinese characters for Hong Kong village names used in this book can be found in *A Gazetteer of Place Names in Hong Kong, Kowloon, and the New Territories* (Hong Kong: Government Press, 1969). Personal names, except for those of early ancestors (pre-1750) and historical figures, are pseudonyms. Terms followed by (C) in the Glossary are in colloquial Cantonese, Yale romanization system. All other Chinese terms are in Mandarin, standard Wade-Giles romanization.

1

Inequality among brothers

of the hamlet wall. These towers command a view of the surrounding rice plain and once served as an early warning system against bandits.

From the outsider's point of view, the houses of Sik Kong Wai all look alike.[2] Of course, some are better maintained than others, but the differences are minor and might easily be overlooked. The visual evidence suggests that there are no great economic differences among the residents of Sik Kong Wai.

Two hundred yards west of Sik Kong Wai, across open fields, is the hamlet of San Wai. Little is left of the wall that once encircled San Wai's houses and ancestral halls. The old entrance gate now stands in the middle of the hamlet. Whereas Sik Kong Wai gives an impression of social uniformity, San Wai is a community of striking contrasts.

Like Sik Kong Wai, the hamlet of San Wai has its share of small, dimly lit, poorly ventilated houses. But unlike those in Sik Kong Wai, these humble dwellings are overshadowed by spacious ancestral halls[3] and an ornate temple. To the west of the hamlet, near the largest of the halls, are two rows of substantial houses. Their size and mode of construction provide a stark contrast to the dwellings of Sik Kong Wai. These San Wai houses are built with four to six ample rooms linked by a central reception hall; the foundations are constructed of huge granite blocks – not the gray bricks that one sees in humbler dwellings. Inside, the furniture is made of teak and rosewood, inlaid with marble. The walls are hung with scrolls of beautifully executed calligraphy and paintings of illustrious ancestors. These houses open into roomy patios and wide lanes.

From the owners of these substantial homes one learns that their grandfathers and great-grandfathers were scholars, respected leaders, and men of affairs. The houses, they will tell you, were built over 200 years ago, and they have been occupied by the descendants of the original owners generation after generation. An examination of the local land records shows that the men who lived in these houses were not only scholars – they were also landlords.

The contrast between the hamlets of Sik Kong Wai and San Wai is apparent to even the casual observer. Yet for all their obvious physical differences, these two hamlets are part of the same community, and their household heads all acknowledge descent from a common ancestor. Along with 9 neighboring hamlets – which, incidentally, resemble Sik Kong Wai far more than San Wai – they

---

2 Nearly all the houses within the walls of Sik Kong Wai are small and old. However, in recent years villagers have built two-story houses just outside the hamlet's walls, and while I was living in Ha Tsuen 2 houses were built within Sik Kong Wai itself. In the future there will probably be more differentiation of housing style both inside and outside the walls of Sik Kong Wai.

3 These are branch ancestral halls. By "branch hall" I refer to buildings that belong to a segment or estate within the lineage. Some of these halls contain ancestral tablets; others do not. Some are large, and others are modest, one-room affairs. In the past these halls were often used as schools, and they continue to be used as recreation and banquet centers for their members.

Introduction

make up the village of Ha Tsuen (see Map 3). Together these 11 hamlets encircle some of the best rice land in the Hong Kong region. Except for a handful of shopkeepers, the males of Ha Tsuen share the same surname (Teng) and form a close-knit religious and ritual community. The focus of this spiritual community is the village's main ancestral hall, which houses the soul tablets of Ha Tsuen's founding settlers.

The visitor to Ha Tseun soon learns that nearly all of its male residents are descended from a scholar-official, Teng Fu-hsieh, who settled in this part of China over 900 years ago, and that two of their more recent ancestors founded the present village in the 1360s. From my very first conversations with Ha Tsuen men, they emphasized the fact that they were both neighbors and kinsmen. "We are all brothers," they would say; "we are of the same *tsu* [patrilineage]." As one lineage elder told me, "In the eyes of the ancestors we are all the same." The Teng share these sentiments with other Chinese. Although Fan Chung-yen, one of China's most famous commentators on lineage themes, lived nearly a thousand years ago, the Teng would find themselves in complete agreement with his views on the lineage. Writing of his agnatic kinsmen, Fan (989–1052) remarks:

Some among them are close, and others distant, relatives. Yet, if we regard them from the viewpoint of our ancestors, all are equally descendants without distinction of the degree of relationship. How should I not feel shame over their suffering from cold and hunger? Moreover, virtue has been accumulating from our ancestors for more than a century, but has for the first time brought forth its fruits in myself. Now that I have achieved high office, if I should alone enjoy my riches and honorable position without thought for my fellow clansmen, how shall I in future days be able to face our ancestors in the next life, and how should I be able to enter the ancestral temple? (quoted in Twitchett 1959:100)

A sixteenth-century writer, T'ang Shun-chih, echoes these thoughts when he argues that members of a *tsu* (lineage) should treat each other "as parts of a single body, like bone and sinew, hand and foot." Within the lineage, he continues, the rich should share with the poor; there should be "no over-abundancy and no deficiency ... no wealthy and no poor families" (quoted in Dennerline 1979–80:46).

These lineage ideals of brotherhood, sharing, equality, and cooperation are commonly expressed by the Teng (see especially Chapter 3). Yet it is obvious that all Teng are not equal and that there is both "over-abundancy" and "deficiency" among agnates. For generations the Teng lineage has been dominated by a small group of wealthy men. These men, who live in San Wai, own much of the agricultural land that surrounds Ha Tsuen. Until recently they dominated local politics and marketing, and controlled crucial links to the outside world.

How, then, are we to understand the statements that the Teng make about brotherhood and equality? Is it simply a matter of the inevitable conflict between how things should be and how they really are? Are lineage ideals merely empty rhetoric?

Inequality among brothers

This study is an attempt to understand how a relatively small group of landlords and merchants dominated a "community of brothers." More than this, it attempts to show the dynamic relationship that exists between class and kinship in China's powerful lineage villages. The important point is not the rather obvious one that lineage ideals are in conflict with economic and political realities. Rather, this book focuses on the complex links between a system of descent and a set of economic and political relations.

Lineage and class in China

It is important to remember that Chinese lineages are not all identical; they are not carbon copies of one another. The term *lineage* has been applied to a wide range of phenomena in Chinese society.[4] This study is concerned with descent groups that are localized, highly segmented, and maintain large corporate holdings of land. In the literature on China, such descent groups have been labeled "elite" or "dominant" lineages.

Maurice Freedman's work on the Chinese lineage (1958, 1966a), together with the findings of many who followed him (e.g., Ahern 1973; Baker 1968; Cohen 1969; Pasternak 1969, 1972; Potter 1968; J. Watson 1975b) have demonstrated beyond any doubt that descent groups can play an important role in a highly stratified society like China. Considering the amount of research that has been done on the Chinese lineage (and given the class-based nature of Chinese society), it is somewhat surprising to find that the relationship between class and the system of descent has remained largely unexplored. Many anthropologists have ignored the question altogether, and others have maintained that economic divisions were not significant in the Chinese countryside and that hence the problem of class and lineage did not arise (see, e.g., Baker 1979:134; Hsu 1949). The work of those who did consider the question often implied that the system of descent was in fact opposed to the practical dictates of life in a class-ordered society. Freedman refers to this opposition when he concludes his first book on lineage organization by asking, "Up to what point of increasing social differentiation could [large-scale, corporate lineages] survive?" (1958:140).

To understand why the relationship between descent and class in China has

---

4 Some lineages are localized; others are not. Some are highly segmented and have large corporate holdings; others have few segments and own little property. In China, lineages vary from the highly populous, with thousands of members living in a single village and dominating the surrounding territory, to those that have fewer than a hundred members living in a small village or in a section of a multilineage community. Maurice Freedman discussed variations in Chinese lineages in terms of an A to Z continuum (1958:131–3; see also Ahern 1973:75–88). According to Freedman's scheme, those lineages that are least differentiated in social status fall on the A end of the scale, and those that are most differentiated cluster at the Z end. According to this criterion, the Teng lineage falls near the Z end of the continuum.

Introduction

received so little critical attention, it is necessary, I believe, to return to the anthropology of the 1950s. In 1958 Maurice Freedman published *Lineage Organization in Southeastern China*. With the appearance of this book, the Chinese *tsu* was incorporated into the fold of social anthropology and its preoccupation with descent. China became yet another conquest for the descent theorists. Of course, China was more complex, more heterogeneous, and more hierarchical than other "descent societies," but this only proved the explanatory power of the descent paradigm (see, e.g., La Fontaine 1973:35). For their part, sinological anthropologists were quick to seize on the vocabulary and concepts of the descent model in their attempts to "make sense" of Chinese society; the match between sinology and anthropology seemed ideal.

There is little doubt that the application of descent theory to Chinese society produced important insights. However, there is at least one serious drawback to applying this model to the Chinese lineage. Because the model was developed from studies of relatively homogeneous, acephalous societies, researchers are not encouraged to explore problems of economic and political inequality. In fact, when applied to China the descent model tends to mask those aspects of social life.

At this point it is perhaps necessary to say something about what I have called the descent model. In the 1950s, when Maurice Freedman was writing his first book on Chinese lineage organization (1958), descent theory was still very much under the purview of the Africanists. Freedman was greatly influenced by his Africanist colleagues and in particular by the work of Meyer Fortes, who in 1953 published his classic essay "The Structure of Unilineal Descent Groups" (see, e.g., Freedman 1974:69). In a general discussion of lineage theory, Adam Kuper notes that Freedman applied the Africanist model with a minimum of adaptation (1983:89).

During the past twenty-five years the Africanist model of descent has been attacked, altered, and adapted by anthropologists working in many different parts of the world (for a review of this literature, see Kuper 1983). China anthropologists, however, have rarely participated in these debates. My goal in this study is not to "save" lineage theory, but to understand the complex intertwining of kinship and class in Chinese society. However, in order to do this the Chinese system of descent must be freed from the concepts, language, and implications of the Africanist lineage model. Because the differences between Chinese and classic African lineages have not been adequately clarified, it is necessary to begin this discussion at the beginning.

In order to understand the ideas that have influenced and continue to influence the study of the Chinese lineage, it is essential to reexamine Fortes's original essay.[5] I do this not because Fortes was the only or the most recent contributor

---

5 For a more recent discussion of Fortes's views on unilineal descent groups, see Fortes 1969:276–310.

Inequality among brothers

to descent theory, but because his work has had a profound impact on the development of lineage studies in China.

I take Fortes's model of descent to have three basic characteristics. First, membership in a unilineal descent group is determined by birth, through the application of a clear principle of descent. Second, the group is corporate, in that it may be described as "a single legal personality" (Fortes 1970 [1953]:78). Lineages have a continuity over time; they form a perpetual corporation (79);[6] and their members share in a set of defined rights, duties, offices, and social tasks (79–80, 84). The third characteristic of unilineal descent groups, or lineages, is that they are internally differentiated, and this differentiation "follows a model laid down in the parental family" (86). According to Fortes, "It is on the basis of the ties and cleavages between husband and wife, between polygynous wives, between siblings, and between generations that growth and segmentation take place" (87). Thus, "Complementary filiation appears to be the principal mechanism by which segmentation in the lineage is brought about" (87). Related to these three basic characteristics are at least two other aspects of the model that are particularly important when considering the Chinese lineage. According to Fortes, a high degree of political centralization and economic inequality is unfavorable to the growth of descent groups (78–9, 91). Furthermore, the model assumes an ahistorical bias; to know that a society has a descent system and that segmentation occurs according to the principle of complementary filiation is enough to explain the appearance and development of lineages. One need not look to history to understand lineage formation and development.

In the following pages I show that lineage membership, the concept of corporation, and differentiation all operate differently in China from the way Fortes's model suggests. The failure to understand and clarify these differences, I argue, has led to confusion in studying the Chinese lineage and especially in appreciating the relationship between class and descent. As demonstrated in Chapter 2, Chinese lineages do not simply appear; they are not the "natural" outgrowth of a patrilineal system. To understand lineages in China one must be aware of the historical context within which descent groups are formed and develop.

In this study, descent, along with marriage and affinity, is taken to be part of the system of relations by which the economic and political order is reproduced. In other words, descent is here viewed as a crucial element in the set of structures and values that makes it possible for one class to dominate another, generation after generation. It is argued that the interconnections between descent and class, and between affinity and class, are of central significance in understanding economic and political relations in those parts of China where large, wealthy lineages have predominated. In the following pages I trace the often complicated relationship between a specific set of class and kinship relations.

6 For a general discussion of the use of the concept of corporation in anthropology, see Fried 1957.

Introduction

This book explores the relations between people who were members of the same lineage but represented two distinct social classes. The dominant class was composed of landlords and merchants, who never constituted more than 10 percent of the Teng population. The bulk of the lineage were representatives of what I call a smallholder-tenant class. In what sense were these groups classes?

Until recently, Ha Tsuen was predominantly an agricultural community, and land was, therefore, an essential resource (see Chapter 4). The landlords of Ha Tsuen controlled most of the best agricultural land. They did not engage in farming themselves but lived off their land rents. Over 90 percent of village households were either landless or land poor, and therefore those who worked the land (until recently this included most village households) rented all or a portion of the land they farmed. For most villagers tenancy was a way of life. Although not everyone in Ha Tsuen fell into these two classes – there were of course a few households that owned all the land they farmed, and a small number ran local shops or worked as sailors or farm laborers – most villagers were either landlords or tenants. It is the relationship between these two classes that concerns me here.

To some extent this entire study is an attempt to understand class not in some formal, abstract sense but as a "lived-in" system of ideas and activities. Understanding class relations in a village like Ha Tsuen is not simply a matter of determining who owns the land and who does not. It is important to know that Teng landlords dominated local marketing and monopolized political power in Ha Tsuen and in the surrounding area. Landlord-merchants followed a different system of affinity from their tenants; they lived in larger houses, ate better food, and had higher levels of education than their poor agnates. In the following chapters the structure of class relations in Ha Tsuen is discussed in detail; at this point I will simply note that differences in landownership, political power, and life-style all played a role in distinguishing Ha Tsuen's landlord-merchants and smallholder-tenants.

Fieldwork and historical sources

The history of the Teng lineage and of the region surrounding it is an important aspect of this study. I have relied on both information that I collected while living in Ha Tsuen (in the hamlet of Bao Wai) and on historical documents. Much of the historical evidence used in this book was not gathered in libraries or archives but rather from genealogies and local histories that are in the hands of villagers themselves. Other evidence comes from personal observations and from discussions with individual Teng. To the Teng the past is fascinating, and they enjoyed unraveling historical puzzles as much as I did. Although they may not express themselves in exactly these words, they would certainly agree with the view that to understand the present we must understand the past. My discussions with Teng elders and their wives, my explorations of local temples,

Inequality among brothers

my walks through local markets with village friends acting as guides were as important to my understanding of the past as were the written genealogies and gazetteers that I consulted.

As with most villages in China, the historical documentation for Ha Tsuen is uneven. Some periods and some topics are well documented, whereas others are seldom mentioned in the records. Sadly, the elaborate parish records found in many parts of Europe do not exist in China. It appears that Chinese chroniclers and local historians were primarily concerned with affairs of state and devoted little attention to the mundane concerns of their neighbors. The situation is further complicated by the fact that even when historical records do exist, they may be unavailable or inaccessible. In Ha Tsuen historical documents are usually held by private individuals. The men who control these records do not see themselves as the custodians of community documents but as their owners. They are often loath to open these precious possessions (which can give those who control them considerable power over their neighbors) to the prying eyes of outsiders.

Although record keeping improved with the coming of the British in 1898, information on local communities still remains spotty.[7] The historical record for the New Territories is not as incomplete at it might seem, however. Numerous historical sources on village life do exist. One of the most important sources of local historical information are lineage genealogies. These, in the case of the Teng, are hand-written lists of the names of lineage members (males), organized according to lines of descent. The Teng have several copies of their genealogy, most of which also contain brief histories of the lineage. Genealogies provide the names and often the birth and death dates of hundreds or even thousands of men, together with wives' surnames, accounts of illustrious ancestors, burial locations, and records of special titles or degrees conferred. Another major source of information on Ha Tsuen are the British colonial land records, which date from 1905. These records have proved invaluable for this study.

In addition to genealogies, the Teng keep local histories of their lineage and community. Most of these were compiled by educated men for their own personal gratification. A few have been published in commemorative booklets (referred to as "Festival" in the citations in this study) that are issued at the time of decennial rituals of community purification. Stone inscriptions recounting temple and ancestral hall histories are also extremely helpful. Tomb inscriptions proved particularly useful in my attempts to reconstruct lines of descent and estate

---

7 On the island of Taiwan the picture is different, primarily because of the presence of a Japanese colonial administration. In 1898 the Japanese annexed Taiwan, and from that date until 1945 the Japanese police kept remarkably complete records on Taiwanese family and household composition. As a consequence, it is possible to do detailed demographic analyses of individual Taiwanese households (see Wolf and Huang 1980). Unfortunately for the historian, British colonial officials did not attempt to register the local population in Hong Kong, and they did not keep records on individual households.

Introduction

membership. The architecture and layout of temples, markets, shops, and houses also provide valuable historical clues. The physical remains of Ha Tsuen's local market give mute but nevertheless striking testimony to the fact that the Teng once had considerable economic influence in the region. The style and location of village houses allows the observer to make independent judgments about the age and settlement histories of various neighborhoods (or hamlets).

County gazetteers (*hsien chih*) exist for most parts of China. These are printed histories compiled by imperial officials and county notables. Unfortunately the quality of gazetteers in China varies enormously. The one that covers the Ha Tsuen region (Hsin-an County of Kwangtung Province) has depressingly little information about Ha Tsuen itself. However, it does provide some extremely useful material on the history of the region as a whole. The last edition of the Hsin-an gazetteer was published in 1819; an earlier version is dated 1688. In Chapter 2 I have made extensive use of the 1819 edition. British colonial records and sources kept by villagers themselves refer mostly to the nineteenth and twentieth centuries.

Obviously, some historical periods are better documented than others. During the late seventeenth and early eighteenth centuries a series of dramatic events occurred in the Ha Tsuen region. The coastal area that incorporates the village became a center of resistance to Manchu rule (the Ch'ing dynasty was established by the first Manchu ruler in 1644). As a consequence, this transitional period is well documented in official and unofficial sources. Fortunately for the purposes of this study, the foundation of the Teng lineage dates from this period. There is, of course, a great deal of information from both Chinese and British records on the late half of the nineteenth and twentieth centuries. In addition, informants' accounts become an important source of information for the period beginning with the British seizure of the New Territories in 1898. These oral accounts, coupled with land records, colonial files, and local histories, allow us to reconstruct the recent history of Ha Tsuen with a considerable degree of confidence.

As a fieldworking anthropologist I have relied heavily upon my conversations with the villagers themselves. Villagers enjoy recounting the history of their community and lineage. Of course, many of these accounts are clouded by nostalgia (and in a few cases by bitterness). As a consequence, documentary sources were especially valuable for cross-checking what I was told by my informants. However, I would not wish to minimize the role that oral history has played in this study. The villagers own accounts of the past were particularly important in fleshing out documentary material and in providing insights into many aspects of local history.

The many stories and legends that villagers told me were valuable not only because of the information they contained about local history but also for the deeper level of understanding that these accounts made possible. Conversations about the past gave me important insights into how Teng men and women viewed their place in their village and society and what it was that villagers valued – or disliked – in their community. "Talking history," I found, often became a way of talking about conflicts and cleavages that could not be openly discussed. I will take up this point in later chapters, but for now I will simply note that discussions of the past often revealed a level of discourse and meaning that it might not be possible to approach in any other way.

Thus far I have emphasized the problem of historical documentation, but I would not want the reader to gain the impression that present-day Ha Tsuen has no place in this study. Discussions of contemporary lineage organization, politics, and class relations play an important role in this book (see especially Chapters 3, 8, 9, and 10). These discussions are based on the hundreds of hours of conversations that I had with villagers, on the many rituals and feasts that I attended, on the visits that I made with village friends to local temples and neighboring communities, and on the formal interviews that I conducted with political leaders and government officials. A local election was held while I was living in Ha Tsuen, and during the month-long campaign that preceded the election I learned a great deal about local leadership, the nature of factionalism, and ordinary villagers' views on political involvement. In the winter of 1978 I conducted a household census in two hamlets (Sik Kong Wai and Bao Wai, numbering 73 households in total), and this has been an invaluable source of information on present-day family life, marriage patterns, occupations, and migration.

In my research I tried to combine historical material with anthropological fieldwork. In a historically conscious and highly literate community like Ha Tsuen, both the questions I asked and the villagers with whom I lived pushed me in that direction. This study covers 300 years of Ha Tsuen's history. During those years tremendous changes have taken place. Villagers have experienced dynastic change, outbreaks of piracy and banditry, persistent interlineage fighting, and colonial rule. Until the 1950s most of Ha Tsuen's residents worked the land, but by the 1960s the agricultural base of the community had begun to crumble. Industrial enterprises and industrial earnings have come to play an increasing role in Hong Kong's rural society. Today land is valuable not because of the crops it can produce but as potential sites for factories and housing developments. Given these new sources of income, the old class differences, based on landownership and tenancy, no longer have any real meaning. Today the population of Ha Tsuen is made up of wage laborers, the chronically unemployed, a small number of nouveaux riches entrepreneurs, and the descendants of the original landlord-merchants. These recent changes provide an important perspective on the relationship between class and kinship in Ha Tsuen. Although Ha Tsuen's political scene is vastly different from what it was before the 1950s, the lineage still plays an important, albeit diminished, role in local politics. The Teng lineage is not in danger of imminent collapse. Lineage ideology and the worship of common

Introduction

ancestors continues to unite the Teng into a ritual community. In the eyes of the ancestors, and in the conduct of the ancestral rites, the Ha Tsuen Teng are still "brothers."

2

The development of the Teng lineage: Ha Tsuen's early history

According to Teng genealogies, three men surnamed Teng (two brothers and a close agnate) and their families settled in what is now the northwestern New Territories in the 1360s. Over the years the descendants of these first Teng founded a number of hamlets near the original settlement. Gradually the Teng expanded their hold over the surrounding territory so that by the nineteenth century, perhaps earlier, they controlled a considerable area that included their own hamlets as well as 14 villages belonging to their non-Teng neighbors. These neighbors remained under the political and economic dominance of the Teng well into the twentieth century. Today the Ha Tsuen Teng are commonly regarded as one of the most powerful lineages in the New Territories.

The Teng were not, however, always so powerful and well organized. Although groups of Teng households were established in their present-day village site as early as 1400, the available evidence indicates that these households were not drawn into a unified lineage until the mid–eighteenth century. Why did Teng men join together to form a corporate lineage, and how did they come to dominate the surrounding countryside? Two events are crucial to understanding this dual process of lineage formation and territorial domination: one was the construction of a walled market in Ha Tsuen (to be discussed in Chapter 4), and the other was the endowment of an ancestral hall, Yu Kung T'ang (or "Hall of Fraternal Reverence").[1]

Yu Kung T'ang was established in 1751, and since its creation it has so dominated community life that it is impossible to write of the "Ha Tsuen Teng" without also discussing Yu Kung T'ang. The villagers are immensely proud of their hall, which, unlike many similar buildings in other parts of the New Territories, is carefully – one might say lovingly – maintained. Yu Kung T'ang is a temple raised to the cult of the dead, and as such it is the ritual center of the lineage. Yu Kung T'ang is also a landholding corporation, and it serves the Teng

---

1 Parts of this chapter have appeared in my article "The Creation of a Chinese Lineage: The Teng of Ha Tsuen, 1669–1751," in *Modern Asian Studies* 1982, 16(1):69–100, and are reprinted by permission of the publisher.

Development of the Teng lineage

as a framework for organizing large-scale economic and political activities. The care of local waterways and paths, the management of the local market and piers, and, perhaps most important, the organization of local defense all fall under the purview of Yu Kung T'ang, its managers and accountants. The hall controls the lineage's security force that for generations has guaranteed Teng domination of a 15-square-mile territory (the *hsiang*, or district) surrounding Ha Tsuen.

Lineage development in China

Underlying many anthropological studies of Chinese patrilineages is the assumption that lineage development is unproblematic. For most anthropologists working on Chinese society, lineages are simply considered to be part of the social landscape, part of the preexisting nature of things. As I have already noted, this disinclination to examine the historical dimension is in part due to the lineage models that sinological anthropologists borrowed from their Africanist colleagues, who were working in societies where historical evidence was scanty and often unreliable. If the process of Chinese lineage development is considered at all, it is discussed either in the most general terms or in a highly technical manner.[2] In either case the social and economic context within which specific lineages are formed and expand is rarely considered.

Lineages are said to develop by a "natural" process of fission: A man leaves his community and sets up a domestic unit that grows and eventually becomes a new lineage (see, e.g., Baker 1979: 49–52). Maurice Freedman writes: "I think we must assume that the desire to form a single lineage in one village territory is a motive in the system. Where there is enough land, a nucleus of agnates strive to build themselves up to form a large homogeneous settlement" (1966a:8). According to this view, demonstrated descent and common residence[3] are sufficient, given the availability of land, to "explain" the formation of patrilineages (Freedman 1966a: Chapters 1, 6). Although there can be little doubt that some lineages in China were formed by fission and migration, the patterns of lineage development are more complicated than Freedman suggests. The

---

2 The arguments over the relationship between lineage development and irrigated rice agriculture (see Freedman 1966a:159–62; Potter 1970:132–3, 138) or lineage development and frontier areas (see Freedman 1966a:162–4; Pasternak 1969; J. Watson 1975b:33–6) are examples of such general approaches. Other studies are concerned with the minutiae of specific cases of segmentation or fusion. Aside from these discussions, anthropologists have given little attention to either the regional conditions or the specific political and economic contexts within which lineages were established.
3 For a discussion of residence (or locality) and descent in Taiwanese lineages, see Ahern 1976. Although Ahern stresses the importance of residence to lineage organization, it is important to remember that in China not all lineages are localized.

Inequality among brothers

creation of the Teng lineage at Ha Tsuen does not fit the scenario outlined by Freedman. In the case considered here, common descent and common residence long predated the foundation of a unified lineage. Only after three centuries of settlement did large numbers of Teng householders unite to form a corporate descent group.

In this chapter I am not attempting to determine the origins of the Chinese lineage system, nor do I seek to present a model of lineage formation that will fit China as a whole. Rather, in examining the history of a specific lineage, I hope to say something about the role that lineages play in Chinese society. How do lineages affect local politics and local economic relations? How do they relate to changing economic conditions? In this discussion I focus on the political and economic context within which the Teng established themselves as a dominant lineage. The Chinese patrilineage is not the domestic unit writ large, as some anthropologists (e.g., Baker 1979:49–50; Hsu 1963:60) have maintained, nor is it the "natural" outgrowth of a system of patrilineal descent. In her study *Land and Lineage in China* the historian Hilary Beattie succinctly states the problem: "The question to be asked is ... why some kinsmen descended from a common ancestor organized themselves effectively in this way [into large lineages] and not others. It is all too often taken for granted that the Chinese lineage was a product of 'natural growth'" (1979:112).

The formation and development of the Teng lineage, I argue, was in large part a response to a new set of circumstances in the regional economy – and not to forces inherent in the Chinese descent system. In the long term, the relationship between the development of localized lineages and the regional economy is very complex, because the economic and political environment both affected and was in turn affected by the presence of powerful descent groups. However, if we are to understand the process of lineage development among the Teng, this complicated relationship must be unraveled. What were the economic and political conditions of the seventeenth and eighteenth centuries when Teng householders were establishing their lineage? What was the regional environment in which Teng lineage builders found themselves?

Before addressing these questions it is important to know something about historical work on the Chinese lineage. If anthropologists have been reticent to examine the historical development of lineages in China, their historian colleagues have not been so hesitant. This work provides both a useful comparative perspective for understanding lineage building among the Teng and, at a more general level, it highlights the dynamic relation between descent and class in Chinese society.

Those who work on Chinese kinship are blessed – some would say cursed – by an abundance of historical data. The study of the Chinese lineage is particularly well served by the historical record. Although China specialists may bemoan the lack of records on family or domestic organization, the same cannot be said for extradomestic kin groups (lineages, clans, and surname collectivities). There

Development of the Teng lineage

is, in fact, an embarrassment of riches in the form of genealogies, county histories (*hsien* gazetteers), and countless treatises on lineage themes. It may be surprising to learn, therefore, that until recently these historical resources have been little used by those interested in the Chinese lineage.

In the late 1950s Denis Twitchett was one of the first historians to cast a critical eye on the development of the Chinese lineage. According to Twitchett, the lineage, with its corporate property and written genealogies, "is to a very large extent the product of Sung times" (1959:97–8; see also D. Johnson 1983). For many historians, the Sung dynasty (960–1280) marked an important turning point in Chinese history; in fact some scholars date the appearance of modern Chinese society from the Sung. Twitchett argues that the descent group, with its large landholdings, developed as a response to two basic changes in Sung society: (1) The old aristocracy with their inherited privileges had disintegrated, and (2) competitive examinations, rather than aristocratic status, became the key to government service (1959:101; see also Twitchett 1961). Lineages, Twitchett maintains, were useful in building stable local institutions upon which solid government could depend. Furthermore, lineages served to consolidate the position of the "official class" that could no longer rely on hereditary privilege (Twitchett 1959:101). Twitchett does not suggest that the idea of the lineage suddenly appeared upon the Chinese scene fully formed. Rather he spells out how preexisting social and cultural elements, not the least of which were Confucian ideas of the family, came to be reformulated as the ideological basis of modern descent groups.[4]

Twitchett was one of the first social historians to see the Chinese descent group within a specific social and economic context, but nearly 20 years elapsed before other historians took up this line of analysis (for a discussion of recent studies, see J. Watson 1982a). Recent historical studies of specific lineages focus primarily on central eastern China during the sixteenth and seventeenth centuries (see, e.g., Beattie 1979; Dennerline 1981; Zurndorfer 1981). Unfortunately, terms like *lineage*, *family*, and *clan* are not always carefully defined in these analyses, and comparison therefore becomes difficult. However, in general these studies do show that lineage formation and development were closely related to specific economic and political conditions. Like Twitchett, Beattie, in a study of T'ung-Ch'eng County in present-day Anhwei Province, stresses the role that successful lineage organization played in maintaining the position of the elite, in Beattie's case a local elite. "Intensive efforts at lineage organization," she

---

4 For example, Twitchett notes that Confucian and Buddhist ideas about family relationships were an important element in formulating descent ideology (1959:100). He also notes that the landed corporations held by Buddhist monastic communities in the T'ang dynasty were very likely a model for the estates that were to play such an important role in the Chinese lineage (Twitchett 1959:102). For further discussion of preexisting social and cultural elements that came to be associated with lineages in the Sung and later, see also David Johnson 1983:363–4.

writes, "came in the mid seventeenth century, when the elite found themselves faced with unprecedented threats, not only from violent revolts, but also from tax changes that drastically reduced their accustomed financial privileges. Henceforward it was even more difficult for a family or wider kinship group to rely on the protection of a few degree-holding members; they had in addition to protect their interests by building up the corporate wealth and authority of the lineage" (1979:129).

Zurndorfer, working on the Hui-chou Prefecture in a different part of Anhwei from Beattie's site, also points to the effect that political upheavals and taxation had on lineage development. Zurndorfer further notes that demographic pressures and Hui-chou's unusual agricultural system were important factors in the formation and growth of local lineages (1981:213).

Dennerline's study of a single county in the Yangtze delta during the sixteenth century emphasizes the important role that lineage ties had for local leaders in constructing links between themselves and powerful bureaucrats (1981:98). However, according to Dennerline, lineage organization was not a dominant feature in the lives of nationally prominent scholar-officials, who preferred to cast their networks further afield than a group of locally based agnatic kinsmen (104–11, 113). Dennerline also notes that lineages rarely emerged in the cotton-growing areas of the Yangtze delta (111, 130). Although this interesting line of inquiry is not developed, Dennerline's analysis does suggest that cotton production did not lend itself to the formation of long-standing corporate estates that play such an important role in Chinese lineage organization. The volatile land market in cotton areas no doubt contributed to the high turnover of landownership and hence presumably discouraged the development and long-term existence of ancestral estates.

This brief summary cannot begin to do justice to recent historical work on the Chinese descent group, but it does illustrate that lineages are not found in all parts of China and that they are not the automatic consequence of a patrilineal system. Although nearly all Chinese order some of their relationships according to patrilineal principles, only a part of the population belong to unilineal descent groups. In effect, the Chinese have a concept of descent that exists outside the confines of the patrilineal descent group. Anthropologists have long recognized that descent ideologies do not necessarily correspond to group membership (see, e.g., Barnes 1962; Sahlins 1965; Scheffler 1966; Schneider 1967; Strathern 1972) nor do they always imply descent groups. In his book on the Hagen people of New Guinea, Andrew Strathern points out that "patrilineal dogmas" may operate in societies where recruitment to groups is not necessarily, or even primarily, according to patrilineal principles (1972:1–5, 213–22). In China, recent work on kinship during the Han (206 B.C.–A.D. 221) and T'ang (618–907 A.D.) dynasties suggests that patrilineal ideas played an important role among the aristocratic elite, although lineages were not evident (Ebrey 1978; D. Johnson 1977:97–8, and 1983). If the lineage in China is defined by the possession of a

Development of the Teng lineage

common estate, by recruitment through demonstrated descent from a common ancestor, and by a sense of ritual unity (cf. J. Watson 1982a:594–602), then according to the available evidence lineages in China were a post-T'ang development.

Even though many Chinese are not members of lineages, they belong to a society that has a definite patrilineal emphasis and ideology – what Scheffler has called a "descent construct" (on the distinction between descent constructs and descent groups, see especially Scheffler 1966). Patricia Ebrey has argued that many neo-Confucian scholars of the Sung believed that the simple compiling of genealogies that set out the exact relationships among agnates would improve individual behavior and establish social harmony (1983:24). Obviously, underlying this idea is the belief that patrilineal descent itself carries a considerable moral force, regardless of the existence of corporate groups. In China much importance is attached to the belief that a father and son (and by extension those who trace descent from a common ancestor) share a special relationship. Sometimes they are said to share the same essence, breath, or bone (Shiga 1978; J. Watson 1982b). Chu Hsi, one of the most respected philosophers of neo-Confucianism, argued against the adoption of daughters' sons because, he said, father and adopted son would not be of the same breath, or *ch'i* (quoted in Ebrey 1983:22).

Shuzo Shiga, in a discussion of Chinese inheritance, summarizes what he considers to be the crucial element of patrilineal descent in China. A son, Shiga writes, is seen as "a continuation of his father." According to Shiga, "In one's descendants one sees one's own ancestors, and to those descendants one commits one's ancestors' lives as well as one's own"(1978:125). Hugh Baker makes a similar point: "The individual alive is the personification of all his forebears and of all his descendants yet unborn. He exists by virtue of his ancestors, and his descendants exist only through him" (1979:26–7). In Chinese society the individual male thus represents, in his own person, the fragile link between the past and the future. Because a man is linked to his ancestors through a series of agnatic ties (they are said to partake of the same *ch'i*), he shares with all of his ancestors' descendants a special relationship – consisting of duties and privileges. As Cheng I, an important Sung thinker, asks: "How much divides your son and your brother's son? They both are the offspring of your father!" (quoted in Ebrey 1983:10).

In many parts of prerevolutionary China where the descent group did not exist or was relatively undeveloped, patrilineal principles had great meaning to individual Chinese. Patrilineal descent was central to the richly complex system of ancestor worship and to inheritance (property passed in the male line; ideally, brothers inherited equally). Patriliny also played a role in residence and in household organization and ritual. Economic and political networks, patronage relations, and the distribution of imperial privileges tended to adhere to patrilineal principles (R. Davis 1980). The operation of patrilineal principles did not, however, imply or depend on the presence of the unilineal descent group.

Inequality among brothers

According to available historical research, lineages (as defined earlier) have not been part of Chinese society since time immemorial, nor was China a "lineage society" in the sense that local organization was necessarily, or even usually, lineage-based. Lineages are found in some areas of China but not in others: they seem to be concentrated in the Southeast.

Early History of Ha Tsuen

After this brief discussion of the spatial and temporal distribution of lineages in China, let us return to an examination of Ha Tsuen's history and the conditions within which the Teng lineage was created and developed. The Canton delta complex of which Ha Tsuen is a part (see Map 1) came under Chinese rule during the Han dynasty, although it was not until the great southward expansion of the Sung and Southern Sung dynasties that the delta was populated by ethnic Chinese (Han people) in any great numbers (see Fitzgerald 1965:183–6; Wiens 1967:183–4). By the Ming period (1368–1644), ethnic Chinese – mostly descendants of migrants from northern China – and sinicized aboriginals were largely in control of the region. For hundreds of years Ha Tsuen was an integral part of Hsin-an County (*hsien*), which forms one of the administrative divisions of Kwangtung Province. Until 1898, when a large part of Hsin-an County was leased to the British, Ha Tsuen fell under the administrative umbrella of Kwangchou Prefecture, which was managed from the city of Canton. Canton, which is about 50 miles from Ha Tsuen, has been an important commercial center for more than a millennium (Wakeman 1966:43). The delta that stands between Canton and the coast has often enjoyed considerable spillover from the city's commercial expansion.

The ancestors of contemporary Teng first settled in the New Territories region in the early part of the twelfth century (for a discussion of Teng history in Hsin-an, see Sung 1973, 1974). Teng Fu-hsieh, an imperial degree holder, was appointed a county magistrate in Kwangtung during the reign of Emporer Ch'ung Ning (1102–6). According to a Teng family history, Fu-hsieh was so taken with the beauty, and with the geomantic possibilities, of the southern coast of Kwangtung that he decided to settle there upon his retirement from official life (Kam Tin Teng Chia-p'u, n.d.). He returned to his native Kiangsi Province and exhumed the remains of his great-grandparents, grandparents, and parents and removed them to what was then Tung-kuan County (Hsin-an County was not made into a separate administrative unit until 1573, when Tung-kuan County was divided into two parts). Fu-hsieh set up residence near the present-day village of Kam Tin (see Map 2), which was to become the parent community for most of the Teng in Hsin-an County.

Although the area into which Fu-hsieh moved was a frontier, it had been influenced by the metropolitan center of Canton. By the time Teng Fu-hsieh had settled in Hsin-an, salt production and pearl fishing were already important

Development of the Teng lineage

industries in the area (see, e.g., Lo 1963:5–7). As early as the T'ang dynasty (618–907), Tuen Mun (on Castle Peak Bay, which is only about five miles from Ha Tsuen) was Canton's outer port and a meeting place for foreign and Chinese vessels. For many decades Tuen Mun played an important role in China's trade with southeast Asia and beyond. During the T'ang dynasty trade was expanded, and a garrison of regular troops was stationed at Tuen Mun (Lo 1963:21), and in the Sung dynasty an officer whose duty was to pursue and arrest bandits was added to the garrison (Lo 1963:23). During the Ming dynasty, Tuen Mun was invaded and occupied by the Portuguese (1514–21), but eventually the Portuguese moved across the delta, where they established Macao. Gradually Tuen Mun was eclipsed by Nam Tao (the capital of Hsin-an County) and, of course, by Macao itself (Lo 1963:27).

As I have already noted, the two Teng brothers (Hung-hui and Hung-sheng) and their agnatic kinsmen (Hung-chih, their father's father's brother's son's son [FFBSS; see Figure 1]) had all moved to the Ha Tsuen area in the 1360s. However, shortly after their arrival, one of the brothers – Hung-sheng or some of his descendants (present-day villagers are themselves uncertain about this point) – went to reside in the vicinity of Tung-kuan City, about 20 miles to the north, where other Teng kinsmen were already living. Later, some of Hung-sheng's descendants returned to Ha Tsuen, but for reasons that will be discussed below they have never been fully accepted into the lineage or the community. When the Teng themselves speak of the "Ha Tsuen Teng," they refer only to the descendants of Hung-hui and Hung-chih.

While the Ha Tsuen settlement was taking shape, another group of Teng were establishing the neighboring village of Ping Shan (Potter 1968). The Ping Shan Teng (see Map 2) and the Ha Tsuen Teng both trace descent from Teng Fu-hsieh, who first settled near Kam Tin village. The two communities are, along with Kam Tin, members of one of Kwangtung's largest higher-order lineages.[5] The patrilineal link between Ha Tsuen and Ping Shan has not, however, tempered the enmity that has characterized relations between members of the two communities for most of their history. The Ping Shan Teng, like the Teng of Ha Tsuen, have organized themselves into a dominant lineage that controls a hinterland of smaller villages inhabited by non-Teng. The two lineages constantly encroached on each other's lands, and many battles were fought across the small river that divides their respective territories (on armed conflicts between Ping Shan and Ha Tsuen, see Potter 1969:13).

The origin legends of Ha Tsuen suggest that the Teng were not the first Chinese to settle in the northwestern Yuen Long plain. Although the Teng managed to force at least one set of villagers out of the area, they were never able to free themselves completely from competitive neighbors. They had to contend with

---

5 For a discussion of higher-order lineages, see Freedman 1966a:20–1; J. Watson 1982a:608–9; Woon 1979.

Inequality among brothers

the Teng of Ping Shan, and by the mid–sixteenth century a number of farming communities had grown up along the fringe of Teng territory. To the south of Ha Tsuen was a complex of hamlets that were settled, according to present-day informants, by people of the surname *T'ao* during the middle of the Ming dynasty. A mile to the east and west of Ha Tsuen were the non-Teng villages of Ngau Hom and Shek Po, which, according to a history compiled by the Yuen Long District Office, were first settled in 1456 and 1531, respectively (Yuen Long History 1962). However, there is little doubt that once Teng landholders gained control over the territory immediately surrounding their settlements, they never relinquished their hold.

Unfortunately, little is known about fifteenth-century Ha Tsuen. Beginning with the sixteenth century, however, there is a marked change in both the quality and the quantity of information about the village and its residents. Villagers still recount a number of myths and stories about their sixteenth- and seventeenth-century Teng ancestors, and documentary evidence is much improved. Local documents relevant to Teng history include temple inscriptions, genealogical accounts, and the Hsin-an County gazetteer, which was published in 1688 and revised in 1819. According to the 1819 edition, the population of Hsin-an County numbered just under 34,000 at the end of the sixteenth century (Gazetteer 1819:269).[6]

The sixteenth century constituted a period of considerable economic growth in most parts of China. Macao, located about 40 miles from Ha Tsuen across the Pearl River estuary, became an important center for the importation of silver during the 1500s (Atwell 1977). How this lucrative trade affected the hinterland of the estuary remains to be documented. However, the historical record does indicate that during this period there was an increase in piracy along the whole coastal region of southern China (Lo 1963:33; Gazetteer 1819:369). Piracy was finally contained, at least temporarily, in the 1660s, but not before the most drastic measures were imposed by imperial authorities.

The seventeenth century was marked by dynastic decline, and the people of Hsin-an were forced to undergo great hardships during this period. The Manchus had invaded China from the north and eventually overthrew the last of the Ming emperors in 1644. The decades prior to the Manchu seizure of power were characterized by a steady decline in Hsin-an's population, caused, according to the local gazetteer, by disease, famine, and banditry.

Accounts of the seventeenth century read like a catalogue of misfortune and disaster (Gazetteer 1819:363–9; for discussion of this era, see R. Watson 1982).

---

6 It is difficult to know how accurate the population figures presented in the gazetteer are, but I would suggest that they provide an indication of population trends. For a detailed discussion of population figures during the Ming and Ch'ing dynasties, see Ho Ping-ti (1959).

Development of the Teng lineage

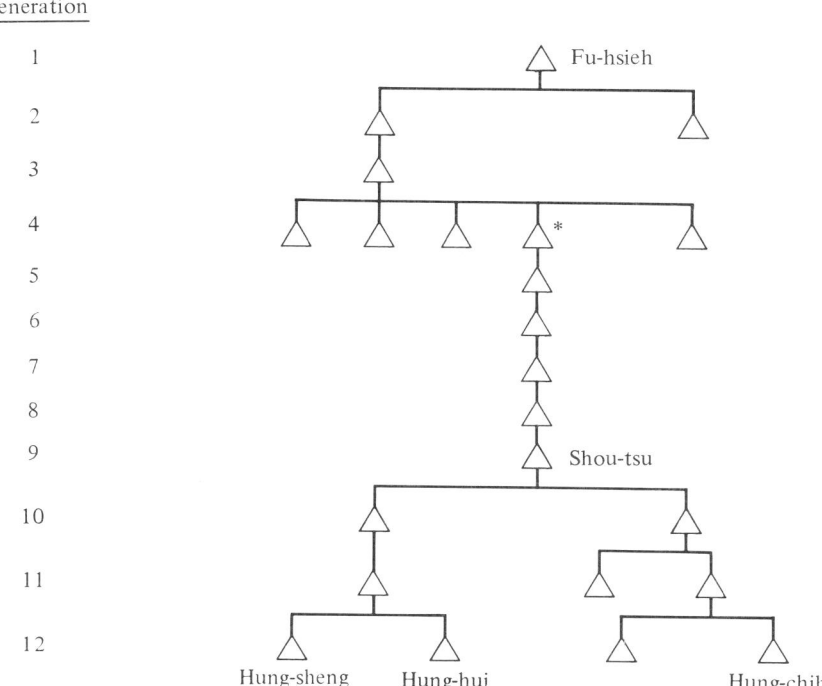

Figure 1. Outline of Teng genealogy. Note: Ha Tsuen and Kam Tin Teng are all descended from the ancestor marked with asterisk.

The population of Hsin-an is given as 33,971 in 1573. By 1643 this figure had dropped to 17,871, and during the period from 1662 to 1669 the population fell to an incredibly low 2,172 (Gazetteer 1819:269–70). It is not surprising that many of the fortifications and walled villages that one can see today in the New Territories were built in the immediate aftermath of this disruptive period (see, e.g., Baker 1968:30; Hayes 1974:118; Mathias 1977:15).

In 1662 a devastating blow fell on the people of Hsin-an and many other coastal areas in southern China. In an attempt to quell the pirates, who by this period had come to include increasing numbers of people loyal to the previous Ming dynasty (Baker 1968:30; Hayes 1974:118), the K'ang-hsi emperor ordered coastal communities to evacuate their homes and move inland (Hsieh 1932). This "scorched earth" policy caused great hardship, and many people died during the retreat. In 1669, due to the intercession of two imperial officials (Baker 1968:30; Hsieh 1932), local Hsin-an people were allowed to return to their homes. Although this forced migration created severe dislocation, it appears that some

Inequality among brothers

villages and families were more severely affected than others.[7] According to Ha Tsuen people, many of their ancestors sat out the evacuation among their kinsmen in nearby Tung-kuan City. Obviously those who could remain in the area or stay nearby were in a good position to guard their property and interests; they were also well placed to occupy new territory once the evacuation was lifted.

During the period immediately following the evacuation, returning Ha Tsuen landowners had to reassert and strengthen control over their holdings both because of the threat from interlopers who had drifted into the area and, perhaps more important, because of the encroachments of powerful neighbors like the Ping Shan Teng. Hugh Baker suggests that in some parts of Hsin-an a scramble for land developed in the aftermath of the evacuation (1968:41; see also Kamm 1977:60–1). During the late seventeenth and early eighteenth centuries, there was heavy immigration into Hsin-an from many parts of Kwangtung (Hayes 1974:120; Gazetteer 1819:270–1; Lo 1963:101–5), and the population began to rise again.

Elsewhere I have argued that during the century following the evacuation, an economic and political structure developed in southern Hsin-an that was to continue well into the twentieth century (R. Watson 1982). During this period a few lineages came to dominate the region, each of which had in their membership a small core of wealthy merchants and large landowners who made up a regional elite. These landlord-merchants were a major political force both in their own communities and in the region as a whole. I do not mean to suggest that after 1669 a group of wealthy men and a number of dominant lineages suddenly appeared on the scene and proceeded to impose their will on neighbors. Obviously, this was not the case, for there is little doubt that some large landowners and some lineage organizations predate the evacuation. What I do wish to stress, however, is that the structure of dominance (the particular combination of institutions and practices) found in nineteenth- and twentieth-century Hsin-an can be traced to the period of great prosperity that followed the dislocation of the evacuation. Most of the institutions (for example, corporate estates, ancestral halls, markets, temple committees) that a few lineages used to establish their power and authority over others date from, or were substantially expanded during, the late seventeenth and early eighteenth centuries.

The evidence suggests that for a 100-year period beginning in 1669 a handful of the area's lineages (sometimes called the "Five Great Clans," Baker 1966) consolidated their control over the region, and the elite of these lineages began to cooperate with each other on a regular basis. In writing about the history of the dominant Liao lineage, Hugh Baker has emphasized the importance of the postevacuation period. He suggests that those who returned to the area in 1669

---

7 The 1688 edition of the gazetteer notes that 24 villages in the affected area of Hsin-an were given special dispensation, and the inhabitants were not evacuated (Ng and Baker 1983:112). Unfortunately the gazetteer does not list the 24 villages.

Development of the Teng lineage

were able to use their knowledge of the region and their previous position and contacts to lay claim to large areas of good land. Baker writes: "The evacuation and return may well have helped the [Liao] lineage to consolidate its position as a major power and land-owner in the area" (1968:41).

When it came to tightening their hold over neighboring villages and lands, the Hsin-an Teng were in an especially advantageous position. By using official connections or their kinsmen in Tung-kuan as a safe haven, many Teng were able to avoid some of the worst effects of the evacuation. Furthermore, the Teng had been established in Hsin-an longer than others. All of this, coupled with the wealth of some individual families, gave the Teng a competitive edge over their more recently settled and less well-connected neighbors. Genealogies and local inscriptions suggest that during this period there were a number of wealthy and educated men in the area.[8] These men were in a position, therefore, to act as spokesmen for Teng interests within government circles. In fact, there is some suggestion that the villagers of Kam Tin did not suffer as much as their neighbors because of the intercession of one of their number, Teng Pao-sheng, an important leader who eventually attained the rare distinction of holding the highest imperial degree, *chin-shih* (Sung 1974:171–3). Few other lineages had such advantages, and it is not surprising, therefore, that after their ordeal the Teng were in a good position to make substantial economic gains. These gains were often made at the expense of their less fortunate neighbors.

It is helpful to compare the situation in Hsin-an after the traumatic events of the evacuation with Hilary Beattie's description of T'ung-ch'eng County (Anhwei Province) after the rebellions of the 1630s and 1640s (1979:44–8). Beattie remarks that after the rebellions that devastated the area, members of the local elite had little difficulty in reestablishing themselves and taking over the property of their deceased neighbors (47). The similarities between Hsin-an and T'ung-ch'eng counties are striking in some respects. Prior to the mid-seventeenth century both counties had communities in which patrilineal descent was important but not yet central to local organization. Only after the disturbing events of the middle 1600s did the large corporate lineages that we associate with the eighteenth and nineteenth centuries come into their own.[9] In both cases the dislocations of

---

8 For examples of Teng degree holders in the Ming dynasty and later, see Sung 1974:170–2.
9 According to Beattie, "The first manifestation of the Chang's corporate existence" was the compiling of a genealogy in the first decade of the seventeenth century (1979:91). The man who was responsible for compiling the genealogy also provided his lineage with 26 *mou* of land to be held in a corporate estate to finance ancestral sacrifices and to aid members (Beattie 1979:91). Beattie refers to the Chang lineage in the 1620s as "embryonic" (1979:91). After the rebellions of the 1630s and 1640s, large amounts of land were added to the lineage's estates (Beattie 1979:93, 98), shrines were established at ancestral graves (98), and the genealogy was updated and greatly expanded (95).

Inequality among brothers

the mid-seventeenth century were followed by an elaboration of lineage organization and structure. Beattie, in the following statement, could just as well be speaking for Ha Tsuen when she writes, "When the survivors returned it quite probably seemed imperative to them to find ways of reasserting their threatened position in the locality ... To strengthen their lineage organizations may very likely have appeared to be one means of achieving this" (93). Beattie reports that lineage rules were strengthened and more rigidly enforced after the rebellions of the mid-seventeenth century, and corporate holdings were greatly expanded.

The last three decades of the seventeenth century were the beginning of an era of great prosperity for China as a whole. Fortunately for the people of Hsin-an County, the Canton delta had a large share in that prosperity. Although the Hsin-an County gazetteer abounds with accounts of disasters in the seventeenth century, there are only a few hints of such hardships in the eighteenth, and these refer mostly to outbreaks of piracy and banditry, twin scourges to which Hsin-an County was prey until the 1940s. As C. P. Fitzgerald remarks, foreign missionaries found eighteenth-century China "most splendid" and the "equal, if not the superior ... of their native France" (1965:547). Trade with the West greatly increased during this period. Pritchard, in his study of Anglo-Chinese relations, details the tremendous expansion of foreign trade with China in the latter half of the eighteenth century (1936:115, see also Fairbank 1953:39–57; Rhoads 1974:100). After 1757 this trade was conducted solely through the port of Canton (Pritchard 1936:128). From the early 1700s to 1842 (the year in which Canton ceased to be the sole foreign trading port in China), the Canton delta reaped the benefits from both the legal and illegal commerce that passed through the area. This was the age of the great schooners laden with legal cargoes and with contraband. Smuggling was rife, and there were opportunities for making money on both sides of the law (Hayes 1974:121–6). It is important to remember that the main sea route for this lucrative traffic with Canton passed within a short distance of Ha Tsuen.

Hsin-an County after 1669

The history of Hsin-an County does not, of course, begin with the evacuation and its aftermath. We have already seen that the port of Tuen Mun was important to China's trading interest as early as the T'ang dynasty, and that salt making, pearl fishing, and agriculture were lucrative economic activities during the Sung. Long before the hardships of the evacuation, educated and wealthy men from southern Hsin-an had established local schools and served in China's imperial bureaucracy (see Sung 1973, 1974:170; Baker 1968:44). Clearly, local history did not start in 1669; nevertheless there is little doubt that the 1660s constituted an important turning point for the people of Hsin-an.

The formation and growth of the Teng lineage of Ha Tsuen can be seen, I argue, as part of a general regional development in which the interests of a few

Development of the Teng lineage

powerful lineages came to dominate local affairs. Many of southern Hsin-an's important markets, temples, and large corporate descent groups trace their beginnings to this period. The development of these organizations created a milieu in which local elites could further both their own interests and the interests of their localized lineages.

The 1819 gazetteer lists three markets for the area that presently make up the northern New Territories (Gazetteer 1819:83). Of these three markets, all were established in the 100-year period after 1669, and all were founded by a dominant lineage (or by a member of a dominant lineage). The market of Yuen Long was established during the early part of the reign of K'ang-hsi (1662–1723) by Teng Pao-sheng of Kam Tin (Teng Shih Tsu P'u, n.d.; see also Hayes 1977:36; Sung 1974:173). Yuen Long became an important market for Kam Tin, Ping Shan, Ha Tsuen, and many other smaller villages in the area. Local people whose families have been involved in Yuen Long Market for centuries say that Ha Tsuen families owned some of the boats that called at the market. If this is true, it suggests that Ha Tsuen people were involved in coastal boat traffic by at least the late seventeenth century. During the nineteenth century the ownership of boats was an important source of income for Ha Tsuen's wealthy residents. Two other large markets, Shek Wu Hui and Tai Po, were also founded in the late seventeenth century, and, like Yuen Long, they too were controlled by dominant lineages (Baker 1968:190; Groves 1964:17; Hayes 1977:36).

These markets all serviced, and continue to service, the fertile rice lands of what is now the northern New Territories. The development of the market towns of Yuen Long, Tai Po, and Shek Wu Hui is proof not only of the new-found prosperity of the postevacuation period but also of the increasing power of the area's localized lineages. These markets were not free and open trading centers; they were, in fact, monopolies of the large lineages (see, e.g., Groves 1964; Skinner 1964–5:36–7). They were controlled by certain individuals, or later by ancestral estates. In the end one lineage dominated each market, controlling access to it, claiming a percentage of sales, and charging a "protection fee" to shopkeepers. This control was backed up by the lineage's self-defense corps. Control over a market both enhanced a lineage's prestige and, on a more practical level, it provided new sources of income both to individual lineage members and to the coffers of the lineage's ancestral estates.

The creation of markets was not the only consequence of the newly found prosperity; large temples were also being founded (or renovated) during this period (for discussion, see R. Watson 1982:83). Markets and temples in China played an important role as a springboard for organizing and sustaining contacts among the rural elite. After the work of G. William Skinner (1964–5), it is hardly necessary to point out that markets are not just concerned with the exchange of goods. Skinner writes,

The standard marketing community can be seen as the locus of such intercourse as petty traders have with the peasantry on the one hand and with the local elite (primarily through

Inequality among brothers

the mechanism of market control) on the other. But its primary significance pertains to the relations between peasantry and "gentry" . . . Every standard marketing community included in traditional times a number of so-called "gentry" families. And it was in the market town that these elitist families exerted "social control." (41)

Similarly, one might note that rural temples are not only religious centers (see also Skinner 1964–5:38). A good example of the use of temples for political and economic ends is the foundation of a temple commemorating the two officials who interceded with the central government to end the evacuation in 1669 (see Baker 1966:38, 1968:194–5). A group of dominant lineages, including the Liao of Sheung Shui and the Man of San Tin, came together to build this temple in the market town of Shek Wu Hui during the late seventeenth or early eighteenth century. Each lineage contributed to a central fund, and the money was then used to build the temple and buy land to cover maintenance expenses. Some of the contributions were used to buy a ferryboat, which made it easier for members of the share-holding lineages to travel to the large market at Sham Chun. Baker reports that elite members of the share-holding lineages met for an annual feast at which temple business and, one assumes, many other things of mutual interest were discussed.

If recent ethnography is an indication, it is very likely that a number of seventeenth- and eighteenth-century temple committees played a political as well as religious role in local affairs. During the twentieth century, large temples (and markets) have been managed by committees whose membership reads like a *Who's Who* of the New Territories. These committees provide an important but informal framework within which members of the local elite can meet, exchange information, and make decisions that often have a direct impact on their home communities. There seems little doubt that in the past, when formal political institutions in rural areas were less developed than they are today, such informal organizations played an important role in interlineage (and intraelite) relations (see, e.g., Faure 1981).

Considering the extensive building that went on during the late seventeenth and eighteenth centuries, it is not surprising to learn that many of the area's large ancestral halls also date from this period. The central ancestral hall at Sheung Shui was built in 1751 (Baker 1968:31); Kam Tin's oldest hall was established in 1701 (Sung 1974:179); and the T'ao hall in Tuen Mun district was completed in 1718 (J. Watson, personal communication). These halls and the corporations they represent are the ritual, economic, and political nerve centers of the lineages to which they belong. It is by means of these institutions that concerted action is organized and carried out (see Chapter 4). To determine whether the construction of these halls marks the creation of new lineages (as was the case with Ha Tsuen) or whether they served to strengthen preexisting but perhaps more loosely organized lineages (as with the Liao of Sheung Shui, discussed later in this chapter) requires more research. However, we can be certain that the construction of these elaborate and enormously expensive build-

Development of the Teng lineage

ings suggests at the very least a decisive strengthening of the organizational framework and powers of the area's major patrilineages.

Elite interests, especially those of the Teng, were well served by the construction of a large ancestral hall in Tung-kuan City. This hall, Tou Ch'ing T'ang, served Teng living throughout Hsin-an and Tung-kuan counties. It was built in 1709 under the patronage of Teng Pao-sheng and a number of other wealthy Teng (Teng Shih Tsu P'u, n.d.; see also Sung 1973:114). The growth of Tou Ch'ing T'ang owes as much to the affluence of the period as it does to the experience of the evacuation that brought many Teng together, perhaps for the first time. This hall provided the Teng of Tung-kuan and Hsin-an counties with an institutional framework for united activities. Nearly 300 years after this hall was built, the kinship unit that Tou Ch'ing T'ang represents continues to play an important ritual and political role in the lives of many Hong Kong Teng.

Higher-order lineages like that focused on Tou Ch'ing T'ang were organized and run by members of the regional elite. Not surprisingly, the Kam Tin scholar-official Teng Pao-sheng was a driving force behind the construction of Tou Ch'ing T'ang, although he did not live to see the completion of the hall (Kamm 1977:60). The very location of Tou Ch'ing T'ang in Tung-kuan City suggests that this hall was primarily an elite institution. Very few Teng farmers would ever have ventured so far afield as Tung-kuan City, which lies about 20 miles north of Ha Tsuen. Furthermore, it is very unlikely that ordinary members of the lineage would have been involved in the actual management of the hall or in its rituals. In many clan or higher-order lineage halls of this type, only the wealthy and literate elite were responsible for rituals and worship (J. Watson 1982a:608–12; Woon 1979:25).[10]

During the eighteenth century, large-scale nonlocalized lineages like that centered on Tou Ch'ing T'ang became a powerful force in Chinese society. Eventually they became a matter of some concern to the imperial government, which took the view that kinship organizations of such magnitude were a possible threat to central authority. In his study of rural China during the Ch'ing dynasty, Hsiao Kung-chuan says that by the late eighteenth century "the imperial government was thoroughly convinced of the dangers of extended clan organizations, whether they were composed of bona fide clansmen or persons unrelated by blood. It appeared to the Ch'ien-lung emperor at least that large clans were more likely to cause trouble than small ones" (1960:355). There followed a series of edicts that attempted, on the whole unsuccessfully, to curb the influence of large clans and lineages.

Aside from the growth of temple and lineage organizations, there are other

---

10 Clans are more than collections of people who bear the same surname. The constituent units of clans are lineages, not individuals. Clan organizations are usually based in county or provincial capitals (on clans in China, see Baker 1977; J. Watson 1982a:610–12).

Inequality among brothers

indications that dominant lineages were expanding their power and wealth during the eighteenth century. The increasing number of men from southern Hsin-an County who gained imperial honors or degrees is one such indicator. Hugh Baker, who has made a study of this, shows that the Liao of Sheung Shui had the greatest number of honor holders in the period from 1704 to 1771, reaching a peak in the year 1738 (1968:44).

Ha Tsuen after 1669: background to unification

Although the Ha Tsuen Teng were not noted for their scholarly achievements, they were very much involved in the general social and economic expansion of the eighteenth century. Two large village temples (dedicated to the god Yang Hou) were greatly expanded during the second half of the eighteenth century, and in 1751 the central ancestral hall, Yu Kung T'ang, was completed. Although these buildings have undergone many renovations, they continue to serve as highly visible symbols of Ha Tsuen's dominant position in the area.

Local accounts, including those given by villagers and those provided in genealogies and local inscriptions, suggest that during the 1700s the Ha Tsuen Teng were being pressured on many sides. Teng Pao-sheng, who lived in Kam Tin, established a firm bridgehead in an area near Ha Tsuen when he built Yuen Long Market. To the east of Ha Tsuen was the ever-present threat of the Teng of Ping Shan, and to the south was a group of communities linked in a political alliance but largely controlled by the T'ao of Tuen Mun. There was also increasing population pressure. In 1732 Hsin-an had only 7,289 inhabitants, but by 1773 the number had reached 30,373. In 1818, if the local gazetteer is to be believed, the population had reached the staggering level of 225,979 (Gazetteer 1819:270–3).[11]

As for Ha Tsuen's own immediate hinterland, many non-Teng settlements were being established during this period. As noted earlier, two neighboring villages (Ngau Hom and Shek Po) are said to date from the period before 1600, but by the time the gazetteer was published in 1819 six more villages had been founded (these villages are listed in Gazetteer 1819:94). If these documents are correct, by 1819 eight non-Teng villages had been established near Ha Tsuen. The Teng, no doubt, kept a careful watch over these communities. The determination of whether these non-Teng settlers came into the area as dependent tenants of the Teng or whether the Teng made them into economic and political clients after they had already established their villages awaits further research. What is clear is that by the nineteenth century these villages had become de-

---

11 In 1898 the population of the New Territories was estimated to be approximately 100,000 (reported in Baker 1968:3). The British leased only a portion of Hsin-an County, and the large towns remained in Chinese territory. It is therefore possible that the population of the entire county could have been in excess of 200,000 in 1819.

Development of the Teng lineage

pendent satellites of the Ha Tsuen Teng. Control over Ha Tsuen's agricultural hinterland, or *hsiang*, was in fact an essential ingredient in Teng success. The Ha Tsuen Teng jealously guarded their control over these satellite communities against the encroachments of their powerful neighbors in Ping Shan.

At the same time as the Teng were confronting these neighbors, the regional economy was booming. Residents of Ha Tsuen were in a good position to exploit the opportunities offered by their location on the coast and their control over the *hsiang*. The increased level of trade in the Pearl River and its estuaries gave their local economy, including both commercial and agricultural/fishing enterprises, a tremendous boost. In fact it was during this period, according to the villagers, that Ha Tsuen's oyster industry was established.

Evidence suggests that during the eighteenth century Teng families living in the Ha Tsuen area were not only competing with their neighbors but were also competing with each other. Two lines, whose descendants in 1978 were still treating each other with considerable distrust, are most often mentioned in local accounts as direct competitors in the 1700s. Both of these lines are descended from the same founder, Teng Hung-hui. A member of one of the families, Teng Tso-t'ai, is credited with being the main force behind the establishment of Yu Kung T'ang, whereas a member of the other family, Teng Wei-yü, is said to have been instrumental in the creation of Ha Tsuen Market. According to local stories, the competition between Tso-t'ai and Wei-yü was so fierce that each plotted the other's murder. Tso-t'ai, I was told by one of his descendants, was saved from certain death by his slave (*hsi min*), who managed to ward off his attackers. It appears that Tso-t'ai's brother, Tso-wen, and his five sons (called the "five tigers of San Wai") eventually tipped the balance in favor of Tso-t'ai and his family. These five brothers are notorious among the descendants of Wei-yü, who still shake their heads in disgust over the stories of their swaggering ways and bullying tactics.

By the mid-eighteenth century the descendants of the three men who originally settled in the Ha Tsuen area were scattered in seven small hamlets (see Map 3), all of which are listed in the 1819 gazetteer (92). These hamlets, which are in some cases separated by only a path or a small rice field, were and are discrete social units. To a large extent the descendants of the three original settlers remained geographically distinct. From current residential patterns and from what villagers have told me, I gather that the descendants of Hung-chih lived (and continue to live) in Tung Tao Tsuen, whereas Hung-sheng's descendants were (and are) concentrated in the hamlet of Sik Kong Tsuen, which they shared with Hung-hui's descendants. The remaining five hamlets were primarily the preserve of the descendants of Hung-hui.

Although at least one dominant lineage in the area (the Liao of Sheung Shui) was, according to its own account, united into a corporate landholding group in the seventeenth century, there is no indication that the Teng of Ha Tsuen were so unified. Among the people of Ha Tsuen, I found no legends or documents

Inequality among brothers

that would suggest that they were organized into a unified lineage prior to 1751– the date when their ancestral hall was completed.[12]

During the expansive period of the eighteenth century, the advantages of unification must have been apparent to Teng living in the Ha Tsuen area. By the 1740s some communities in the area were already organized into large patrilineages with corporate estates and ancestral halls (for example, ancestral halls were built by the Kam Tin Teng in 1701 and by the T'ao in 1718). The Teng, for a variety of reasons, may well have encountered more obstacles to their unification than did their neighbors. First of all, there was intense competition among families and lines, although this was no doubt a problem in other communities as well. Second, Ha Tsuen's residential clusters divided rather than integrated the major kin groups. That is, the descendants of the three founders tended to live in separate enclaves. The greatest difficulty of all, however, was the absence of a focal ancestor around whom these disparate families, lines, and residential clusters could join together. Unlike most of their neighbors, the people of Ha Tsuen had not one founder but three.

In a society like China there were, of course, many forms that Teng unification could have taken (for example, they could have united around temples or irrigation societies; see Pasternak 1972). Patrilineal descent was, however, very much a part of their conceptual system; the Teng, of course, did not invent the patrilineage. We have already seen that some of Ha Tsuen's neighbors provided examples of successful lineage organization. Furthermore, the people of Ha Tsuen were lineally related. To use Morton Fried's phrase, they could "demonstrate" their ties of descent to one another (1957, 1966), in this case by using Teng Fu-hsieh as their focal ancestor. It is not surprising, therefore, that the Teng should unite on the basis of patrilineal descent.

The evidence I have collected suggests that the Teng remained a loose collection of households and small residential groups until the eighteenth century. It appears that the Ha Tsuen Teng had no corporate identity until Yu Kung T'ang was completed in 1751. As noted above, in contrast to some other dominant lineages in the area the Teng had some difficult problems to overcome before they could hope to emulate their neighbors. Unfortunately there is little detailed information available on the formation of specific lineages in Hsin-an. There is some material, however, on the early history of the Liao lineage at Sheung Shui. It might be useful at this point to review that history in order to place the Ha Tsuen data in a comparative perspective.

Baker reports that the Liao's founding ancestor came to Hsin-an in the four-

---

12 A stone set in Yu Kung T'ang does make a vague reference to an earlier ancestral shelter/shrine, *tz'u yü*. Significantly, the term *yü* and not *t'ang* is used in this context. In local usage *yü* refers to a minor shrine. The stone does not make clear who among the Teng used this *yü*, nor does it give the name of the *yü*. There is, in fact, no supporting evidence (architectural remains, records, or oral traditions) that corroborates the existence of this shrine.

Development of the Teng lineage

teenth century, about the same time that the founders of Ha Tsuen settled in the Yuen Long plain. The Liao newcomers and their early descendants did not remain in one community, and gradually as the years passed they became scattered throughout the region. However, in the eighth generation (counting from the first settler in Hsin-an) a Liao decided to unite his kinsmen into one settlement, Sheung Shui, which was established around 1600. An ancestral estate, based on agricultural land, was formed and dedicated to the fourteenth-century founder who first came to Hsin-an. While Baker notes that the Liao lineage as a unit really dates from 1600, "The Liaos themselves date it from the Founding Ancestor, whose trust [estate] it is which forms the basis of the group's unity" (1979:52). Clearly the Liao had an advantage over the Teng in that they could focus on a single ancestor whose corporate estate provided an organizational framework for their unification.

In order for the Teng of Ha Tsuen to find a common ancestor around whom a corporate estate could be formed, it would have been necessary to choose as their focal ancestor a man who had lived in another village, Kam Tin. That is, they would have had to go back three ascending generations to find a common ancestor (namely, Teng Shou-tsu; see Figure 1) and this of course would have taken them back to Kam Tin. It is possible that a corporate ancestral estate dedicated to Shou-tsu existed before the eighteenth century, but such an estate very likely would have included both the Teng living in the Ha Tsuen area and those living in Kam Tin as well. Whatever the situation may have been, there is no doubt that an ancestral estate in which the focal ancestor is shared by those from whom one wishes to differentiate oneself cannot be a very effective mechanism for declaring one's independence of that larger group. As Maurice Freedman has pointed out, ancestral estates are a means of differentiation (1958:77–80; see also Ahern 1976). In forming an ancestral estate a new unit is set off from other units. The Teng in the Ha Tsuen area were prisoners of the fact that they had three founders, only two of whom were brothers (the third being their FFBSS). In addition to this, their very proximity to the parent village of Kam Tin (about six miles away) must have made it even more imperative that they clearly differentiate themselves from their kinsmen, the Kam Tin Teng. To show their independence, both ritual and economic, they needed to create an institution that did not compromise but rather proclaimed their independence.

Of course, it is possible that although the Teng had no kin-based groups that united the descendants of the original settlers prior to 1751, they may have had some form of ancestral estates that united a few households. There is only one piece of evidence relating to this matter. A brief history of the lineage is recorded on a stone inscription that was set in Yu Kung T'ang at the time of its construction (and can still be found there). In this account, reference is made to the landed properties of Hung-hui and Hung-chih, who by 1751 had been dead for nearly 300 years. Unfortunately the stone does not provide enough detailed information to permit us to determine the exact nature of the "groups" that owned these properties. The groups themselves are not referred to by the term *tsu*, which villagers use when designating corporate ancestral estates. Instead, the general term *fang* is employed, which in this context simply denotes two similar but opposing groups or units. Hence, although the inscription clearly states that the properties were held in the names of Hung-hui and Hung-chih, the use of the term *fang* suggests an absence of corporation. It is significant that the two *fang* are not listed as subdivisions of a larger named corporation of any kind. Had there been such an overarching organization, the Teng certainly would have noted its existence.

The inscription was, of course, prepared for public consumption after the lineage had been consolidated. There is, I think, reason to suggest that the authors may have tried to give themselves, the descendants of Hung-hui and Hung-chih, a more illustrious history than they in fact possessed (by claiming to have extradomestic kinship organizations that predated Yu Kung T'ang). The terminology used supports this view. The point needs to be made that even if the people of Ha Tsuen were in some manner organized into two separate groups prior to 1751, this does not imply any overall unity, and it does not imply the existence of a corporate lineage. Furthermore, the *fang* divisions would only have accentuated the differences among the various groups (or units) of householders. Although at this point we cannot be sure of the exact nature of local organization in Ha Tsuen prior to 1751, the evidence from the stone, I believe, supports my contention that at the mid–eighteenth century the Teng who lived in the Ha Tsuen area were not organized into a unified lineage.

Foundation of Yu Kung T'ang

In 1751, according to the stone inscription found in Yu Kung T'ang, the Teng established their ancestral hall, and with its construction the Ha Tsuen Teng proclaimed both their independence from other Teng communities and their active membership in the region's economic and political elite. With the inauguration of Yu Kung T'ang, the Teng of Ha Tsuen became one of the most populous and powerful lineages in southern Hsin-an, with all the features that an organization of this type implies in China: corporate property, demonstrated descent, written genealogies, and ritual unity.

Significantly, Yu Kung T'ang was not built within the confines of any particular hamlet. It is situated on what villagers consider to be neutral territory facing an open expanse of tidal marshes. According to the stone inscription found in Yu Kung T'ang, funds for the construction and maintenance of the hall came from three sources. First, there were rents from the "properties of Hung-hui and Hung-chih." Second, there was a general subscription of all Teng who were descendants of the two founders. And third, 48 men each contributed 20 *liang* of silver to complete the construction. These men are referred to as *p'ei hsiang chu*, or "benefactors." Inscribed on the stone are the rights and privileges that

Development of the Teng lineage

the various members of Yu Kung T'ang enjoy. The descendants of the 48 named benefactors have special rights to rental income, and every year the descendants of these men are to receive extra shares of sacrificial pork at the Spring and Autumn Rites held in Yu Kung T'ang. According to the inscription, it took 2,900 *liang* of silver to build Yu Kung T'ang. Money left over from the construction fund was used to buy land that was set aside (in a corporate estate) to finance community projects and the worship of lineage ancestors.

For reasons that are now unclear, Hung-sheng's descendants did not contribute to the construction of Yu Kung T'ang. Therefore they are not members of the hall, which means that their descendants remain outside the effective boundaries of the lineage itself. To this day they do not share in the benefits of the hall or its estate. Even though Hung-sheng and Hung-hui were brothers and shared a common genealogical relationship to a number of Teng ancestors, and even though descendants of these two brothers still reside in Ha Tsuen, they and their descendants are not members of the same localized lineage. Membership in a hall like Yu Kung T'ang is based on descent *and* voluntary financial support. It must be emphasized, however, that this element of choice is exercised only at the foundation of an ancestral hall or estate. Once the estate has been established, male descendants of the original contributors are members by right of birth.[13]

I suggested in the beginning of this chapter that Maurice Freedman's writings imply a specific model of lineage formation in which there is a logical progression from original settlement by one man, the focal ancestor, to the development of nesting estates through a process of segmentation. According to this view, the localized lineage is unified from the very beginning by having a founding (or focal) ancestor, whose estate becomes the material foundation of the organization. Freedman's scenario suggests that all males living in a community thus formed would be descendants of a single ancestor and hence members of the localized descent group. Research in Ha Tsuen, coupled with studies in other parts of China, clearly suggests, however, that there is no uniform process of lineage formation in China.

The localized descent group of the Ha Tsuen Teng was created by a process

---

13 Emily Ahern argues that full lineage membership, by which she means incorporation of one's tablet into the ancestral hall plus of course the usual criteria (a share in corporate property, participation in rituals), is not automatically ascribed by the principle of descent. She maintains that incorporation of one's tablet into the ancestral hall "turns on whether the people involved have contributed in certain ways to the wealth and size of the lineage" (Ahern 1973:116). In the case of Ha Tsuen I would not go so far as to say that only those whose tablets were in Yu Kung T'ang were full members of the lineage. In fact, very few Teng have their tablets in the main hall (see Chapter 3). If we used Ahern's criteria, we would have to exclude most of the Teng from full membership. However, Ahern's discussion does show that, at least in some lineages, "The right to full participation in the lineage is not simply ascribed automatically to males by birth or to females by marriage into the lineage" (1973:116).

Inequality among brothers

involving the amalgamation of previously separate units. The Teng are by no means unique in this respect. For example, the Liao of Sheung Shui, as we have seen, have a similar pattern of development, as do many Taiwanese patrilineages. Pasternak and Cohen, in their studies of nonlocalized agnatic groups in Taiwan, have shown that fusion can play an important role in lineage formation (Pasternak 1969, 1973; Cohen 1969; see also Woon 1979:25). In writing about Hakka communities in Taiwan, Cohen remarks: "In the past, fusion was indeed the process whereby small agnatic groups formed themselves into larger units" (177).

Aside from the question of fusion, the Teng lineage of Ha Tsuen differs from Freedman's model in a number of other important respects. The corporate property of the Teng is held in the name of a hall (*t'ang*), not in the name of a focal ancestor. In effect, owing to the fact that they would have to share an apical ancestor with another localized lineage (the Teng of Kam Tin), the Ha Tsuen Teng have no recognized focal ancestor at all. Finally, an analysis of the formation of Yu Kung T'ang shows that genealogical relationship may not be the only criterion for membership in a lineage such as the one under study. Those who made special contributions toward the construction of the hall are set apart from their fellow agnates in lineage ritual and in their entitlement to extra shares of estate income. Although Hung-sheng's descendants lived in the Ha Tsuen area at the time Yu Kung T'ang was built, they did not contribute to its construction, and therefore they are not part of the lineage. In Ha Tsuen the criteria for membership are demonstrated descent as well as financial subscription. This is an important point; the Teng themselves are fully conscious of the distinction. The localized lineage in Ha Tsuen is organized, to some extent, along the lines that one associates with voluntary associations, not unilineal descent groups.[14]

The work of the historians Denis Twitchett and Hilary Beattie suggests yet another process of lineage and estate formation. In both the cases that Twitchett and Beattie describe, previously distinct units (or loosely organized units) are brought together (fused) into a single lineage organization with common property and focused on a common ancestor. The lineage estates that resulted from these unions were not, however, named in honor of an ancestor, as Freedman's model suggests, nor were they formed by subscription as was the case in Ha Tsuen. Rather, the corporate holdings of these lineages were established by a gift of land to the lineage. A wealthy agnate donated some of his own property to the lineage (for a similar case in Taiwan, see Pasternak 1973:268). These charitable estates were then used for the benefit of the entire lineage membership (Twitchett

---

14 Unilineal descent groups are usually thought to be closed – that is, groups in which membership is not a matter of choice but is determined by genealogical relationships. In China this distinction is sometimes hard to draw. For example, Myron Cohen reports cases of "dispersed lineages" in which membership is primarily determined by financial contribution (1969:180).

Development of the Teng lineage

1959; Beattie 1979:42, 91). All those who traced descent from the lineage's perceived focal ancestor shared in the estate. Membership was determined by genealogical relationship based on a written genealogy, and not by material contributions as in Ha Tsuen.

From these cases we can delineate at least two basic processes of lineage formation. One is characterized by fusion or aggregation of smaller units. The other is characterized by a process of growth in which the founder produces sons who in turn produce more sons; eventually property is set aside for the worship of a deceased father or grandfather, and a lineage develops. In those cases involving fusion, a number of units are joined together within one institutional framework. In Ha Tsuen this was done by building a hall and endowing it with land. The corporate holdings of such a hall are not strictly ancestral estates at all. That is, the property is not held in the name of a focal ancestor but rather by a corporation of shareholders. There is some question as to whether the Ha Tsuen Teng constitute a unilineal descent group or a voluntary association posing as a unilineal descent group. On one point there is little doubt, however; the Ha Tsuen Teng, whatever the technicalities of their group status, see themselves as a unified lineage (*tsu*) and refer to themselves as such.

Common residence and shared descent did not in themselves unify Teng households into an effective patrilineage. Only after the Teng had been settled in the Ha Tsuen area for over 300 years did they form a corporate lineage (even then, not all Teng residing in the area were included). The Teng lineage at Ha Tsuen is not the result of some dynamic that is inherent in the kinship system itself; rather it was created by a group of eighteenth-century Teng who were responding to a particular economic and political environment. Like the people of T'ung-ch'eng studied by Beattie, the Teng were facing increasing threats to their control over crucial resources. The unification of the Teng into a single patrilineal descent group gave them the organizational basis to compete successfully in a region where competition over agricultural land, territory, water, and markets was fierce and unrelenting.

3
Lineage organization and ideology

In this chapter, lineage organization and lineage ideology are discussed in detail. In particular I am concerned with the relationship between an ideology that emphasizes lineage solidarity and a socioeconomic system that is based on clear economic inequalities. In Chapter 2 I discussed the early history of the Teng lineage; the present chapter is concerned with the lineage during the twentieth century, although the patterns described are very likely representative of earlier periods as well. The data presented in the following pages are based upon conversations with lineage elders, personal observations, and analyses of the many lineage rituals I attended. Lineage genealogies also provide an important source of information.

In Ha Tsuen the representations of the system of descent are complex and even contradictory. In some contexts the unifying aspects of descent are emphasized; in other contexts differences among agnates are stressed. The image of an undifferentiated lineage is one that the Teng are quick to express in conversation and thus remains a conscious ideal. The other view of the lineage emphasizes the differences among agnates and is most clearly reflected in rituals associated with the ancestral cult.

Anthropologists who work on lineages in other parts of the world will find little that is surprising here, for it is well known that all unilineal descent groups have within them unifying and differentiating tendencies. However, in the Chinese context differentiation has a special meaning. In China, descent groups have been imbedded in a class-based, bureaucratic state system for centuries. From their very inception, large lineages like the one under study here have incorporated people from nearly every stratum of society – from the very rich to the very poor. In this milieu the differentiating aspects of the lineage are of a different order than those found in the acephalous, classless societies of premodern Africa (see, e.g., Fortes 1945, 1970). In such societies differentiation "follows a model laid down in the parental family" (Fortes 1970:86). For example, men who share the same father but have different mothers are thereby differentiated; married brothers are distinguished by their possession of a wife and children; age and generation differentiate one agnate from another. In the Chinese case,

Lineage organization and ideology

differentiation is based on many of the same criteria, plus wealth. That is, to have any structural significance, differentiation within the Chinese lineage must be based on the incorporation of property, usually land, into ancestral estates (*tsu*).[1] To establish a new segment a man must do more than marry and produce sons; he and his descendants must have enough personal property to endow an estate. The Chinese lineage is internally segmented into distinct property-holding corporations. Some men may belong to dozens of these estates, others may belong to none (a situation that Freedman [1966a:37] referred to as asymmetrical segmentation). In this chapter I argue that economic differences among agnates, far from being opposed to or in conflict with the Chinese system of descent, are in fact of fundamental importance to that system.

Descent in Ha Tsuen is clearly an expression of unequal property relations, but it also expresses the ideals of fraternal cooperation and group solidarity. How then, does the Chinese system of descent manage to bridge what appears to be an insurmountable contradiction? What, we may ask, kept the Teng lineage from dissolving into discrete resource-holding units, each attempting to dominate its less affluent agnates? Why did the rich not deny their relationship with the poor or subordinate and enserf them, as sometimes happened among agnates in Indian society? (see, e.g., Fox 1971: 76–7).

As was demonstrated in Chapter 2, the Teng lineage, from the time of its formation in 1751, had both rich and poor members. In the foundation stone of Yu Kung T'ang itself a distinction was drawn between "benefactors" and ordinary members. Just as rights to lineage-owned land differentiate lineage members from outsiders, so rights to corporate property define groups within the lineage.

Although property is thus a crucial factor in Chinese lineage organization, I do not wish to reduce descent simply to a matter of property relations. In Ha Tsuen, descent also provides the Teng with a framework for thinking about their relations with each other and with the world outside the lineage. Many anthropologists have emphasized the importance of examining descent as a conceptual or ideological system (see, e.g., Parkin 1978; Scheffler 1964; Schneider 1967). This approach does not imply that descent should be seen as a set of rules to which the Teng more or less adhere. The relations between descent as a conceptual system and everyday social interaction are extremely complex. One of the things I wish to stress here is the way the Teng themselves think about their lineage. In this chapter I examine the values, ideas, and principles that underlie lineage organization among the Teng.

---

1 The observation that unilineal descent groups and the transmission of rights in property are closely related phenomena is certainly not new (for a discussion of this point see Goody 1962:354, 433–5). However, what makes the Chinese case different from most other descent systems is the importance of private property.

Inequality among brothers

Descent as a conceptual system

As I have already noted, patriliny is an important organizational principle throughout Chinese society, although it is, of course, more elaborated in the Southeast. Patrilineal descent plays a crucial role in inheritance and marriage. It is particularly important in the formation of social groups; in fact, even groups that are not based on kinship are often organized on lineage principles. Voluntary associations (Fried 1953), religious orders (Topley 1958), and secret societies (F. Davis 1971) all make implicit use of the lineage as a model for organization. While some societies may use the idiom of territory, marriage, or caste as a way of ordering social relations, the Chinese emphasize descent and agnation. The Chinese also make affinal alliances, maintain ties of patronage, and unite on the basis of territorial or residential proximity, but among the Chinese, patrilineal descent is a dominating cultural theme.

It is difficult, perhaps impossible, to say that descent can be reduced to one set of principles or that it has one basic meaning to which all other meanings relate. Descent in Chinese society is not just one idea but many different ideas, some of which appear to be in conflict with each other. Among the Ha Tsuen Teng, patrilineal descent provides a structure for a whole series of religious, economic, and social relations; it sets the context for group action. In later chapters I will discuss the political and economic aspects of lineage organization. Here I wish to emphasize some of the underlying principles of the descent system as it is found among the Teng. One way of approaching this problem is to examine those aspects of the lineage that the Teng themselves consider important and around which a great deal of symbolic elaboration is evident. The central ancestral hall, corporate estates, and ancestral graves are some of the more visible expressions of descent in Ha Tsuen, while lineage ritual and beliefs regarding the dead provide more abstract expressions of that system.

It may be helpful to begin this examination with a discussion of those descent ideals that the Teng themselves express on countless informal occasions. What kind of language do the Teng use in discussing their lineage? In Ha Tsuen, common descent is thought to be the basis of a special relationship that stresses fraternal equality and mutual cooperation. If one asks about relations within the lineage, a common response is: "Our founding ancestors gave us life; they fought against our enemies so that we might enjoy security and wealth. We must show that we can work together so that we do not disgrace our forebears." Men linked by common descent are said to be like brothers, while all those not so related are called "outsiders" (*wai lai jen*, lit. "those who come from outside"). A man expects cooperation from his brother, whereas outsiders are to be treated with calculation and suspicion. The representation of the lineage as a group of brothers is significant, for in Chinese society brothers are similar but not the same. Brothers, for instance, are distinguished by age; that is, the younger must observe certain forms of respectful behavior toward the elder. However, brothers

Lineage organization and ideology

by custom inherit equally, and there is no principle that endows one brother with jural authority over his male siblings. It is therefore interesting that the Teng themselves should stress not some abstract concept of equality but the idiom of brotherhood, an idiom that emphasizes similarity but leaves room for individual differences.

From one perspective the formal organization of the lineage appears to be remarkably egalitarian. There are no formal positions in the lineage save for that of "lineage master" (*tsu chang*), the oldest man in the most senior generation. Although the lineage master is a ritual leader, he has no political power as such. Men over sixty years also have a special place in lineage ceremonies, and they often receive special portions of sacrificial pork. However, these "elders" (*fu lao*) do not constitute a managing elite. Elders are given respect, but they wield no political power by virtue of their age alone. There is no senior line in the Chinese lineage, and segmentary divisions play no role in lineage rituals. Agnates worship as a unit. During lineage rituals, for instance, there is no way for the onlooker to determine segment affiliation. All elders wear the same style of clothes – gray or black gowns – and the Teng who belongs to the wealthiest estates in the lineage will stand with his generation fellows who may not belong to any estates at all (except for that of Yu Kung T'ang, that is). Generation alone defines the order and position of worshippers.

In this context, members of the lineage are seen as a clearly demarcated group of men whose relations are characterized by fraternal cooperation and equality. There is, however, another representation of the lineage that suggests that some Teng are more equal than others. As noted in Chapter 2, the 48 benefactors who provided more money than their neighbors for the construction of Yu Kung T'ang are singled out in the inscribed stone that is set in the foundation of the hall. Considering the ideals of unity and brotherhood, it is somewhat disconcerting to learn that these men and their descendants receive special recognition in two important lineage rituals (the Spring and Autumn Rites). During the Spring Rites in 1978 I was surprised to discover that certain men received more than the usual share of sacrificial pork. When I asked people about this, most could offer no explanation other than "This is the custom of our lineage." The fact that no one could explain these differences is particularly striking because at other lineage rituals pork divisions are meticulously evenhanded (with equal shares weighed out on a scale). One elder suggested that the differences might have something to do with the hall's ancestral tablets; those whose ancestors were represented by tablets, he ventured, might receive an extra share. On checking, however, I found that there was no correlation between tablets and special shares. Finally one of the more knowledgeable men in the village suggested that this unequal distribution of pork might relate in some way to the list of founders' names that appears in Yu Kung T'ang's stone inscription. After examining the stone I discovered that the extra shares went to descendants of the 48 benefactors who had helped build the hall in 1751. This shows clearly

Inequality among brothers

that age and generation are not the only distinguishing principles among agnates. Although the lineage is often presented as a fraternal and undifferentiated group, agnates are distinguished by wealth and by genealogical connection to the benefactors. Lineage ritual itself gives expression to this dual image: equality among agnates is stressed, on the one hand (no differentiation by segment, ranking by generation only), but on the other hand the division of ritual pork highlights inequality (distinguishing the descendants of benefactors from regular members).

In the remaining sections of this chapter, I examine a number of ancestral rites with a view toward better understanding these contradictory images of the lineage. However, before we begin it is important to know more about Yu Kung T'ang, the building in which many of these rituals are performed.

Yu Kung T'ang and lineage ritual

In many dominant lineages the grave of the founding ancestor plays an important ritual and symbolic role. In these communities, rites at the founder's grave are the primary means of expressing group unity. Because the Teng do not have one founding ancestor but two, and therefore not one grave but two, their central ancestral hall is probably of greater significance than is the case for their neighbors. For the Teng, Yu Kung T'ang is the visible manifestation of their lineage.

The hall, which is the largest structure in the community, is constructed of brick and faces an open plaza. Except for its tiled, steeply pitched roofs, Yu Kung T'ang has rather an austere appearance. This simplicity of line and general lack of decoration is typical of most ancestral halls in the region and stands in stark contrast to the ostentation of the local Taoist and Buddhist temples. Yu Kung T'ang measures approximately 120 feet by 50 feet and is divided into three distinct chambers. An iron gate and a set of large wooden doors guard the hall's only entrance.

Upon entering Yu Kung T'ang, one's gaze is immediately arrested by an enormous and highly carved wooden altar. This altar, which holds the lineage's ancestral tablets, is the only piece of furniture in the hall. Yu Kung T'ang's altar displays 103 tablets arranged in 6 rows. It is believed that each of these wooden tablets contains one aspect of an ancestor's soul. On each tablet is carved the ancestor's surname, generation name, and personal name (three characters) followed by a set phrase, "the place of the spirit" (*shen chu wei*, lit. "spirit host seat"). The ancestor's generation number, titles (if any), and wives' surnames are also included.

Once the tablet is placed in the hall, it becomes part of the generalized body of lineage ancestors. Unlike the ancestors' graves or the domestic tablets in the home (discussed later in this chapter), the hall tablets are not the focus of individual or household worship. Tablets in a hall are normally worshiped by the lineage as a collective unit; they are rarely singled out for special attention. Whereas the ancestor in his grave is thought to have direct links with his own

Lineage organization and ideology

descendants, the ancestor in his hall tablet is of generalized importance for the lineage as a whole. Once the ancestor enters the hall, he becomes part of the undifferentiated but revered lineage dead (Freedman 1958:84); he no longer belongs to any one family.

There is, at least in the New Territories, some feeling that if the ancestors in their tablet form are respected and well cared for, the lineage will prosper, although there is little elaboration of how this will come about. In the village of San Tin, members of the Man lineage parade offerings, which will later be taken to the founding ancestor's grave, before all the tablets in their central ancestral hall. They do this, they say, "so that the ancestors can all see how wealthy and strong we have become." In Ha Tsuen, village men often remark that it is important that attendance at hall ceremonies be high and that rituals be conducted properly, for "the ancestors will see what we do."

In Yu Kung T'ang, the men who are regarded as founders of the lineage, Teng Hung-hui and Teng Hung-chih, have the place of honor on the ancestral altar. Their tablets and the tablets of their ancestors (who lived in the village of Kam Tin) are arranged on the top row of the altar, with those of Hung-hui and Hung-chih in the center. Each generation follows in succession, with the bottom tier including tablets of several twenty-second generation Teng (in 1978 the lineage was in its twenty-eighth generation). According to villagers, new tablets are placed in a hall only at the time of its initial construction or during major renovations, which usually occur every 50 to 100 years. Theoretically, all male descendants of Ha Tsuen's two recognized founders may have their tablets placed in Yu Kung T'ang. In fact, however, only 103 out of several thousand eligible ancestors are commemorated in this way. The tablet's place (*wei*, "seat") on the altar must be purchased at the time of renovation. The cost of these seats is high, thereby excluding poor members who might wish to include their own or their ancestors' tablets in the hall. A distinction based on wealth is thus incorporated into the very structure of the lineage's most important collective representation. Viewed from one perspective, the tablets represent the generalized body of all lineage ancestors, whose worship promotes the well-being of the entire lineage. However, if we examine the tablets from another perspective, we find that only a few ancestors are allowed into the hall, a privilege for which they or their immediate descendants pay dearly.

I was told that only those ancestors who died for the lineage by protecting it against bandits or enemy neighbors or those who made a name for themselves as scholars and government officials had tablets placed in the hall free of charge. In order to have a tablet in the hall, therefore, most Teng were dependent not only on the financial resources of living descendants but also on their memory and affection. Over a period of years, many ancestors may have become too far removed from their descendants to warrant the cost of a tablet. One way that a man could ensure his entry into the hall was to buy his own seat and tablet during the hall's renovation. Tablets of living people are sometimes placed in

Inequality among brothers

ancestral halls, and covered with a red sheath until the men concerned died. The wooden tablet does not become imbued with a spirit until it is "dotted" 100 days or more after the owner's death. This is done by literally adding a dot, or stroke, that completes one of the characters of the tablet: 王 ("king") becomes 主 ("host"). The substantial fees that are charged for the place on the altar usually go into the hall's renovation or construction fund.

The tablets in Yu Kung T'ang are the focus of some of the lineage's most solemn and elaborate rituals. The daily care of the tablets and hall is left to a non-Teng, a caretaker hired especially for the job. The Teng maintain that they have always hired outsiders to watch the hall because it would not be seemly for a member of the lineage to hold such a menial and servile position. The caretaker is also responsible for doing much of the heavy work involved in the preparation for lineage rituals.

Ha Tsuen's ritual calendar is based on the lunar cycle and begins with the lunar New Year festivities. Most New Year observances take place in the household or hamlet, but a few are celebrated in Yu Kung T'ang. On New Year's Eve, men who will reach the age of 61 during the coming year go to the hall to make their first offerings as elders. Dressed in their long gray or black gowns and carrying offerings of fruit and meat, they present themselves to the ancestors.

On the tenth day of the first lunar month, Yu Kung T'ang is decorated with huge painted paper lanterns. This is the festival of *k'ai teng* ("lantern lighting"), which marks the formal acceptance of "new males" (*hsin ting*) into lineage membership. The "lantern festival" is the least austere and most joyous of the many lineage rituals held in the hall. Each father of a male child born in the previous year places a small oil lamp on the altar below the ancestral tablets, "so that," they say, "the ancestors can see how the lineage is growing." After the fathers have presented their offerings to the ancestors, the infants' names are entered in a large book called the "Record of New Males," which is kept by Yu Kung T'ang's business manager. (The book contains the baby's personal name or *ming*, his father's and grandfather's names, his mother's surname, his mother's father's lineage and village, plus the exact time of birth.) Needless to say, the book is guarded very jealously by the Teng; entries can be cited as legal proof of lineage membership in property disputes.

After the names of new males have been recorded, a raw pig is divided, and shares are given to each infant. Receiving a share of pork and 10 Hong Kong dollars (HK$10) in cash (or about $2.20, in U.S. currency) "from the ancestors," as the villagers put it, marks the boy's membership in the lineage. Throughout a man's life this acceptance of pork and money reaffirms his ties to the lineage and to the ancestors. The proper way of asking whether a person belongs to a particular lineage or segment is to inquire, "Do you have a share?" (Cantonese: *Neih yauh mouh fan a*?). The division of sacrificial pork is scrupulously even-handed; even the pig's tail and ears are divided into as many pieces as there are new males. Although the emphasis in this pork division is on equality, the infants

Lineage organization and ideology

are differentiated according to age. The first boy born in the previous year has the largest lantern, and his father is expected to bear the responsibility for the practical organization of the ritual.

During the second lunar month, the Spring Rites are held in Yu Kung T'ang (this set of rites is again repeated in the autumn). In contrast to *k'ai teng*, these are the most formal of all the lineage rituals held in the hall. All elders try to attend this ceremony, which is conducted with a precision that is generally lacking in most village rituals. During this ritual elders stand in generational rows near the interior screens that mark off the hall's altar area. The oldest man in the most senior generation, the lineage master, actually makes the offerings to the ancestors, while the rows of elders look on. After the master has presented the offerings, each elder comes forward, bows three times before the altar, and pours out cups of wine to the ancestors. A record (or *chi wen*) is read for the benefit of the ancestors, informing them of the lineage's growth and general well-being. The ritual ends with the division of raw pigs. In 1978, 4 pigs, purchased out of Yu Kung T'ang's funds, were divided among 84 participating elders. These pork shares are then taken home and consumed without further ceremony. It is in the Spring Rites that the distinction between benefactors' descendants and ordinary members is most forcefully made. The benefactors' descendants each receive an extra share of pork. The rental income from lineage lands is no longer distributed, but in the past the descendants of benefactors were also entitled to a larger share of this income. Again the themes of equality and inequality, of unity and separation, are expressed.

Yu Kung T'ang is not only the ritual center of the lineage; it also plays an important role in the life of the entire community. A number of secular celebrations are held in the first of the hall's two courtyards – well away from the ancestral altar, it should be noted. Lineage members may host banquets celebrating the marriage of a son or the birth of a grandson in the hall. The importance of Yu Kung T'ang as a community center is dramatically highlighted by one community event that is held each New Year season (on the fifteenth of the first lunar month). This is a community-based (as opposed to lineage-based) division of pork in which men, women, and children pay a small fee and receive a few ounces of pork and dried duck. The fathers of the previous year's new males organize this community ritual, which is a very lighthearted affair. Even resident outsiders (usually shopkeepers) and unmarried Teng daughters are allowed to participate. When I moved into the village, one of the first things people mentioned was that I must be certain not to miss this colossal pork division. Even I, they said, could participate and have a share. The sight of row upon row of neat little piles of pork and duck (in 1978 there were 2,297 shares in all) is an image that is dear to the heart of every Ha Tsuen resident. Nearly everyone in the community turns out to witness and participate in this division. Shareholders' names are read out from a roll of red paper over 100 feet long; it is considered bad luck not to be mentioned, and parents of emigrant sons make sure that those

Inequality among brothers

who are not able to attend are included on the list. This is the only occasion in which Yu Kung T'ang plays host to an entire community, Teng and non-Teng alike.

Until the 1950s, Yu Kung T'ang was used as a school for lineage boys, and it has always been a gathering spot for lineage men. Men still discuss lineage and community affairs in the hall, and disputes are sometimes settled there as well (see Chapter 5). Although it is easy to see that Yu Kung T'ang is a powerful symbol of unity, we must not lose sight of the fact that it also expresses division and inequality. The selection of hall tablets and the distribution of pork at the Spring and Autumn Rites highlight the differences that exist among lineage members, differences that are ultimately based on an unequal access to wealth.

The formation of estates

The Teng lineage is made up of more than 80 segments (or corporate estates, called *tsu* and *t'ang*)[2] of varying size and significance. Some are very wealthy and powerful, but others are of little relevance even to their own members. Rivalries between the major segments are sometimes fierce and in some cases have lasted for centuries. I have heard Teng elders talk about intersegment disputes as if they had happened yesterday, only to learn later that they were referring to some slight or incident that occurred over 200 years ago.

In Ha Tsuen, segments are formed around an ancestor whose personal property (or the property of his descendants) was placed in a corporate estate. The rental income from this property pays for the offerings to the ancestor and for the maintenance of his grave; any funds left over are divided each year among the surviving descendants. Estates, villagers say, honor the ancestors, but there is little doubt that they also compensate the living.

In Chapter 2 I noted that in Chinese lineages there is no expectation that two brothers will become the foci of two different segments. It is the ownership and transferal of property through inheritance that mark off one man and his descendants from their agnates. Without property there can be no estates or hall tablets, and without estates and tablets the deceased cannot become a lineage ancestor. In her book *The Cult of the Dead in a Chinese Village*, Emily Ahern points out that among the Chinese ancestor worship is not simply a matter of obligations among agnates created by descent (1973:154). Ahern stresses the vital role that the inheritance of property plays in obligating the living to worship the dead. According to Ahern, it is only when the dead leave property that the

2 The term *t'ang*, is should be noted, has a variety of meanings. For example, it can refer to an estate, a corporation of shareholders, or a building (a hall or temple).

Lineage organization and ideology

living are unquestionably bound to their ancestors.[3] "In every other situation," Ahern writes, "there is room for interpretation, contention, and debate" (155).

Maurice Freedman, writing about lineage organization in southeastern China, observes that ancestral estates are formed when a new group (usually brothers) divides off from a larger group. According to Freedman, agnates form new ancestral estates in an attempt to differentiate themselves from their fellow kinsmen. In this way the localized lineage grows asymmetrically by a process of segmentation (Freedman 1958:47–50, 1974), and new localized lineages may be formed by fission.[4] However, as outlined in Chapter 2, evidence from Ha Tsuen clearly shows that lineages and segments can also develop by a process of aggregation or fusion. Such lineages are formed by aggregating units that were once separate and distinct. Estates formed by segmentation emphasize separation and distinctiveness, while those formed by a process of aggregation place more stress on unity.

Estates formed by a process of segmentation normally incorporate the focal ancestor's personal property soon after his death. The ancestor's descendants all have shares in this estate. In segments formed by fusion, men pool their resources and choose a common ancestor in whose honor they can form their estate. Shareholders include only the descendants of those men who provided funds to form the estate. Those who can trace descent from the focal ancestor have no automatic right to membership unless they are also shareholders. This, it will be recalled, is the way that Yu Kung T'ang was formed in 1751.

Although Yu Kung T'ang is the most important estate formed by fusion among the Ha Tsuen Teng, it is by no means the only one. Another such estate is focused on a fourteenth-generation ancestor called Teng Fei-wu, who lived during the seventeenth century (see Figure 2). According to one of Fei-wu's descendants, this estate was established in the 1930s by a group of about 100 men who all trace descent from Fei-wu. Each descendant was asked to contribute a specific amount of rice, which was then converted to cash and used to purchase land. The rental income from this property underwrites the expenses of worshiping Fei-wu. Members of the estate pointed out that one line of Fei-wu's descendants refused to contribute toward setting up the estate. They therefore have no share in this particular estate and do not participate in the group ancestral rites dedicated to Fei-wu.

In considering this example it is important to understand why an estate was formed at the fourteenth-generation level and why Fei-wu became the focus. When asked, the villagers themselves give only religious reasons for their de-

---

3 In a discussion of ancestor worship and inheritance in two West African societies, Jack Goody emphasizes the obligation that the transmission of property creates between ancestor and descendant (Goody 1962:399–404).
4 Freedman distinguishes segmentation, which he argues is a process of internal division within a lineage, from fission, which, according to him, involves the formation of a new, independent unit (1966a:27–8).

Inequality among brothers

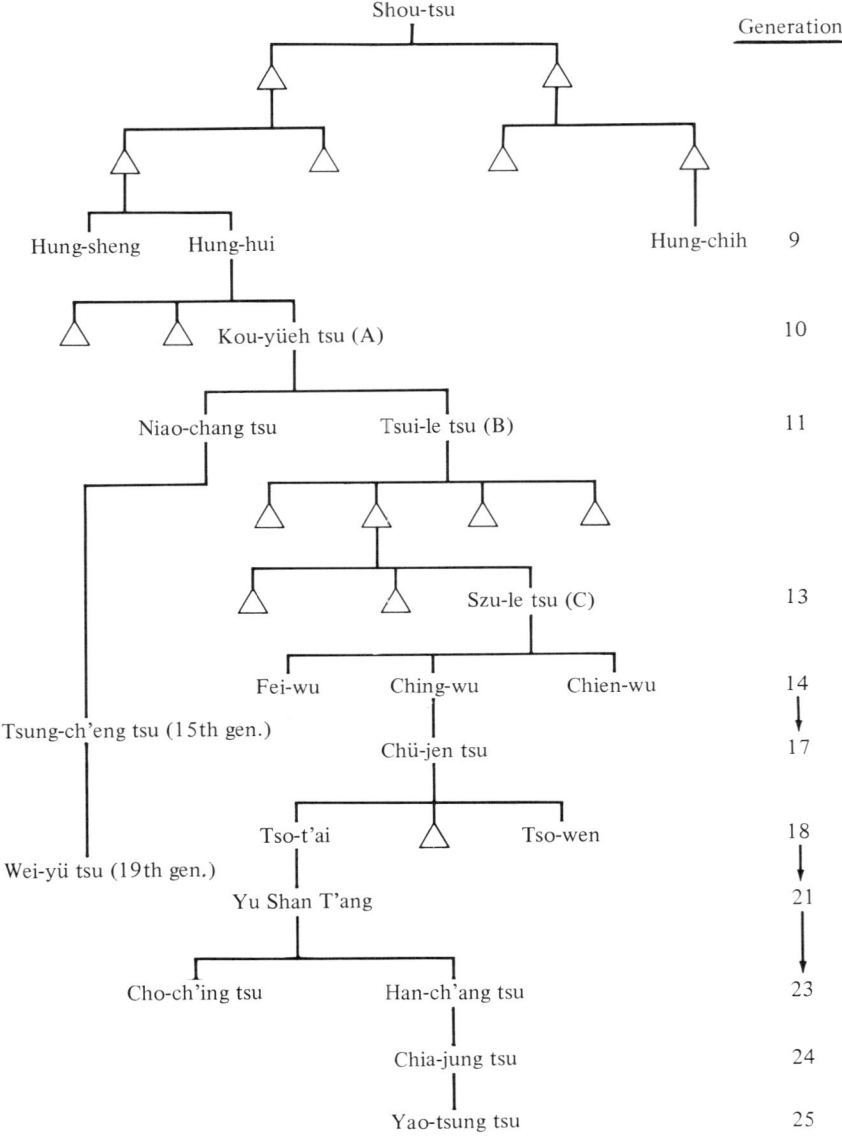

Figure 2. Outline of major segments in the Teng lineage.

Lineage organization and ideology

cision to form an estate: "We wanted to show our respect for Teng Fei-wu," they say. An examination of the segmentary system of the Teng lineage, however, gives an important clue as to why this particular ancestor and not others was chosen (see Figure 2). Kou-yüeh *tsu* (generation 10, *A* on Figure 2), Tsui-le *tsu* (*B*) and Szu-le *tsu* (*C*) are among the wealthiest ancestral estates in the lineage (in 1905, according to the Land Records, their combined holdings were over 62 acres of good rice land). These estates are closely linked, and in recent years a single accountant has served all three estates.[5] The ancestor Szu-le had three sons, and from the middle son, Ching-wu, are descended the wealthiest families in the entire lineage (the landlord-merchants of San Wai; see Chapter 4). The fact that the descendants of Ching-wu are rich and are themselves organized into a number of wealthy estates gives them great economic and political power in the community. They tend to speak with a unified voice when decisions are made about the running of the three estates. Their control over segment resources is informal, but that does not make it any less effective. One way in which Szu-le's unorganized descendants could redress this imbalance was for them to form an estate. In this case, it appears that men living in the 1930s went back over 300 years to find an ancestor around whom they could rally in order to compete with their wealthier kinsmen.

It is interesting to note that those descendants of Szu-le who are not organized into an estate (the descendants of Chien-wu) are among the least prosperous families in Ha Tsuen. In fact, it is they who live in the poorest section of San Wai. They have no effective voice in running Szu-le *tsu* and certainly have no say in administering any of the larger estates in which they have an interest. Because they were poor, unorganized, and largely illiterate (until recently, that is), they have had little control over the properties and funds of the larger estates to which they belong. Of course, even after the formation of an estate, Fei-wu's descendants are still at some disadvantage vis-à-vis the wealthier Ching-wu branch. Nevertheless, their unification into an estate does give them more cohesion and visibility than the descendants of Chien-wu. During my stay in the village a member of Fei-wu's estate was serving as accountant for all three of the larger estates (that is, for Kou-yüeh *tsu*, Szu-le *tsu*, and Tsui-le *tsu*).

Obviously, the process of forming estates by fusion or aggregation constitutes an important organizational tool in the hands of the unorganized. The pooling of resources and the creation of an ancestral estate is one method of counterbalancing the political power of the few. It allows a group of men to speak with one voice and makes it possible for them to unify for cooperative action. How-

---

5 Each of these estates has a different manager, who usually serves for life. In recent years, a single accountant who serves a one- or two-year term has taken over the accounts of the three estates. The accountant looks after the financial details of the estate; the manager is legally responsible for the estate's activities and selects the tenants who farm estate land.

Inequality among brothers

ever, it must not be imagined that only the poor formed estates by fusion. In fact, one of Ha Tsuen's wealthiest estates, Yu Shan T'ang (see Figure 2) was established in this way. The existence of a corporate estate is important, but it is not in itself enough to make the members of that estate powerful. To be effective an estate must have substantial lands to rent out, for these lands provide both a supplement to estate members' income and a loyal following in the form of tenants.

We have discussed the formation of estates by aggregation or fusion. What about other processes of estate formation? Many estates in Ha Tsuen were formed by a straightforward process of segmentation. These estates are usually formed around the personal property of the focal ancestor. Let us assume that a man, X, dies leaving 40 acres of land to his two sons, Y and Z. These sons may each take 15 acres and place the remaining 10 acres in an ancestral estate (a corporation) named in honor of their father. The 10 acres are then registered in the land records under the title of "X *tsu.*" Initially some funds from the corporate estate may be used to construct a brick tomb for their father's remains. Each year part of the proceeds from the estate pays for the cost of a sacrifice at the grave. The remaining income is then divided in half, each brother taking his share. It is possible that the brothers may share the management of the property or, more likely, that the position of manager will rotate between the two brothers. If they decide to manage the estate in turn, one brother, after paying the expenses of grave worship, may be given sole use of the estate's remaining income for a year. At this stage, management of the estate is relatively straightforward. However, as the number of descendants increases, problems often arise. One brother (Y) may have six sons and the other (Z) one son. According to the local custom of *per stirpes* division, therefore, the six sons of Y share among themselves one-half of the estate's income, whereas their cousin, the only son of Z, receives the other half. The estate at this point has been divided into two sections, or what the Teng call *fang* ("branches" or "sections"). Over time this inequality may become more pronounced, with perhaps a handful of men sharing one-half of the estate's income and dozens or even hundreds sharing the other half. In this situation there may be pressure from the larger group to change the basis of division from a *per stirpes* system (based on *fang* divisions) to a per capita one. There is, in fact, a famous court case regarding just such a dispute among the Teng of Ping Shan (Potter 1968:110–11). The internal organization of estates formed by segmentation and fusion are similar, although the latter usually maintain per capita divisions. This is particularly true of those estates like Yu Kung T'ang that do not have a focal ancestor.

Like lineage ritual, estate formation mirrors the two sides of the lineage. In estates like Yu Kung T'ang or that of Fei-wu, the emphasis is on unity and the cooperative pooling of resources; however, estates formed by segmentation tend to emphasize the separation of agnates. Of course both types of estates isolate a discrete group of agnates, but whereas one does this through unifying kinsmen

Lineage organization and ideology

and aggregating resources, the other does it by separation. Both forms are, of course, based on wealth, and both ensure their focal ancestors a kind of immortality. In both types of estates, the income from corporately owned property pays for an annual rite at the ancestor's grave.

The Chinese ancestor survives only so long as he is worshiped, and he is worshiped only so long as "his" estate produces an annual income. In the following section I relate estate formation to the system of ancestor worship among the Teng. The theme of economic and social inequality is nowhere more evident than in the Chinese cult of the dead.

The cult of the dead

The cult of the dead is at the very core of the Chinese system of descent, and therefore it must be considered if we are to understand the underlying principles upon which the lineage is based. The living and the dead are bound to each other by reciprocal ties (on this point, see also Ahern 1973:91, 161; J. Watson 1982b). The living provide sacrifices to the dead and thereby immortalize them, while the ancestors in their graves provide worldly benefits for their descendants. The bonds of reciprocity are, however, rather one-sided. The ancestors are more fully dependent on their descendants than the descendants are on the ancestors. The ancestors must be cared for by the living if they are to survive as individual spirits in the afterlife. Descendants who neglect their ancestors run the risk of losing the geomantic advantages that accrue from a well-placed ancestral grave. But, the ancestor's retribution is generally not thought to be life threatening, although it can be harmful to the prosperity of living descendants. The belief that the dead can affect the living is largely tied to the cosmological system that the Chinese call *feng-shui* (lit. "wind and water") often translated as "geomancy."

According to Chinese eschatology, the dead have not one soul or aspect but many (Freedman 1958:86; Jordan 1972: 31–2). In the New Territories the treatment of the dead implies a threefold division of the soul; one aspect of the soul can be found in the grave, one in the ancestral tablet, and the third in the underworld. Immediately after death the spirit of the deceased remains close to the living. The dead are very dangerous during this period, and many of the mortuary rites that are performed by Taoist priests and Buddhist nuns are concerned with the safe separation of the soul from the realm of the living. Prior to burial the deceased is given constant attention and helped along on the journey to the underworld. The soul must be equipped with money and food so that it can survive and, most important, so that it can bribe its way through the more unpleasant aspects of hell. The Chinese conception of hell is a mirror of their conception of human society (Ahern 1981; A. Wolf 1974:145); it is a world in which the bribery of authorities is often a key to success. The funeral, burial, and end-of-mourning rites are primarily concerned with the soul's wanderings

Inequality among brothers

and difficulties in hell. However, in time this aspect of the soul declines in significance as it recedes from the world of the living.

In Ha Tsuen the deceased is first buried in an unmarked, hastily chosen grave in the hills behind the village. Usually the dead are buried within 24 hours of death. At this stage little attention is given to the choice of burial site because it is assumed that this is not the permanent resting place. On the one-hundredth day after death the deceased's soul is incorporated into the collective ancestral tablet of the household, the so-called domestic tablet. This ceremony is also conducted by a Taoist priest. In Ha Tsuen, households do not keep individual tablets for each ancestor, as in the hall; rather the names of a family's immediate ancestors are written on a large sheet of red paper that is displayed on the household's "spirit altar" (*shen t'ai*). After each death the paper is changed: the names of the household's most distant ancestors are gradually deleted and new ones inserted in their place. Most households list only five generations of ancestors on their domestic altars. Although most ancestors cease to be part of the domestic ancestral cult after five generations, they can escape extinction by having a tablet placed in an ancestral hall or by becoming the focus of a corporate estate or segment within the lineage.

Southern Chinese, including of course the Cantonese, practice a system of burial in three stages. After the deceased has been buried for a period of approximately seven years the remains are exhumed, and the bones are cleaned by a mortuary specialist. These bones are then put into a large pottery urn, referred to as a "golden pagoda" (*chin t'a*). In Ha Tsuen this urn is placed in the hills behind the village but not reburied, although it may be partially surrounded with earth so that it is secured. Later – perhaps decades or even centuries later – the bones may be placed in a permanent brick or stone tomb. The tomb is marked by a stone inscription giving the name of the deceased and date of death. Sometimes a husband and his wife or wives are buried in the same tomb. It is important to emphasize that not all people go through the three stages of interment. In fact, very few achieve the final stage of a marked tomb. The earthen graves or bone urns of most people are visited only as long as kinsmen remember their locations. Over the years and generations these places of interment that have no permanent markers may be forgotten. Many ancestors are "lost" in this way. As Maurice Freedman points out, "The humble dead . . . never reach a final grave, their bones being left to lie in the urns which, in great numbers, can be seen to dot the New Territories landscape, at the end of their career being toppled, split and desolate" (1966a:121).

For the Teng, mortuary rites are often a very expensive proposition. In 1978 a funeral might cost as much as $2,000, about half of a factory worker's annual income. In order to prepare for this expense, some villagers join funeral associations, which operate as a kind of savings bank. Over the years members invest small sums of money, some of which will eventually be used to defray their

Lineage organization and ideology

own funeral expenses. These associations also guarantee that a respectable number of mourners will be present at a member's funeral, and that the mortuary rites will be properly carried out. Both people with and without heirs join these funeral associations, which, incidentally, operate in present-day Ha Tsuen much as they did in the past.

In Ha Tsuen, death in old age is not a topic from which people shrink. Old people often buy their own coffins, storing them under their beds until they are needed. The material preparation for death is a topic of everyday conversation, especially among older women. In fact, some of them positively delight in telling people about the quality of their coffins and the manner in which they are dispersing possessions as they prepare for their own demise. If the mortuary rites are properly conducted, if one has a natural death, and if one has a male heir, a Teng can expect to become a respected ancestor. However, although many achieve the status of ancestor for a time, few attain the kind of immortality they seek. Eventually most ancestors are lost; their names are taken off the domestic tablets, and their graves are forgotten. What saves an ancestor from such an ignominious end?

The deceased's chances of "survival" are greatly increased if he has left enough property to form an estate in his name. With an estate the ancestor's continued "existence" no longer depends so completely on the vagaries of human memory or emotion. There is little doubt that the wealthy have a better chance of attaining immortality than do the poor. It is, of course, possible that descendants may form an estate in honor of an ancestor who is long dead (as with Fei-wu); however, such events are rare and require both resources and organizational skill.

In 1905 there were, according to the colonial land records, 82 ancestral estates in Ha Tsuen. These estates account for about 50 percent of the land owned by the Teng in Ha Tsuen *hsiang*. The largest estates incorporate up to 40 acres of choice rice land. It may be asked why people allow precious land to be tied up in this way. What do the living gain by forming ancestral estates? There is, of course, great prestige attached to creating estates. The descendants are acting in a highly praiseworthy and filial manner, for they are making their ancestor immortal. By honoring their ancestor in this way, they are also separating themselves from their fellow agnates and reserving to themselves alone the often considerable supernatural, economic, and political advantages that membership in an ancestral estate entail. It is also important to emphasize that the proceeds from an estate formed by incorporating the ancestor's personal property, excluding the cost of ritual observances, are not lost to the ancestor's immediate descendants. In the first generation, each son's personal share may not differ appreciably from what it would have been had no estate been established. As for estates like Yu Kung T'ang, the cost to each contributor is usually not great, while the prestige and political benefits that accrue are often considerable. The

Inequality among brothers

political and economic aspects of ancestral estates are given further attention in later chapters. Here I wish to call attention to the values and ideas that underlie estate formation.

The ancestor in his grave is at the heart of a religious and cosmological system that the Chinese have believed in, or at least honored, for millennia (see Freedman 1966a:118–54). According to Stephan Feuchtwang, the term that the Chinese use for this cosmological system, *feng shui* "stands for the power of the natural environment, the wind and the airs of the mountains and hills; the streams and the rain; and much more than that: the composite influence of the natural processes ... By placing oneself well in the environment *feng-shui* will bring good fortune" (1974:2). The link between the ancestor in his grave and his descendants is a strong and consequential one. The ancestor's bones are the conductors of the forces of nature. The proper placement of these bones in the landscape has direct consequences for the worldly success or failure of descendants. The grave (or tomb) must be located so that the ancestral bones can partake of the efficacious constellation of "wind and water" in the local environment, and so link the living to these natural forces (cf. J. Watson 1982b).

To the Teng the hills around their village are intimately known. The major burial sites, of which there are dozens, all have geomantic names that evoke for the villagers the power and meaning of the site. For example, one site is called Jade Woman's Hall and another is known as Sleeping Tiger by the Stream. Although villagers enjoy passing the time in discussions about the *feng shui* of their area and many, in fact, seem quite knowledgeable about the local arrangements of "wind and water," they do not trust themselves with the important task of siting their own ancestor's grave. For this, a "wind and water gentleman" (*feng shui hsien sheng*) is employed. These specialists receive large fees for locating graves and buildings. The construction of a tomb is an expensive affair. One small tomb that was built during my stay in Ha Tsuen cost over $2,000 (this figure includes the geomancer's fee, which was $800). If the ancestor has left enough property for a tomb plus the geomancer's fee and regular offerings, he will be among the few who survive beyond the four or five generations that most ancestors enjoy. And, if his descendants are careful in their treatment of his bones, they can expect to achieve worldly success.

The graves of those who are the focus of ancestral estates are visited each fall in the ninth lunar month (this ritual is called *chung yang*). In Ha Tsuen these grave rites go on for nearly two weeks, and they are much enjoyed by the Teng. Everyday one sees groups of men trooping off to the graves in the nearby hills accompanied by one or two young men whose job it is to carry the offerings of pigs and other food up the steep paths. As soon as they arrive at their destination the elders don their long silk gowns and kneel before the grave while a report (or *chi wen*) is read to the ancestor, informing him of the year's events. After the ancestor has "savored" the essence of the offerings, the segment members

Lineage organization and ideology

divide the pig offering. Each man may carry his pork share home, or the group of worshipers may find a scenic spot where they cook the pork over an open fire. Thus the day may end in a picnic at which old men spend the afternoon admiring the beautiful siting of their ancestor's grave and comment disparagingly on the grave sites of their neighbors.

The *chung yang* festival reaches a crescendo in a series of rites at the graves of the first Teng to settle in Kwangtung's Hsin-an County. The Ha Tsuen Teng share these ancestors with their agnates from other Teng villages (Kam Tin, Ping Shan, Lung Yeuk Tao, Tai Po Tao, and a few smaller Teng communities). The ceremonies at such major graves are elaborate and may involve hundreds of elders from many different communities. On these occasions the large brick tombs of the major ancestors are decorated with banks of potted flowers and beautifully arranged food offerings. In 1977 the Teng offered eight pigs to their founding ancestor, Fu-hsieh. These pigs were divided at the grave site, and each Teng in attendance took home a portion of the sacrifice. It is believed that the pigs offered at a grave absorb some of the power of the grave site by association with the tomb's *feng shui* (see J. Watson 1982b), and by sharing in this offering one is in touch not only with one's ancestor but also with the power of the grave site itself.

The ancestor in his tomb is the visible focus of lineage segments in Ha Tsuen. But the tomb does not ensure the ancestor's immortality. To achieve immortality the ancestor must be nourished by the living, and to be nourished he must become the focus of a continuing group of worshipers with a recognized and institutionalized economic base, usually in the form of land. Just as hall-based rituals reflect two conflicting principles of organization, so too do grave rites. In the cult of the dead, one principle celebrates unity (grave worship unites a group of agnates), and another emphasizes division (the grave separates agnates into discrete resource-holding corporations). Ancestors represent fraternal unity, while at the same time they remain very much part of a system of economic and social inequality.

In discussing internal lineage organization, Maurice Freedman makes the important point that many of the jural elements that one finds in African lineages are missing in China. For example, Chinese patrilineages do not have a senior line, nor do lineage or genealogical principles determine positions of economic or political importance. Social status, power, and authority are given to men on a nonkinship basis, and there is no particular kin-ascribed status that conflicts with this. It should also be remembered that one's status and authority in a lineage community like that of the Ha Tsuen Teng did not depend on age alone. Authority was always linked to one's position in the wider political and economic system. As Freedman points out, one of the major keys to understanding the internal organization and external relations of the Chinese patrilineage is to appreciate the interlocking of lineage elites and the national bureaucracy

Inequality among brothers

(1958:138). Leadership in the lineage rested not on principles of age or genealogy or agnation but on wealth, power, and status gained in the world outside the lineage.

What seems to be a conflict of principles in the Chinese lineage may be seen at another level as different solutions to two different problems. It is important that the lineage be presented as a unified corporation to the outside world and, perhaps even more important, to lineage members themselves. Nevertheless, the lineage existed in a highly stratified society. In order to survive, lineages required literate and sophisticated leaders who moved easily in business and government circles, men who could act as mediators with the regional and national elite. And yet the economic and political integrity of the lineage depended on the support, often in a physical sense, of all members, irrespective of wealth or class. There is little doubt that the egalitarian ideology of the lineage plays an important role in bridging the gap between rich and poor.

4
Economic organization: the land and the market

This chapter and the next are concerned with the structure of economic and political relations in Ha Tsuen during the late nineteenth and early twentieth centuries. Unfortunately the century that followed the formation of the Teng lineage in 1751 is not well documented for Ha Tsuen. However, beginning in the 1860s and 1870s more and better information is available. Local histories, government records, architectural evidence, and informants' accounts combine to give a fairly detailed picture of Ha Tsuen from the 1860s to the Japanese occupation in 1941. Most of the following discussion will therefore relate to those decades, although where possible I will include information on the earlier period.

In the first section of this chapter the patterns of landownership and the livelihoods of Ha Tsuen's people are discussed. Until the 1960s, when the Teng began to take up factory jobs, most villagers made their living from the land. Rates of landownership and tenure arrangements therefore reveal a great deal about the nature of economic relations among the Teng. The second section is concerned with the development and eventual decline of Ha Tsuen's market. The history of this market is closely intertwined with the history of Ha Tsuen's landlord-merchant class during the nineteenth and twentieth centuries. In the last part of this chapter the economic activities of one of the wealthiest landlord-merchant families in Ha Tsuen are explored in detail.

Land tenure during the nineteenth century

For most of Ha Tsuen's history, land has been an essential resource. Land tied Teng tenant to Teng landlord, and the lineage's propertied estates formed the basis of powerful groups. Until recently, landownership was the key to local class relations; control over land was crucial to the success of the landlord-merchant class. In stressing the importance of landownership, there is, of course, a risk that the nonagricultural pursuits of Ha Tsuen villagers may be ignored. Later in this chapter we will see that money lending, manufacturing, mercantile activity, and fishing played an important role in the local economy. However,

Inequality among brothers

if we are to have any understanding of economic and social relations in Ha Tsuen, we must first turn to the system of land tenure.

Unfortunately it is not possible to determine with any great accuracy the pattern of landholding among the Teng prior to the British takeover of southern Hsin-an in 1899. Imperial Chinese land records were notoriously inaccurate. According to Stewart Lockhart, one of the first British officials to investigate the New Territories, half the area's agricultural land had never been registered with the Chinese government (Lockhart 1899:540). Apparently many local residents had managed to avoid paying substantial amounts of land taxes for generations. All of this was to change, however, when, soon after the British took control of the area, the new administration began a massive land registration program that was completed in 1905.

Although there is no way of determining the exact distribution of agricultural land before the British takeover, the available evidence does suggest that Hsin-an had high rates of tenancy during the late Ch'ing dynasty. In a discussion of the agricultural economy of Hsin-an during the eighteenth and nineteenth centuries, John Kamm argues that most farmers were tenants. Kamm writes: "In general, ownership of productive resources (agricultural fields, fishing grounds, oyster beds, quarries, and salt pans) were concentrated in the hands of landlords who leased them to tenants ... In short, Hsin-an during the Ch'ing was essentially a tenant economy" (1977:56).

Tenure arrangements in the pre-British era were extremely complex. There were, in fact, two or perhaps three systems of land tenure operating at the same time (for a general discussion of land tenure in the New Territories, see Wickberg 1981a; J. Watson 1977). As noted in Chapter 2, by the mid–nineteenth century and probably earlier, the Teng controlled, either in the form of ancestral estates or as private landowners, most of the land in Ha Tsuen *hsiang*. What did this control entail? There is little doubt that the Teng had full title to a large portion of the land they controlled. That is, they had written proof of ownership. However, it appears that the Teng did not have title deed to all of the land from which they extracted rent. Their claims to this land had no legal standing, and yet because of their power in the region they were able to enforce "rent collections." By the early 1800s eight non-Teng villages were established in Ha Tsuen *hsiang* (see Gazetteer 1819:94), and by 1900 there were 14 of these communities. Because the Teng farmed the best land, many of these newcomers had to settle in agricultural fringe areas where land was hilly and subject to salt water flooding. It is over this land controlled by the Teng but farmed by non-Teng that claims were often substantiated not by legal ownership but by coercion.

Prior to the British takeover, wealthy men from dominant lineages claimed the right to collect rents or taxes from large areas of land in southern Hsin-an. As the British were to learn in 1905, the question of land taxes is not an easy problem to unravel. A great deal of land was unregistered, and therefore the "taxes" that were collected did not go to the government but were pocketed by

Economic organization

the "tax collectors" (sometimes called "taxlords") themselves. In an article on land tenure in the New Territories, Edgar Wickberg refers to these extractions as "protection money" and argues that this arrangement was not based on documented landownership but on the local balance of power (1981a:27).

When the British entered the scene in 1898, tenants claimed that they had been paying land taxes to members of the dominant lineages for generations. However, the men who collected the tenants' money maintained that this money was rent paid to them as landlords (see, e.g., Shepherd 1900:222). Lockhart writes:

> The greater part of the land claimed by ... [lineages] was never registered and, as a rule, it appears that no land tax was ever paid on this land to the Government. The cultivators, who have paid rent for years to the ... [lineages], in view of the fact that the land had not been registered, were afraid to dispute the rights of ownership, as they anticipated it would result in the land being resumed by Government, and they would then be deprived of their right of cultivation. (1900:19)

Not all so-called taxes were pocketed by the "landlords"; in some cases local men did act as genuine tax collectors. The Chinese government had a policy of farming out the right to collect taxes, and it was wealthy men of the area's dominant lineages who were usually successful in bidding for this right. G. N. Orme, a colonial official who dealt with land tenure in the early 1900s, provides a good description of the way in which many wealthy men gained their income: "Before the New Territory was taken over, many ... [*pen-ti*, or "native"] villages were living on their capital or 'squeezes' from their neighbours, and on pay received from the Government for collecting taxes" (1912:44). Stewart Lockhart, a contemporary of Orme, notes that four-fifths of the land taxes paid in the New Territories passed through the hands of intermediaries (1901:574).

Prior to the colonial period, rents were usually collected under the so-called perpetual lease or hereditary tenancy system. Lockhart notes in one of his reports that "a large proportion of the land is held on perpetual lease" (1901:576; see also Wickberg 1981a:25–6). The perpetual lease system (sometimes called permanent tenancy or "one-field, two-owners") was in fact common throughout large parts of southern China (Kamm 1977; Rawski 1972; J. Watson 1977; Wickberg 1981a, b). In this arrangement the "landlord" is often said to have ownership rights to the subsoil (or "earth bones," *ti ku*); for a specific sum he leased the rights of cultivation to another party. The latter had rights to the topsoil (or "earth skin," *ti p'i*). As long as the original leaseholder or his descendants continued to pay the fee required by the subsoil owner, the cultivator could then lease to others his rights to the topsoil. In this way long chains of sublessees might develop.

The yearly payments to the landlord (or subsoil owner) were often very low (Kamm 1977: 62; Hayes 1977:49–50), and with the perpetual lease the landlord had little control over what the tenant did with the land. He had to be content simply to collect his rent, which, once fixed, was seldom changed. As Kamm

Inequality among brothers

remarks, over the years the "cultivation value" of the land became separated from the "rent value" (60). Lockhart discusses this system as it related to southern Hsin-an and comments on the

> ignorance of the landlords regarding their own land. For generations landowners have been content to collect their rents without ever having taken the trouble to inquire into the land itself, which has been left entirely under the control of the tenants. These tenants have changed from time to time, subleased the land, sold the right of cultivation or mortgaged that right, without consulting the landowners, who were quite satisfied so long as the rent was regularly paid. (1900:255)

Aside from the "tax collection" and perpetual lease arrangements, there appears to have been a system of land tenure by short-term contract that gave the landlord more control over his land. The contract, which may have been either written or verbal, specified the rights and duties of each partner and of course laid down a specific period during which the arrangement would be valid (usually 3, 5, or 10 years). The landlord was free to change tenants at the end of the contract period. As with the perpetual lease, rent was often paid in kind.

Chen Han-seng, in a survey of Kwangtung landlord–peasant relations during the early twentieth century, reports that some counties operated both the perpetual lease and the short-term contract system of tenancy, but other counties had only contract arrangements (1936:51). Studies of Taiwan also suggest that during the nineteenth century both perpetual and contract tenancy were present. Edgar Wickberg notes that by 1900 the perpetual lease system "was becoming less common [in Taiwan] as a consequence of tenant competition" (1981b:216). As land became scarce and population increased, tenants were forced to compete for land. This competition led to the gradual demise of the perpetual-lease system in Taiwan and tipped the balance between landlord and tenant toward the landlord (on this point, see also Chen 1936:42–53). Whether a similar pattern can be established in southern Hsin-an remains to be seen. Unfortunately there is little published work on land tenure in this area.

Prior to 1905 the Teng of Ha Tsuen were involved in all three of the tenancy arrangements outlined above. However, there is no evidence to suggest that "tax collecting" was an important source of income for Ha Tsuen's landlord-merchants. How did the systems of tenancy described above work in Ha Tsuen *hsiang*? I would suggest – and this is an hypothesis to be tested rather than a statement of fact – that the short-term contract system was more likely to be found when both landlord and tenant were Teng and the perpetual-lease system when a Teng landlord rented his land to non-Teng tenants. This is supported by the work of J. L. Watson in the New Territories village of San Tin (1977). Watson suggests that the perpetual lease system, which he refers to as hereditary tenancy, played an important role in the relations between a dominant lineage and dependent neighbors. In this arrangement the tenants lived in satellite villages that were economically and politically dependent on the dominant lineage. The tenancy rights (earth skin) passed from father to son in the satellite villages.

Economic organization

Obviously not all satellite villagers had perpetual leases, nor did all Teng have short-term contracts; there was certainly some intermixing of the two. Nevertheless, we might expect to find that within the dominant lineages tenancy arrangements tended to be short-term and contractual, whereas relations that cut across lineage barriers were long-standing and much more likely to involve direct forms of coercion.

Lockhart emphasizes the powerlessness of the landlord in the perpetual lease system. However, there was no doubt some variation in the actual conduct of landlord–tenant relations under this system. When the land was distant from the landlord's residence or in cases in which the landlord simply wanted a steady income, Lockhart's description is probably accurate. However, when the land involved was near the landlord's own village, when competition over land was intense, and when tenants were not only economic dependants but also political subordinates, as was the case in Ha Tsuen, we might expect the landlord to exert considerable control over his land and his tenants. Clearly the perpetual lease system did have its harsh side.

British colonial land policy: 1905

The history of colonial land policy has yet to be written, but there is little doubt that the land registration of 1905 had a profound effect on the region's economic and political structure. As I have noted earlier in this chapter, prior to 1905 much of the land in southern Hsin-an was unregistered. In many cases landlords did not have a proper deed to their holdings, even though they had been collecting rents or taxes on them for generations. When, in 1905, colonial officials registered this heretofore unregistered land, they often established the cultivator as legal owner.

Lockhart explains how the land registration program was carried out:

A district is chosen and marked out by boundaries and a notification then calls upon all land-owners to present their claims to the Court before a given date. All lands claimed are surveyed and particulars of ownership entered on the demarcation books, while claimants are summoned to attend the Court where the proper forms are filled in for them by the clerical staff. After the last day for presenting claims all land unclaimed in the district is the property of the Crown. The claims themselves are sorted, undisputed ones being available for the rent roll, while those which are contested are set down for hearing. (1901:568)

Those who had legal proof of ownership (that is, those who held Chinese deeds of ownership called *hung ch'i*), need not fear that they would lose their land, the British claimed. However, in cases where both the landlord/taxlord and the cultivator/tenant claimed the same piece of land but neither had proof of ownership, the cultivator was usually proclaimed the owner.

Although the local elite did suffer some reverses during this period, the sit-

Inequality among brothers

uation was not as difficult as it may at first appear. According to Orme, some of the larger taxlords did receive compensation. Orme writes:

> On the recommendation of the Land Court, the Governor decided that 14 elders of the Northern District [which included Ha Tsuen and Kam Tin] should be compensated for certain "taxlord" rights claimed by them to have existed before the Convention [ceding the New Territories to the British], but not compatible with the principles of British administration, by the grant of 252.33 acres of Crown Land in the Northern District, to be selected by each "taxlord" in proportion to the value of the right claimed by him. (1912:46).

Landholding families in the New Territories claim that they lost large amounts of land in the 1905 registration (Potter 1968:100). Of course, their claims may be exaggerated, but there can be little doubt that this policy had the effect of curtailing some of the economic and political power of the larger landlords. In some cases whole islands and *hsiang* were taken out of the control of the old landlord-taxlord group and given over to the local cultivators (on this point see Blake 1981:30; Hayes 1977:50, 132).

How did the Ha Tsuen Teng fare under the British? I have already noted that "taxlordism" or "tax farming" was not as important to the Ha Tsuen Teng as it was to some Hsin-an residents. Nevertheless, Teng landlords and Teng estates did experience some losses. Two or three Ha Tsuen families claim to have lost lands located on Hong Kong Island and in the area that is now urban Kowloon at the hands of the British. According to J. L. Watson, who has conducted a study of Teng and non-Teng relations in Ha Tsuen *hsiang*, in 1905 Teng landlords lost control over large parcels of land near the satellite villages of Ngau Hom, Fung Kong Tsuen, and Sha Kong Wai. The colonial authorities registered this land in the name of those who cultivated it, namely the residents of satellite villages (personal communication).[1]

Although Teng landlords lost some land during this period, the British were not bent on a policy of radical land reform. Landowners were able to retain land to which they could show clear proof of ownership. The land figures that I discuss below show that Teng landlords continued to hold large amounts of land within the *hsiang*. Clearly the Teng did not lose all their land to their satellite tenants, but colonial land policy did weaken the Teng's control over their *hsiang* dependents. Colonial land policy did not, however, create a revolution in the *hsiang*'s political structure. Some powerful institutions continued to bolster the Teng position, and Teng landlords managed to keep their satellites in subordinate status until after the Japanese occupation. Only when changes in land policy

---

1 It is probable that Teng tenants did not fare as well as satellite villagers under the 1905 British land policy. Teng tenants usually farmed land near Ha Tsuen, land over which Teng landlords were likely to have clear proof of ownership. Under these circumstances landlord claims were recognized, and Teng farmers remained tenants.

Economic organization

were coupled with changes in local political and economic organization did the Teng hold over the *hsiang* begin to crack. In Chapters 5 and 8, the political implications of this new land policy are discussed in more detail.

Land tenure in Ha Tsuen after 1905

Land in the New Territories was officially divided into three classes, depending on the type of crops that it could support. On the basis of the 1905 land records, I estimate that about 60 percent of Teng-owned agricultural land (in Ha Tsuen *hsiang*) was of the high-yield, double-crop paddy variety (hereafter termed *first-class land*). About 15 percent was used for the production of a single crop of rice or vegetables (termed *second-class land*), and the remaining 25 percent consisted of hilly or brushy land on which secondary crops, sometimes pine or fruit trees, were planted (termed *third-class land*). A small portion of Ha Tsuen's land was tidal marsh, and in the past some of this was used for salt production. According to villagers' accounts, however, these salt pans have not been worked in recent times (cf. Lin 1967:138).

The 1905 land records show that whereas most Teng either owned small holdings or were landless, there were in the village a few private landlords with large holdings. Individually owned land was not, however, the only form of landholding. In fact, a large amount of the land in the Ha Tsuen area was corporately owned; in 1905 about half of the land owned by the Teng belonged to corporate ancestral estates.

In the time I had available during my year of fieldwork, it was not possible for me to collect all the land data available for Ha Tsuen. I therefore had to concentrate on certain aspects of the data. I collected data on the landholdings of all ancestral estates in Ha Tsuen for the year 1905. The data on private landownership are based on the land records for two of Ha Tsuen's hamlets. One, the hamlet of San Wai, was selected because it was the residence of nearly all of Ha Tsuen's large private landowners. The other hamlet, Sik Kong Wai, was chosen because it was the hamlet with which I was most familiar. Sik Kong Wai is broadly representative of Ha Tsuen hamlets in general – that is, with the exception of San Wai. I have the complete land records (1905) for the hamlet of Sik Kong Wai. In the case of San Wai, I have searched the records and noted every landholder who owned more than 5 acres of land. Both Sik Kong Wai and San Wai, which are about 200 yards apart, had over 200 households in 1978. It should be noted that the land data refers only to Teng-owned land in Ha Tsuen *hsiang*.

In 1905 the hamlet of San Wai had six major landowners, all of whom owned

Inequality among brothers

Table 1. *Landholdings in 1905, San Wai private landowners with over 5 acres*

Landlord	Total acres owned	Acres of first-class land owned
A	71.00	46.73
B	69.81	46.65
C	62.23	42.93
D	39.95	28.29
E	20.26	14.73
F	7.18	3.24
Total	270.43	182.57

over 5 acres of land[2] (see Table 1 for holdings of the six landlords). One of these landlords owned just over 7 acres, and the remainder each owned more than 20 acres; the largest holding was 71 acres. Altogether these six men owned 270.43 acres, of which 182.57 acres (or 68 percent) was first-class or double-crop paddy land; 49.82 acres (or 18 percent) was second-class land; and 38.04 acres (or 14 percent) was third-class land. Because the data I collected are restricted to holdings in Ha Tsuen *hsiang*, these figures do not provide a complete listing of all the land these men owned. Some of them certainly owned land in or near Yuen Long Market, and villagers told me that a few San Wai families owned land in the neighboring *hsiang* of Tuen Mun. However, this does not alter the basic patterns of landholding that we find in Ha Tsuen *hsiang*. I estimate that the Teng owned about 750 acres in Ha Tsuen *hsiang*[3] and on the basis of this figure I calculate that San Wai's six landlords owned 36 percent of Teng-owned land in the *hsiang*.

2 C. K. Yang defines landlords in the Canton delta village of Nanching as follows: "Measured against the local norm, those possessing over thirty *mou* (about five acres) constituted the landlord class" (1959b:40). Although this figure of 5 acres cannot be applied throughout southeastern China, it does provide a useful marker for dividing landlords from smallholders in the Canton delta (on this point, cf. Chen 1936:20–2; Wickberg 1981a:33; and on landlordism in general, see Hinton 1966:27, 623–26). Ha Tsuen landlords did not work the land they owned.

3 I arrive at this figure of 750 acres by adding the corporate holdings (377 acres) and the holdings of San Wai's large landholders (270 acres) together with an estimate of 100 acres of the private landholdings for the remainder of Ha Tsuen. Because I have complete figures for only the private landholdings for the hamlet of Sik Kong Wai (21.46 acres), this last figure in the equation is an estimate. Sik Kong Wai's pattern of landholding, I argue, is broadly representative of Ha Tsuen's other hamlets, with the exception of San Wai. Based on the Sik Kong Wai data and considering that Sik Kong Wai has a population considerably larger than most of Ha Tsuen's 10 other hamlets (only San Wai and Sik Kong Tsuen are larger), I estimate that these hamlets accounted for about 100 acres of privately owned land. When this is added to the 270 acres held by San Wai landlords and the corporate holdings of 377 acres, we arrive at a figure of 747 acres of Teng-owned land in Ha Tsuen *hsiang* in 1905.

Economic organization

Table 2. *Landholdings in core area in 1905, San Wai private landowners*

Landlord	Total acres owned	Total core area, acres owned (%)
A	71.00	28
B	69.81	28
C	62.23	60
D	39.95	43
E	20.26	62
F	7.18	72

San Wai landholders owned land throughout Ha Tsuen *hsiang* and not just in the "core area" surrounding the village. If Ha Tsuen's core area is defined by the land that is located within a half-mile radius of Ha Tsuen Market, we find an interesting geographical distribution of landholdings. Ha Tsuen's two largest landlords had only 28 pecent of their land located in the core area, whereas the remaining four landowners had from 43 percent to 72 percent of their holdings near the village (see Table 2). Assuming that the farther the fields were from Ha Tsuen, the more likely they were to be rented to non-Teng tenants, these figures suggest that Ha Tsuen's private landlords rented at least some portion of their land to non-Teng farmers. If this assumption is correct, the data on distribution of landholdings suggest that Ha Tsuen's two largest landowners had more of their land rented to non-Teng farmers than did smaller landowners.[4]

Land figures from one New Territories village are important, but their value is considerably increased if they are compared with land data from similar communities. Although there is little discussion of private landownership in the literature on the New Territories, we do have some information on two dominant lineages in the area. Jack Potter notes that in the 1960s the largest private landlord living in the Ping Shan hamlet of Hang Mei owned only 3.9 acres of land (1968:96). Hang Mei, according to Potter, is the home of many of Ping Shan's wealthiest families, and therefore if we are to find any large private landlords, we would expect to find them there. In the dominant lineage village of San Tin,

---

4 This finding seems to conflict with data from other parts of the New Territories that suggest that private or individual holdings were usually located near the owner's residence, whereas more distant holdings tended to be owned by lineage ancestral estates (Wickberg 1981a:38; Baker 1968:171). A survey of Ha Tsuen's corporate land shows that of the larger estates (10 acres and over), only one had nearly all its land outside of Ha Tsuen's core area (it should be noted that nearly all this land was either second- or third-class land). The remaining estates varied from a low of 30 percent in the core area to a high of 88 percent in the core area. Yu Kung T'ang had 43 percent of its holdings within the Ha Tsuen core.

Inequality among brothers

the largest private landholder in 1905 owned less than 17 acres.[5] Compared to these figures, Ha Tsuen, with its largest private landholding of 71 acres, appears to be unusual. There are, of course, differences among these three communities that might account for the disparity. San Tin has an unusual ecological situation in that most of its cultivated land is made up of reclaimed salt fields, and much of this was corporately exploited and corporately owned (J. Watson 1975b:31–8, 1977). Ping Shan has an even higher rate of corporate landownership than San Tin (for statistics, see the discussion of Potter's [1968] figures given later in this section). However, even if these differences are taken into account, the available material on New Territories private landholding does suggest that Ha Tsuen had substantial private landowners and as a consequence may have exhibited a more marked class structure than the dominant lineage villages of Ping Shan and San Tin. Why this should be the case is an interesting question, but it is one that must await further comparative data.

Large landowners (men who owned more than 5 acres), I was told by the Teng, did not farm their land themselves. They preferred to rent out their holdings in an arrangement that held few risks for the landlord, who provided nothing but land. Although Ha Tsuen's large landowners did not work the land they owned, they did continue to reside in the village. They were not absentee landlords. To my knowledge only one landlord maintained a regular residence outside Ha Tsuen during the early twentieth century. This man resided primarily in Yuen Long Old Market, but even he kept a house in San Wai where his two sons (by his principal wife) were both reared.

To assess the significance of private landownership among the Teng, it is essential to determine the rate of tenancy and the level of landholdings for Ha Tsuen's population as a whole. As a step in this direction, I collected and analyzed complete figures on landownership for the hamlet of Sik Kong Wai (in 1905). Significantly, not one of Sik Kong Wai's private landholders owned land outside of the core area surrounding Ha Tsuen. The land that they owned fell within easy walking distance of the hamlet. Because they had no holdings outside Ha Tsuen's core area, it is very unlikely that they owned any land outside the *hsiang* itself. We may assume therefore that these figures give an accurate account of all land owned by the residents of Sik Kong Wai.

Sik Kong Wai had only one private landholder who owned more than 5 acres

---

5 Data are from 1905 colonial land records from San Tin village. In a survey of the Pat Heung area in the New Territories, Edgar Wickberg reports that in 1905 the largest private landowner had 50 acres. Wickberg notes that this was a sizable holding by New Territories standards (1981a:33). Wickberg's findings are difficult to compare directly to Ha Tsuen because they are based on a survey of a number of communities and one does not know the extent of corporate holdings in the village where his largest private landowner lived. However, according to Wickberg (1981a:31), the Pat Heung area as a whole does not have as large a proportion of corporate holdings (35 percent for the entire area surveyed) as Ha Tsuen (with its 50 percent corporate holdings).

Economic organization

Table 3. *Sik Kong Wai private landholdings in 1905*

Size of holding (acres)	No. of owner households	Total acres	Acres of first-class land
Over 5.0	1	5.28	3.26
1.0–5.0	4	4.90	2.70
0.5–1.0	11	8.17	5.25
Under 0.5	16	3.11	2.91
Total	32	21.46	14.12

(for a breakdown of Sik Kong Wai landownership, see Table 3). This man owned 5.28 acres, of which 3.26 acres (or 62 percent) was first-class land. In all there are only 5 holdings in Sik Kong Wai of more than 1 acre (altogether these holdings amounted to 10.18 acres). In 1905 Sik Kong Wai had only 32 private landholdings (for purposes of this discussion, each joint ownership – 11 joint ownerships in all – is counted as 1 landholding household). These 32 holdings totaled 21.46 acres, of which 14.12 acres (or 66 percent) were first-class land. Eleven holdings consisted of from 0.5 acres to 1 acre, and the remaining 16 had less than 0.5 acres (with 6 of these owning less than 0.1 acres).

It is difficult to know with any certainty just how much land a Ha Tsuen family needed to survive in the late Ch'ing and Republican periods. The Canton delta village of Nanching, which C. K. Yang studied in the late 1940s, should, however, provide some indication. Yang found that the so-called middle peasants, or those operating farms of from 1 to 3.3 acres of land (including both owned and rented land), were usually able to meet the minimum expenses of a peasant family (1959b:41, 58). In a discussion of agriculture in Hong Kong, Charles Grant has suggested that in the 1950s a rice farmer required about 1.5 acres of arable land to make a living (1964:56), and Potter found that among the Ping Shan farms he surveyed in 1962, the average size was just under 1.8 acres (1968:65). Of course, these figures do not suggest that because most Sik Kong Wai villagers owned less than 1 acre they lived below the level of subsistence. Most farmers were able to rent land sufficient for their household's needs.

Although detailed records on landownership are available, it is far more difficult to determine the extent of tenancy and landlessness for Sik Kong Wai residents. Unfortunately there are no reliable population figures for 1905, nor is there any precise information on landlessness. However, while the 1905 cadastral survey was being conducted, the colonial government was also surveying the house lots of New Territories hamlets. The colonial survey contains a list of Sik Kong Wai houses by lot number and owner. According to these records, in 1905 there were 107 houses in Sik Kong Wai. If we assume that 1.5 of these houses

Inequality among brothers

represented 1 household,[6] we can then calculate that 39 households were landless (or that out of 71 households, 32 owned land). According to these calculations, 55 percent of Sik Kong Wai households owned no land whatsoever. Of course, this method of calculation can provide only an estimate of the extent of landlessness in Sik Kong Wai. Whatever the rate of landlessness, it is important to remember that even those Sik Kong Wai residents who owned land had very small holdings. In fact, 84 percent of these households owned less than 1 acre, and half owned less than 0.5 acres. If we use Grant's estimate that a rice farmer needed 1.5 acres of arable land to make a living, we find that out of 71 Sik Kong Wai households, 69 did not own the minimum land required. According to these calculations, 97 percent of Sik Kong Wai households would have been forced to rent some of the land they farmed. There is little doubt that most households in Sik Kong Wai were land poor.

Unfortunately there is not a great deal of data on landlessness in the Canton region during the first decades of the twentieth century (for a general discussion of land distribution in rural China, see Esherick 1981). What is available suggests that while Sik Kong Wai's rate of 55 percent may be higher than some communities, it is not improbably high. One of the few studies of prerevolutionary landholding patterns in southeastern China is Chen Han-seng's large survey made during the 1930s. In this study Chen calculates that in Kwangtung "nearly half of the peasant families are entirely landless" (1936:viii). John Lossing Buck, working at about the same time as Chen, reports that in the double-cropping rice area, which includes Kwangtung and large parts of three neighboring provinces, 28 percent of surveyed farmers were classified as tenants who owned none of the land they farmed (1937:196). However, in reporting on another survey in the same area, Buck notes that 46 percent had no land (196). In a study conducted 30 years later, Potter found that of 42 Ping Shan farmers he surveyed, 83.3 percent farmed only rented land, 11.9 percent owned part of their farms and rented the rest, while only 4.8 percent owned all of their farms (1968:80). Potter does not give any estimate of landlessness for Ping Shan, but his extremely high rate of tenancy suggests that considerable numbers of Ping Shan farmers were without land in the late 1950s and early 1960s. Of course in discussing Potter's figures we should keep in mind the fact that Ping Shan, as we have noted, has a particularly high rate of corporate landownership.

Although some communities in the region may have a lower rate of landlessness than Sik Kong Wai, they share with the Teng a common pattern of small holdings and extremely high rates of tenancy. Although authorities may

---

6 In the absence of census data, this figure of 1.5 dwellings per household is no more than a rough guide to the number of households in Sik Kong Wai in 1905. Some households may have owned 2 or 3 houses whereas others may have had only 1. In 1978, when villagers were much better off than they had been in the past (and therefore might have been expected to own more houses), the hamlet of Bao Wai had just under 2 houses per household.

Economic organization

disagree over the extent of landlessness in Kwangtung, there seems to be considerable agreement over the tremendous importance of tenancy in the area. It will be remembered that Kamm, in a study of Hsin-an's economy during the nineteenth century, states that Hsin-an was "essentially a tenant economy" (1977:56). Wickberg estimates that while most village households in the Pat Hueng area of the New Territories (a region near Kam Tin, see Map 2) owned some land in 1905, "90 percent or more of the households were *both* owners and tenants" (1981a:32). For the delta village of Nanching, C. K. Yang found that in the 1940s there were few landless families (20 landless families out of 230 families, or 8 percent; see 1959b:51), but he also says, "We did not encounter a single peasant who did not rent some land from others" (46; on estimates of tenancy in Canton delta, see also Wickberg 1981b:214). One obvious way to account for the high rates of landlessness in Ping Shan and Ha Tsuen is to remember that both communities have a high proportion of corporately owned land (93 percent [Potter 1968:96] and 50 percent, respectively) compared to the lower corporate rates of 35 percent for Pat Heung (Wickberg 1981a:31) and 6.2 percent for Nanching (C. K. Yang 1959b:42). When we consider that 50 percent of Teng-owned land was tied up in corporate estates and that a further 35 percent was in the hands of a few private landlords, it is not surprising to find a high rate of landlessness in Ha Tsuen. Of course it is important to remember that landlessness and small holdings do not necessarily indicate that Ha Tsuen's tenants were desperately poor. A person who rented land from his ancestral estates and from private landlords might be better off than a neighbor who owned an acre of land (see C. K. Yang 1959b:46–7).

The Sik Kong Wai statistics and data from other New Territories communities suggest that tenancy was nearly universal among local farmers. The figures that I examined indicate that there was a clear distinction between Ha Tsuen's landlords and tenants in terms of landownership. In later chapters we will see that landownership was not the only thing that separated Teng landlords from Teng tenants; there were social and cultural differences as well.

Tenure arrangements in Ha Tsuen were similar to those in other parts of Kwangtung. Informants who had been tenants before the Japanese occupation said that they paid their land rent in kind (see also Wickberg 1981a:35–6). Some villagers reported that they handed over a specific amount of rice to the landlord no matter how large or small their crop, although the rent requirement might be reduced during particularly bad years. Other informants said that their rents were calculated as a proportion of their harvested crop. A few maintained that the landlord took as much as 50 to 60 percent of their crop in rent, while others placed the figure at 30 to 40 percent. Wickberg, in his survey of Pat Hueng, writes of rents in 1905: "Typically, the level of rent was an amount of grain that approximated one-half of the year's yield of rice, paid in two installments" (1981a:36). The variations in rates of rent among the Teng may reflect the use of different tenure arrangements (long-term or short-term contracts or perpetual

Inequality among brothers

Table 4. *Land held by ancestral estates in 1905*

Size of holding (acres)	No. of estates	Total acres	Acres of first-class land
Over 20	6	184.27	98.85
10–20	6	85.65	48.45
5–10	7	57.19	30.28
1–5	13	24.57	17.72
Under 1	50	18.01	11.68
Total	82	369.69	206.98

Note: These calculations exclude a *tsu* that held 100.54 acres, of which 100.06 acres was third-class land (see Chapter 4, n. 7).

lease), or they may be due to the fact that men who rented from their own ancestral estates tended to pay lower rates. In any case, the Ha Tsuen figures are considerably higher than the overall Hsin-an rate quoted by Kamm, who calculated that during the nineteenth century 28 percent of the tenant's crop was paid in rent (1977:57). Whether this indicates an increase of rents during the first years of the twentieth century or a pattern of higher rates in the Ha Tsuen area remains an open question.

Villagers reported that they rented most of their land from Teng landlords who lived in San Wai or from Ha Tsuen's ancestral estates. Some local tenants also rented fields on the fringe of Ha Tsuen *hsiang*, in areas where the landlords were from Ping Shan or Yuen Long. In most cases, however, both landlord and tenant resided in Ha Tsuen.

According to the 1905 land records, the Ha Tsuen Teng held a total of 377.64 acres as corporately owned land.[7] Of this total, 7.95 acres belonged to hamlet or religious associations, and the remaining 369.69 acres were owned by ancestral estates. Of the estate land, 206.98 acres (or 56 percent) were classified as first-class land. I estimate that about 50 percent of the land owned by the Ha Tsuen Teng was incorporated into ancestral estates. This figure is in line with a sample survey of Yuen Long area villages, which found that 44 percent of the land was "lineage owned in 1905" (Brim 1970:34).[8] Ha Tsuen's rate is also comparable

7 This figure excluded a *tsu* that held 100.54 acres, of which 100.06 acres was third-class land. This *tsu* has been excluded from the calculation of corporate property because it is highly unusual. It is Ha Tsuen's only ancestral estate with a holding of over 2 acres whose acreage consists almost entirely of third-class land. All of the other major estates have a large proportion of first-class land (see Table 4). To include the holdings of this estate in my calculations of corporate property would, I believe, create a false impression of landowning patterns in Ha Tsuen.
8 I have already noted that Wickberg (1981a:31) gives a rate of 35 percent for "clan-owned" (presumably he refers to lineage-owned) land for the Pat Heung area. This figure is lower than that for the dominant lineages in the New Territories; the Pat Heung area is not noted for its powerful lineages.

Economic organization

with the figure of 52 percent corporate landownership that Baker gives for the Liao lineage of Sheung Shui (1968:171) and J. Watson's estimate of 65 percent for the Man lineage of San Tin (1975b:36). However, all these figures are much lower than that which Potter reports for Ping Shan. Potter states that in one of Ping Shan's eight hamlets (the wealthy hamlet of Hang Mei), a staggering 93 percent of the land is owned by ancestral estates (figures for 1960 [1968:96]). Perhaps one of the reasons Potter's figure is so much higher than those reported for other dominant lineages in the area is that Potter based his calculation on the wealthiest hamlet in Ping Shan, and the one that contains nearly all the community's large ancestral halls (in the land records ancestral estates are listed under the hamlet where their managers live). In surveys made of Kwangtung in the 1930s, Chen Han-seng (1936:34–5) calculates that public land made up about 35 percent of the total cultivated land. Compared to these figures, Ha Tsuen is not unique in its percentage of estate land. The variability in the rates of corporate landownership between the neighboring villages of Ping Shan and Ha Tsuen is significant, however, and this problem warrants further research.

The amount of land held by Ha Tsuen's ancestral estates varies a great deal, with the largest incorporating 40.96 acres and the smallest owning only 0.02 acres (of third-class land). Potter found a similar but more glaring pattern of difference in Ping Shan, where among 30 different estates 37 percent owned less than 1 acre, 50 percent owned from 1.1 to 15 acres, and the remaining estates each held more than 15 acres. The largest estate owned 178.4 acres of land (1968:97).

Ancestral estates were important sources of rental land throughout southeastern China. Potter notes that in Ping Shan estate members who rented from their own estates received a reduction in rent (1968:113). In Ha Tsuen some villagers said that they received reductions, while others claimed that they paid the same rent as nonmembers. For the village of Nanching, C. K. Yang reports that there was "no practical difference in the type of tenancy and the amount of rent charged" between private and ancestral land (1959b:47). Although there was no bar to renting estate land to nonmembers in Ha Tsuen, some villagers claimed that members generally had an advantage over nonmembers in competing for tenancy rights.

Even though some estates produced large rents, few Teng could afford to live off the proceeds of ancestral estates without some other source of income.[9] The

---

9 As a rough guide to the income produced by estates, I can provide some data for 1978. In that year three estates that kept their accounts together (Kou-yüeh, Tsui-le, and Szu-le *tsu*) shared out HK$35,000 among approximately 800 members. Each man received HK$10 from Szu-le *tsu* and Tsui-le *tsu*, and HK$5 from Kou-yüeh *tsu*; men aged 61 to 70 years received HK$20, those from 71 to 80 years received HK$30, and so on. One family, for example, received a total of HK$185 from the three estates, calculated as follows: payment for four sons plus an extra HK$60 for the father, who was 65 years old.

Inequality among brothers

largest landowning estate is Kou-yüeh *tsu*, which in 1978 had a membership of over 800 men. During recent generations, rent from this estate produced a surplus after expenses that was sufficient to pay only a token cash dividend to members. There were, of course, a few estates in Ha Tsuen that in 1905 produced large amounts of rent that were shared among a small membership. These estates are all recent in origin; Han-chang *tsu* was formed in the twenty-third generation (ca. 1880) and Chia-jung *tsu* in the twenty-fourth generation (see Figure 2). In 1905 these two estates, totaling 51.34 acres, had only a few members (in fact they would have included only the sons and grandsons of Han-chang). The yearly dividends from these estates were considerable, but it is unlikely that members lived solely on estate proceeds, for in 1905 these men were among Ha Tsuen's wealthiest landlord-merchants.

Ordinary villagers may have received a few dollars each year from their share of corporate holdings, but they were nearly always alienated from control over the property of the large estates. The real benefits were firmly in the hands of the wealthy, who served as estate managers (*szu-li*). Managers handled, and continue to handle, the business affairs of the estates. They also act as the estates' legal representatives; in the words of a 1910 ordinance, the manager acts "as if he were the sole owner . . . [of the estate land], subject to the consent of the Land Officer" (quoted in Freedman 1966a:52). In Ha Tsuen, once selected, managers usually retain the position for life. Often managers were the sons of previous managers, a pattern that is still repeated. Even today there is no formal procedure for choosing a manager, although the colonial administration has instituted formal guidelines for their conduct. Nearly all the men who become managers, especially of the large estates, are members of the local elite. Potter notes that in Ping Shan, "The last surviving gentry member of Hang Mei village, who died in 1920, was said to have been the manager of all important ancestral land estates in the village" (1968:104). In 1977–8 managers of Ha Tsuen's largest estates were political leaders or wealthy men; often they were both. Among the Teng, managers are always members of the estates that they manage.

There were many ways in which managers could make money and acquire influence during their trusteeship of ancestral property. In Ha Tsuen managers were especially powerful because, as I have mentioned, they served for life terms (see also Potter 1968:105). Potter notes that in Ping Shan the primary way that a manager could take advantage of his position was by loaning out cash from the estate fund. At the end of the year when the accounts were due, he collected the principal and put it back in the estate coffers, keeping the interest for himself (107). Ha Tsuen informants report that managers often received "gifts" of money from prospective tenants or lessees of estate property who wanted to secure the tenancy of badly needed agricultural land. Villagers reported that estate managers often acted toward tenants much like private landlords. At the end of the harvest, informants said, just as the crop from privately owned land was taken to the house of the landlord to be measured and the rent determined, so the crop from

Economic organization

Table 5. *Size of landholdings by major* Tsu *and* T'ang *in 1905*

Name of *Tsu* or *T'ang*	No. of acres owned
Kou-yüeh tsu	40.96
Chü-jen tsu	38.28
Chia-jung tsu	28.79
Yao-tsung tsu	27.59
Cho-ch'ing tsu	26.10
Han-chang T'ang	22.55
Yu Kung T'ang	16.00
Tsung-ch'eng tsu	14.96
Tzu-hou tsu	14.51
Yu Shan T'ang	14.06
Szu-le tsu	13.18
Niao-chang tsu	12.94
Total	269.92

Note: There were a total of 82 estates in the Teng lineage in 1905 (see Table 4). Seventy *tsu* and *t'ang* had fewer than 10 acres. Out of these 70, 63 had fewer than 5 acres.

estate land was taken to the home of the manager, and not to a public area as might be expected. The rent was measured out with the landlord's or manager's own nonstandardized baskets (*tou chung*). This again left room for the manager (and landlord) to maneuver for advantage. Ha Tsuen's exfarmers are convinced that their managers had the biggest rent measures in the New Territories.

In Ha Tsuen it is no secret that the community as a whole, and some ancestral estates in particular, have been badly served by managers. Managers have often been high-handed and dishonest in their dealings. Many Teng believe that Ha Tsuen has lost valuable property and suffered a general political decline as a consequence of the corruption or incompetence of past leaders and estate managers. In particular, villagers point to the decline of their market, darkly suggesting that at best their leaders were outmaneuvered by a group of outsiders and government officials or at worst their acquiescence was for sale (for details, see the discussion in the next section of this chapter).

The usual requirements for becoming an estate manager, especially the manager of a large estate, were literacy, knowledge of the world outside the village, and wealth. It was believed that personal wealth ensured at least a minimal level of honesty because the manager's private property could be confiscated if he strayed too far from acceptable behavior. The importance of wealth in choosing estate managers also ensured that a few men, mostly landlords and merchants, monopolized this source of local power. Effective monopoly over corporate estates was an important element in the set of structural advantages by which Ha Tsuen's landlord-merchant class established and maintained their dominance.

Inequality among brothers

The 1905 land records not only include information on the amount of land held by each of Ha Tsuen's ancestral estates but also list the names of managers for all the large estates. An examination of these records shows that one man, San Wai landlord Teng Cheng-ming,[10] was the manager of 8 estates and that during his lifetime he controlled (either as private owner or estate manager) a total of 193.75 acres. Of the 12 ancestral estates in Ha Tsuen with more than 10 acres (see Table 5) Cheng-ming was manager of 6 (one of which was Yu Kung T'ang), and of the 19 estates with more than 5 acres he was manager of 8. Thus, in his role as manager this one man controlled 52 percent of all ancestral land. According to calculations cited earlier, the Teng owned approximately 750 acres in Ha Tsuen *hsiang*, which means that Cheng-ming either owned or managed over 27 percent of Teng land in the *hsiang*. Villagers still speak in awe of Cheng-ming; they remember him for his philanthropy, his artful settlement of disputes, and of course for his wealth (more will be said about this man later).

Ha Tsuen Market: commerce and manufacturing

In Ha Tsuen control over land is important, but to appreciate the landlord's position in the local community we must also see him in his guise as entrepreneur and merchant. By examining the elite only in their capacity as landlords, many analyses of Chinese rural society have failed to understand the complex foundation upon which the landlord-merchant class rests.

One of the most striking memorials to Ha Tsuen's status as a dominant community is its walled market. Ha Tsuen Market (Ha Tsuen Shi) is more than the usual street bazaar found in other lineage communities of the New Territories. Inside the walls are a number of permanent shops, two factory complexes, and a market temple dedicated to the god Kuan Ti. Ha Tsuen Shi stands as a vivid reminder that Ha Tsuen was not a simple agricultural village.

According to a history written by the clerk of Ha Tsuen's elementary school, the market was built sometime in the mid–nineteenth century (Festival 1974). Other evidence suggests, however, that the market may have been built before the 1850s. Some villagers claim that Teng Wei-yü was the organizing force behind the construction of the market. If this is correct, then the market must have been built sometime in the second half of the eighteenth century, the period when Wei-yü was active. The market is not, however, listed in the 1819 edition of the Hsin-an gazetteer, but this means little. Generally only those markets that were formally recognized by the imperial officials were included in the gazetteer. It is impossible, on the basis of available evidence, to determine whether Ha Tsuen Shi was established in the late eighteenth century or a few decades later.

---

10 Personal names used in this book, except for those of early ancestors (pre-1750) and historical figures, are pseudonyms.

Economic organization

What is certain is that by the 1870s the market was an important commercial center for the Teng.

Although there is some confusion over dating the market, the oral accounts that the villagers gave me concerning the actual construction of Ha Tsuen Shi were consistent. There are some striking similarities between the formation of Yu Kung T'ang and Ha Tsuen Market. Just as Yu Kung T'ang was initially funded by local subscription, so too was the market complex built with community contributions. According to my informants' accounts, those interested in doing business or investing in the proposed market contributed money according to the size of the shops they desired to own once the buildings were complete. Various lotteries, corresponding to the amount subscribed, were then drawn, and shops were assigned in proportion to the investment made and the luck of the draw. According to this description, the market was not built piecemeal but was constructed as a unit. The physical uniformity and architectural composition of the market buildings confirm the oral evidence.

There can be little doubt that the market owes its creation at least in part to the increased trading possibilities of the eighteenth and nineteenth centuries. Ha Tsuen's coastal location was also a factor in the market's success. The hamlets on the northern fringe of the community were connected to the open waters of Deep Bay by a stream that ran through the tidal marshes. Cargo boats were able to use this stream to reach Ha Tsuen. These boats docked at the hamlet of Lo Uk Tsuen, and their cargoes were then transported by carry pole to the market, about 500 yards away. Boats that were owned by Ha Tsuen Teng received a discount in the fee charged for unloading at the Lo Uk Tsuen pier. This pier was owned and managed by Yu Kung T'ang. According to villagers, the boats that stopped at Ha Tsuen also called at the larger market of Yuen Long and at the administrative center of Nam Tao (on the opposite side of Deep Bay). Three of the men who worked on these boats were still living in Ha Tsuen during the period of my research. They report that boats owned by Teng sometimes went as far as Amoy and Canton, although they specialized in local commerce, sailing between Nam Tao and Hong Kong's Western District. Most of these cargo boats were owned by the family of Teng Cheng-ming or his brother.

Ha Tsuen's proximity to Deep Bay was an important factor behind the formation of Ha Tsuen Shi, but this does not in itself explain the existence of a substantial market only three miles from the older and much larger market of Yuen Long. The villagers claim that violence and physical insecurity were the primary reasons for establishing Ha Tsuen Shi. The home of the Ha Tsuen Teng's arch-rivals, Ping Shan, stood directly along the land and water routes to Yuen Long. During periods of active hostility between the two Teng settlements, the people of Ha Tsuen had great difficulty reaching Yuen Long Market, I was told. One suspects that for most periods the threat was more felt than real, although no doubt these fears were real enough to the villagers themselves.

Perhaps a more important reason for establishing a market in Ha Tsuen was

Inequality among brothers

the fact that Yuen Long was under the firm control of the Teng of Kam Tin. Although relations between Ha Tsuen and Kam Tin were generally friendly, the Ha Tsuen Teng certainly did not have free access to Yuen Long Market. Like everyone else they were not allowed to engage in business unless they paid fees to the Kam Tin–controlled market corporation (see Groves 1964, 1969). These conditions served as an ever-present reminder of Ha Tsuen's dependence on Kam Tin. During the nineteenth century some of Ha Tsuen's wealthy families did have substantial business interests in Yuen Long, but this did not stop them from investing heavily in the development of Ha Tsuen Market.

At least four factors were important in the creation of Ha Tsuen Market: Ha Tsuen's unique coastal location, its sense of insecurity, local concern for the symbols of elite status, and of course the pursuit of economic advantage. By the 1870s it is clear that Ha Tsuen's wealthiest families were heavily involved in mercantile and manufacturing enterprises. For these landlord-merchants, Ha Tsuen Market offered a lucrative source of income as well as a protected environment for their commercial and manufacturing enterprises.

Ha Tsuen's walled market is still intact today, although in recent years many of its shops and factories have been converted into residences. The market is constructed in a T-shape, with two main, shop-lined thoroughfares. According to colonial government records, the market had 28 permanent shops in 1905. In addition to these shops, there was a daily market for fresh food and a periodic market for livestock. The periodic market met on a 2, 5, 8 schedule; that is, people gathered for this special livestock market on the second, fifth, eighth, twelfth (etc.) day of each lunar month.[11] Significantly, Ha Tsuen's market schedule did not conflict with that of Yuen Long Old Market, which met on a 3, 6, 9 schedule, making it possible for people to attend both markets.

Villagers told me that prior to the Japanese occupation, Ha Tsuen Shi boasted a number of teahouses, ink and stationery shops, herbal medicine shops, and cloth shops. There were also a number of rice buyers and millers, a sugar mill, a peanut oil factory, a bean curd factory, and a slaughterhouse, and on market days a number of itinerant peddlers would offer their wares in the market lanes (informants maintain that there were nearly three dozen temporary stalls clustered outside the walls in the 1920s). The services of a Taoist priest and a spirit medium were also available in the market.

Although Ha Tsuen Shi offered a large array of goods, Yuen Long shops were larger and had more variety than those of Ha Tsuen (for example, Ha Tsuen did not have a pawnshop or a jewelry shop). Nevertheless, Ha Tsuen Shi was under the firm control of local people, and this was important to commercially minded Teng. According to the land records for 1905, only two shops were owned by non-Teng. Of course, non-Teng may have leased shops, and therefore their names

---

11 Periodic market schedules of this type are very common in China (see Skinner 1964–5).

Economic organization

would not appear in the land records, but there is no doubt that the market was primarily a Teng affair.

Since the 1870s Ha Tsuen Shi was dominated by a peanut-processing factory that was situated on one of the main thoroughfares. Here the peanut oil so important to Chinese cooking was processed and shipped to markets throughout the Canton delta. The oil factory was also used for the processing of herbal medicine and the storage and milling of rice. The factory was owned by Teng Cheng-ming and his brother Teng Cheng-fu, two of San Wai's wealthiest landowners. According to Cheng-ming's daughter-in-law, who now lives in part of the disused factory, Cheng-ming and Cheng-fu inherited a small factory from their father. Sometime in the 1870s the two brothers expanded this factory and then, a decade later, they added sugar to their other interests. Sugarcane was processed into blocks of raw sugar in Ha Tsuen Shi and transported to urban Hong Kong for final refining. In their heyday these two factories are reported to have employed over 50 workers, mostly non-Teng.

Residents of nearby satellite villages had long depended on Teng landlords for access to land, but with the establishment of these factories new relations of dependency emerged. In addition to working in Ha Tsuen Shi, many non-Teng became suppliers of raw materials (peanuts and sugarcane) for the factories owned by Cheng-ming and Cheng-fu. Sugarcane and peanuts are crops that can be grown on poor-quality (second-class) land, which, in Ha Tsuen *hsiang*, means the hills surrounding satellite villages.

Ha Tsuen's market continued to operate successfully until around 1915, when its access to boat traffic was blocked (see Festival 1974). A group of entrepreneurs from T'ai-shan (a district to the south of Canton) received permission from the colonial government to build a dam enclosing the tidal land directly to the north of Ha Tsuen. The land was converted to brackish water paddies (for more information on this conversion, see Grant 1964:56; Wood 1916:J1–2). The entrepreneurs then brought in their own workers and settled them in a company town about a mile from Ha Tsuen. These "new fields" blocked the stream that connected Ha Tsuen with Deep Bay. Access to Deep Bay was of crucial importance to the Teng, for during the early part of the twentieth century boats offered the only feasible method of transporting large amounts of goods to and from Ha Tsuen. The village was some distance from the as yet skeletal road system and from the Kowloon-Canton Railway (which runs along the eastern side of the New Territories). The construction of the dam was a serious blow to Ha Tsuen, but it was not the only problem that Teng manufacturers and shopkeepers had to face during this period.

The market's fate was sealed when European-owned companies began to compete successfully with Ha Tsuen's own local manufacturers. Sugarcane could be grown and block sugar processed much more cheaply by Dutch-run firms in Indonesia than by New Territories companies (see S. G. Davis 1949:172). The final collapse of the local sugar industry came, a Teng elder told me, when the

Inequality among brothers

British-owned Tai Koo Company, the main buyer of Ha Tsuen's sugar, stopped purchasing block sugar from the New Territories. According to the Teng, a similar fate awaited their peanut oil business. As new, highly capitalized factories were set up in urban Hong Kong, the competition increased. An old man who had once worked in the market told me that the Teng could not possibly compete, and so Ha Tsuen's oil and sugar factories ceased operating around 1920. The factory building is still standing, but now its only occupants are the elderly widow and unmarried daughter of Cheng-ming's son, who have made their home in a section of the old factory.

Although Cheng-ming and Cheng-fu's factory in Ha Tsuen collapsed, they do not appear to have suffered a serious setback as a consequence. Ha Tsuen Market was not their only source of income. Besides extensive holdings in land, the two brothers also had flourishing businesses in Yuen Long Market and trading contacts throughout the Canton delta and beyond.

According to a descendant of Cheng-fu, Cheng-fu's father had opened a pawnshop in Yuen Long in the 1850s or 1860s. Cheng-ming and Cheng-fu expanded this firm in the 1890s. The building that once housed their pawnshop is still standing on Yuen Long Old Market's central street. Its rifle slits, thick walls, and heavy doors make it look like a fortress compared to the small shops that surround it. Near the pawnshop is another of the brothers' business ventures, which was also established in the 1890s. This is a large three-story red-brick building that is now used as a warehouse; originally it housed a match factory. The pawnshop is no longer a place of business and is now the home of Teng Yao-feng, Cheng-fu's son, who at 93 years was, in 1978, the oldest surviving member of Ha Tsuen's premier landlord-merchant family. It is ironic that both Yao-feng and his cousin's wife (the widow of Cheng-ming's son) should have decided to live out their last years in the buildings that once symbolized their family's power and position in the region. The pawnshop and the match factory, which are among the largest buildings in Yuen Long Old Market, provide striking evidence of the extralineage, extravillage outlook of Ha Tsuen's leading landlord-merchant family.

Teng Cheng-ming and Teng Cheng-fu were not newcomers to the ranks of Ha Tsuen's landlord-merchant class. They, like most other wealthy villagers, were direct descendants of one of the Teng's leading eighteenth-century figures, Tso-t'ai. They were also members of nearly all of Ha Tsuen's large ancestral estates. In 1905 their combined private landholdings were enormous by local standards, consisting of over 100 acres in Ha Tsuen *hsiang* alone. Figure 3, in Chapter 6, provides a schematic genealogy of this family from about the mid–nineteenth century.

Cheng-ming and Cheng-fu were not, of course, the only landlord-merchants in Ha Tsuen, although they were without doubt the most successful. The family home of these two brothers is still to be found in San Wai's landlord-merchant cluster. Many of the occupants of the neighboring houses were closely related

Economic organization

to Cheng-ming and Cheng-fu, and like them they too were landowners, moneylenders, and boat owners. Some also owned shops in Ha Tsuen and in Yuen Long. One of the brothers' neighbors owned a ferryboat that operated from Sha Kong Pier along the Lau Fau Shan coast. Nearly all of these families belong to Chu-jen ancestral estate, and most were members of Yu Shan T'ang (see Table 5 for landholdings of these estates). Since the early 1900s many men in these families have become professionals. In the 1970s, a dentist, a Western-trained doctor, and a number of teachers were among this group. Most of the large houses in San Wai are still occupied by the descendants of Ha Tsuen's landlord elite. Cheng-ming's and Cheng-fu's grandsons have continued working in the businesses their forebears so successfully established. The political position of the landlord-merchants and the ties that they maintained with members of the regional elite will be discussed in Chapter 5.

Smallholder and tenant livelihood

In contrast to the diversified interests of Teng landlord-merchants, Ha Tsuen's smallholder-tenants were heavily dependent on agriculture. However, they did supplement their incomes with other activities such as fishing, peddling, and casual labor. Although these sources of income might be categorized as supplementary, they were by no means insignificant. For many households, fishing or wage labor might well have meant the difference between having enough to eat and going hungry.

The occupational histories that I collected in two of Ha Tsuen's hamlets (Bao Wai and Sik Kong Wai) reveal that for the 30-year period before 1960, over 85 percent of the households gave agriculture as their primary occupation. Ha Tsuen people grew a variety of crops, but rice was the villagers' major agricultural product until the 1960s. On first-class land (about 60 percent of the total cultivated land in Ha Tsuen) two crops of rice were grown: one planted in spring and harvested in summer, the other planted in summer and harvested in autumn. Older villagers remember when rice grown in the Yuen Long area was highly prized in urban markets.

Male labor is more closely associated with rice growing than with any other crop. Men did all the ploughing and were involved in most stages of the growing cycle. But men, according to many village women, participated far less in the production of vegetables, fruit, and sweet potatoes, Ha Tsuen's other major crops. Some women said that after the fall rice harvest their men spent the winter months in Ha Tsuen Market gambling and relaxing, while the women managed the winter catch crops. After the second rice harvest most of the fields were planted with sweet potatoes or green vegetables. For many families, at least some of the vegetable crop became a source of cash income; vegetables were salted and later sold in Ha Tsuen Market. There are some lichi orchards near Ha Tsuen, and I was told that women and the elderly harvested this crop. Villagers

Inequality among brothers

also kept chickens, pigs, and of course water buffaloes, which were used to plough the fields.

Most peasants relied on rice, sweet potatoes, vegetables, bean curd, and fish for their diet. Older women reported that in the past they had eaten two meals a day, one in the morning and one at night. Sweet potatoes were usually mixed with rice to make a kind of gruel, and when there was no rice, sweet potatoes were eaten alone. One 78-year-old woman told me that when she married into Ha Tsuen in 1918, her husband's family (who were landless) ate sweet potatoes every day all year round. To contemporary villagers sweet potatoes are a symbol of poverty, and they often refer to the past as "the time when we ate sweet potatoes."

The household was the primary unit of production. For purposes of this study, a "household" is defined as a unit that eats together and shares a common budget for consumption (see also Nelson 1969:114). I do not have historical material on the household composition of Ha Tsuen, but according to Buck's 1930 survey of China's double-cropping rice area (which includes Kwangtung), households were composed of an average of 5.9 persons (1937:38). C. K. Yang found that there was an average of 4.8 persons per household in the village of Nanching in the 1940s (1959b:17).

According to villagers, only the more affluent farmers could afford to employ full-time laborers. In fact, the regular employment of laborers seems to have been a mark of status. When married women were asked about their father's occupation, one of the first things some of the wealthier women mentioned was that their fathers had employed one or two full-time farm workers. Buck notes that only 8 percent of the farms surveyed in the Southeast had farm laborers hired by the year; this is the lowest figure reported for all of the eight regions surveyed by Buck (1937:291). Not only were there few permanent farm laborers in Ha Tsuen, but many exfarmers told me that they rarely hired part-time or casual workers, even in peak periods. It would appear that many households were dependent on their own members for labor. The fact that long periods of little work alternated with short periods of intensive labor was a perennial problem in Chinese agriculture.

In the past nearly everyone in the village, except for very small children, was employed in some form of productive work. Many domestic and agricultural tasks were assigned on the basis of sex and age, but others were performed by anyone available. Ploughing, I have already noted, was exclusively the preserve of men. Women spent more time on vegetable crops than did their husbands, and they alone were responsible for such things as carrying water and gathering fuel. Wood was scarce and too precious to burn, so women had to gather dry grass and brush in the hills behind the village. A steady supply of grass was essential to the running of a household, for it provided both heat and cooking fuel and was sometimes sold to produce a little cash income.

In a survey of the New Territories in 1898, Stewart Lockhart emphasized the

Economic organization

importance of fishing to the local population (see also Hayes 1977:33, 38–9). Lockhart noted that stake-net fishing was carried on in the western sectors of the New Territories (which includes Ha Tsuen) (Lockhart 1899:543). "The fish," he writes, "are sorted, salted and sun-dried, and exported to various markets. The trade in salt fish is one of the most important, and employs a large number of persons" (543). The Teng were certainly involved in fishing along the shores of Deep Bay. Men who had themselves regularly fished in local waters told me that they used both stake nets and nets thrown from small boats just off the shore (cf. Hayes 1977:38–9). According to historical records, Yu Kung T'ang obtained a lease to a large part of the Lau Fau Shan coast from the Ch'ing government in the eighteenth century (Festival 1974:28). From that time onward, Yu Kung T'ang controlled access to Lau Fau Shan's coastal resources (see Map 2). In order to fish in this area, I was told, it was necessary to obtain permission from Yu Kung T'ang, which conducted an annual auction for the privilege (open only to Teng). Groups of 10 or more men would bid for the right to net fish along the coast.

Before the Japanese occupation in 1941 there were, according to villagers, 10 permanent fishing stations (points along the coast where stake nets could be placed) that fell under the control of Yu Kung T'ang. Teng who had participated in this form of fishing estimate that between 50 and 60 men were involved. Although it was obviously important as a supplement to agriculture, fishing was not a primary source of income for most Teng. Only a portion of the male population was involved, and fishing was restricted to a few days each month when the tides were right and agricultural responsibilities permitted. Some of the netted fish were eaten by the fishermen and their families, but most of the catch, according to villagers, was sold fresh in Ha Tsuen Market or salted and stored for later sale.

Not all the fish sold in Ha Tsuen Market were caught by the Teng themselves. A few Ha Tsuen people acted as middlemen and retailers of fish that they purchased from boat people who anchored nearby (see Anderson 1972; Ward 1959). During the twentieth century (and perhaps before) boat people sold their catch at a fish market along the Lau Fau Shan coast about a mile from Ha Tsuen. After the rice harvest, according to informants, some Teng bought fish at this special market for resale in Ha Tsuen. In the 1930s, up to 10 Teng, I was told, were involved in this form of marketing (boat people, it should be noted, were not allowed to sell their own fish in Ha Tsuen).

The coastline along Deep Bay is ideally suited for oyster beds. The Teng claim that they took up oyster cultivation in the mid–eighteenth century, when they learned the necessary technology from the oystermen of Sha Jeng, a region farther up the delta (now in the People's Republic). We know from later sources that the local oyster industry was operating successfully in the second half of the nineteenth century. For example, a missionary living in Hsin-an in the late 1850s wrote complaining of the many oyster beds that made navigation in Deep

Inequality among brothers

Bay dangerous (Krone 1967:105). Lockhart, writing 40 years later, makes ρ point of mentioning Deep Bay oysters in his economic survey of the New Territories (1899:543). It is unclear whether Yu Kung T'ang, which held the lease to the coast, was actively involved (through its managers) in establishing local oyster beds or whether the hall merely leased parts of the coast to individual Teng who then developed the new industry themselves. The technology of oyster cultivation is not particularly complicated, nor are large capital investments necessary to establish or maintain the beds. Although Yu Kung T'ang continues to hold the lease over the coast (now, of course, under the purview of the New Territories' administration), the oyster beds are privately exploited.

Most of the harvesting and maintenance of Lau Fau Shan's oysters was done by non-Teng, I was told. However, Teng people did on occasion work in the oyster beds, and families who leased small beds harvested their own oysters (as they do today). The fact that hired labor was a regular part of oyster production in the past suggests that most beds were leased by Ha Tsuen's wealthier residents, who did not harvest the oysters themselves. The Teng were also involved in the production of oyster by-products. Fertilizer made from oyster shells was produced by Teng-owned companies, as was a substance used in incense pots. Oyster sauce was also a local product. In fact, Teng Cheng-ming's family still owns a large oyster sauce business in Lau Fau Shan.

Aside from fishing and oyster collecting, the coastline also provided local people with another source of food and, presumably, cash income. Krone comments that in the 1850s "hundreds of old men, women, and children, may be seen on the extensive flats left by the receding tide, collecting the small fishes, crabs, and other animals which have been stranded" (1967:124). Even today many older women in Ha Tsuen are known for their ability to collect shellfish, a skill that I was told was particularly important during lean times.

Before leaving Ha Tsuen's coast it is important to add that a few Teng became completely dependent on the sea for their living. In the 1930s there were at least three households in the hamlet of Sik Kong Wai whose sole source of income was remittances from sailors. Other families were partially dependent on absentee sailors. Furthermore, as noted earlier, many local men supplemented their income by working on the cargo boats that supplied Ha Tsuen Market. Clearly, the sea, the delta waterways, and the coast have all played an important role in the economic lives of the Ha Tsuen Teng.

Teng farmers were never heavily involved in growing cash crops such as sugarcane and peanuts; these were generally left to their satellite neighbors. The fact that the Teng grew rice instead of cash crops does not imply, however, that the Teng were self-sufficient or isolated from the market. Like everyone else in this part of China they were immersed in a cash economy and had to make regular purchases of essential items in order to survive.

A portion of what Ha Tsuen farmers grew on their land or took from the coast was sold in local markets. Many retired farmers reported that prior to the Japanese

Economic organization

occupation they exchanged their own high-quality rice for low-quality rice in a "catty-for-catty" system whereby 1 catty of unhusked grain brought 1 catty of husked rice (see J. Watson 1975b:40; Hayes 1970:174). Some reported a variation of this system in which they exchanged, catty-for-catty, their higher-grade grain for poor, broken rice plus a cash payment to cover the difference. One 60-year-old man noted that Ha Tsuen's rice dealers preferred to buy only the highest-quality grain, so he usually sold his crop in Yuen Long, where it was possible to get a better price. Sweet potatoes were one of the few crops that were not marketed, but as I have already noted, some vegetables were salted and sold.

Teng households appear to have made extensive use of Ha Tsuen Market. Nearly all the daily needs of a farm household could be acquired there. Aside from the services that I have already mentioned, at the turn of the century the market also housed a metal tool maker, a coffin maker, wine and oil shops, a barber, a tailor, and a house builder. Certain goods (jewelry for dowries, special foods, fancy cloth, and clothes) were not available in Ha Tsuen, however, and had to be purchased in the larger market at Yuen Long. Although Ha Tsuen's factories began to decline around 1915, the market continued to supply most of the everyday needs of the community until a decade or so after the Japanese occupation.

Class differences and economic relations in Ha Tsuen

Access to agricultural land was of vital concern to both Ha Tsuen's landlord-merchants and its smallholder-tenants. The major difference between these two classes was that the smallholder-tenants were heavily dependent on their wealthy agnates. Landlord-merchants controlled crucial resources that Ha Tsuen's smallholder-tenants required for their survival. Tenant households rented the land they farmed from their landlord kinsmen or from Teng ancestral estates that were often controlled by these same landlords; they shopped in Ha Tsuen's landlord-merchant–dominated market for most of their daily needs; and they borrowed money from the pawnshops that their wealthy agnates owned. Some local men worked on Teng-owned cargo boats or in Teng-owned shops and manufacturing firms (although the factories appear to have employed mostly non-Teng). Teng landlord-merchants, on the other hand, were not restricted to their kinsmen for economic support; they had diversified both the nature of their economic interests and the geographical distribution of those interests. Their cargo boat businesses took them throughout the Canton delta and beyond; the goods that they sold in their shops came from Hong Kong Island; they sold their block sugar to urban capitalists and their peanut oil to merchants in Nam Tao. Ha Tsuen's leading families had personal ties, including affinal links, with merchants as far afield as Canton and Amoy (see Chapter 7).

In later chapters we will see that the parochialism of Ha Tsuen's smallholder-tenants extended well beyond the economic realm, for they were also encap-

Inequality among brothers

sulated within a social and cultural world that gave them little knowledge or experience of life outside their lineage. In this chapter I have been concerned to demarcate the smallholder-tenants and the landlord-merchants as distinct economic classes, but in later chapters I shall demonstrate that they can also be differentiated by social and cultural criteria. The marriage and affinal patterns of the two classes were different; they had different levels of education; they lived in houses of different styles, and the social lives of their wives and daughters varied enormously. It is only when these cultural factors are considered together with the economic and political factors that one begins to appreciate the gulf that divided the two classes in Ha Tsuen.

5
Local political organization

In the 1950s the British instituted a new system of local administration in the New Territories. Prior to that period political organization among the Ha Tsuen Teng was not highly formalized. There was no system of political offices, and the only clearly defined political institution was the village guard. Decisions were made and disputes adjudicated by informal leaders, and everyday administration was handled by religious and landholding corporations.

Prior to the 1950s, two institutions were central to local politics in Ha Tsuen. One was the community's "village guard" (*hsün ting*) and the other was Yu Kung T'ang. The village guard (or self-defense corps) was a policing agency and was responsible for the security of the area. The guard did more, however, than defend the local population against thieves and bandits. Ha Tsuen's village guard provided the force that backed up Teng territorial claims, especially the claims of Teng landlord-merchants.

Although Yu Kung T'ang was not an overtly political organization, it was nonetheless deeply involved in local politics. Yu Kung T'ang provided a framework for handling community and *hsiang* affairs, and as a consequence the manager of Yu Kung T'ang played an important leadership role. At the turn of the century, as we have seen, the manager was Teng Cheng-ming, one of Ha Tsuen's leading landowners.

At first examination, Ha Tsuen's political system appears highly egalitarian; this is in fact the way the villagers themselves often present their political arrangements. Because lineage members are also members of Yu Kung T'ang and because Yu Kung T'ang provides the platform for local political activity, we might expect that all lineage members played some role in local politics. However, one need not probe too deeply before realizing that effective power was held by the manager of Yu Kung T'ang and not by the general membership.

This analysis of local politics covers the same period as Chapter 4, the late nineteenth and early twentieth centuries. Although there is not as much detailed information as one could wish, it is still possible to piece together a fairly clear picture of Ha Tsuen's political organization prior to the Japanese occupation in 1941. For this discussion I have relied on what written local sources I could

Inequality among brothers

find (local histories, land records, colonial records), on the memories and oral traditions of my informants, and on data available for other communities. As a preliminary to my examination of the political structure of Ha Tsuen, I will first discuss the regional and national milieu within which that political system operated.

Central government and local political organization

For its entire 600-year history, Ha Tsuen has been imbedded in a centralized bureaucratic state. During all but the last 80 years of that history, the Teng have lived under the authority of China's imperial government. The state did not, however, impinge very often or very directly on China's rural population. In fact, the formal state apparatus did not reach beyond the *hsien* (or county) level. As long as people paid their taxes and fulfilled the occasional obligations that the state required, they were largely free of direct government control. Of course, this generalization should not be pushed too far, for as Hsiao Kung-chuan cautions, the village enjoyed autonomy "not because the government intended to give it something like self-government, but because the authorities were unable completely to control or supervise its activities. Such autonomy, in other words, was a result of incomplete centralization; the government never hesitated to interfere with village life whenever it deemed it necessary or desirable" (1960:263). Even though local communities were not fully integrated into the formal hierarchy of government structures, one should not assume that they were isolated from central government decisions and practices.

Sometimes central authority rested lightly on China's rural population, but at other times its weight was heavy indeed. Certainly one of the most dramatic examples of the effect of imperial control on Hsin-an was the forced evacuation of coastal China in the 1660s. As was mentioned in Chapter 2, this imperial policy had far-reaching implications for the Teng and their neighbors. Central-government policy did not, however, always operate to the disadvantage of villages like Ha Tsuen. Many rural areas benefited from the transportation facilities that central government made possible. These facilities helped create markets for rural products and stimulated economic development in regions like the Canton delta. The existence of a uniform system of writing, a national bureaucracy and army, and a common set of weights and measures shows that China's state system had its positive side.

In most cases, however, the impact of imperial policies on the lives of the Teng was indirect and generalized. Ha Tsuen's leading families were not members of the national elite and so were not directly dependent on the vagaries of imperial favors. Villagers had few direct dealings with government authorities, who tended to remain in the county capital at Nam Tao. The Teng paid their taxes, they fell under the authority of the Ch'ing legal code, and a lucky few sat the imperial examinations, but for most people this was the extent of their involvement with the state. For many, even these contacts with officialdom could

Local political organization

not have been very significant. According to studies of the taxing arrangements in Hsin-an County during the Ch'ing dynasty (1644–1911), the tax burden was relatively small in comparison with other areas of China (Kamm 1977). The actual collection of taxes, as we have already seen, was usually done by local men (landlord-merchants or their agents) who turned over the money to government authorities.

Although all Chinese were subject to a single legal code during the Ch'ing dynasty, the people of Ha Tsuen, in common with other villagers, attempted to keep the judicial branch of the central government at arm's length usually with considerable success. Rev. Krone, a missionary who lived in Hsin-an during the 1850s, reported that

the Mandarins in the Sanon [Hsin-an] district have very little power. The people pay the taxes, but do not allow the mandarins to interfere with their own local government. Lawsuits, differences, and offences are very seldom brought before the mandarins. The mandarin from whom I learnt the preceding facts had not, as far as I know, during a period of several years, more than one case brought before him for decision; in this instance he was both plaintiff and judge, – the criminal being a youth who was caught stealing fruit in his garden. (Krone 1967:125)

Krone goes on to report that disputes were settled by the local elite, or if they could not be settled in this way the disputants, rather than placing themselves at the mercy of the courts, usually resorted to armed conflict. Writing of these conflicts, Krone reports that "in these quarrels, many a bloody battle is fought, hundreds of men perish, and whole villages are destroyed" (125).

Intervillage and interlineage violence was endemic in the Canton delta, and this central fact must be considered in analyzing political organization in Hsin-an County. During the mid-nineteenth century, most of China, including what is now the New Territories, experienced serious outbreaks of violence (see Kuhn 1970; Lamley 1977; Wakeman 1966).[1] The so-called martyr halls of the New Territories date from this period and provide dramatic evidence of the extent of armed conflict in the region (on New Territories martyr halls, see Hayes 1974:128). These buildings, which closely resemble ancestral halls, were built to commemorate those who fought in local battles. The Teng of Ha Tsuen were, according to their own accounts, sorely tried during the nineteenth century. In the middle 1800s their neighbors (the Teng of Ping Shan) joined with another Teng lineage from Tung-kuan County in an effort to defeat the Ha Tsuen Teng. According

---

1 At least some of the violence in the area was due to piracy. The pirate Chang Pao-tsu had his headquarters in the Hong Kong region from 1806 to 1810. In 1810 an amnesty was granted to Chang's followers, and this particular phase of piratical activity came to an end (see Lo 1963:106–18; Murray 1979:114f). The Taiping rebellion also made itself felt in the Hong Kong region. According to S. G. Davis, beginning in 1850 "the rebels and government forces had numerous engagements in and about Kowloon City" (1949:29). Unfortunately I do not know what effect this had on Ha Tsuen.

Inequality among brothers

to local accounts, the Ha Tsuen people survived this challenge because they were able to gain the support of a number of other communities in the Yuen Long area. To this day the Ha Tsuen Teng feel an intense mistrust of the two Teng lineages that attempted to take over the rich lands and coastal resources of Ha Tsuen *hsiang*.

In 1898 the Chinese imperial government was forced to lease part of Hsin-an County to the British. Ha Tsuen villagers report that local people were not properly informed of the agreement between the Chinese and British governments. There was a great deal of confusion, and people in the leased territory were very suspicious of British intentions. The British were thought to be an invading force intent on expansion into China.

In April 1899, British troops and a local Chinese militia met near Tai Po Market (see Map 2). The outcome of these engagements could never have been in much doubt; the British, with their professionally led and trained soldiers, soon overcame the locally mustered force.

The information on the resistance comes from two sources. First there are, of course, the many accounts that the Teng have heard from their fathers and grandfathers who witnessed the British occupation. Second, there are a number of Chinese documents that were captured by British troops in 1899. These documents reveal Chinese plans for mounting a resistance to the British occupiers (Groves 1969; Endacott 1964:263; Wesley-Smith 1980:57–67).

The resistance movement is extremely interesting, because it provides both a clear example of interelite cooperation in the region and some insight into local political organization. According to Robert Groves (1969) and Peter Wesley-Smith (1980), who have written on the organization of the Chinese response to the British take-over, the Kam Tin, Ping Shan, and Ha Tsuen Teng were the major force in organizing and provisioning the local militia (on Chinese militia organization in other parts of the Canton delta, see W. Hsieh 1974; Wakeman 1966). Although Ha Tsuen people appear to have played a central role in this organization (Wesley-Smith 1980:65), the resistance was not solely a Teng affair. In the later stages of planning, held in Yuen Long Market, the Teng were joined by leaders from a number of other Hsin-an communities (Groves 1969:43–58). As Groves notes:

The documents concerning the resistance name 63 people as active in the movement, in that they: (i) took part in the meetings which organized it; and/or (ii) acted as leaders during the fighting. Ten of the 63 leaders are identifiable as members of the gentry, in the sense that they are mentioned in the documents as having [imperial] degrees ... Most of the remainder could be termed "local notables." Some were substantial owners of agricultural land and village houses. Others owned shops in their local markets. (56–7)

The ability to mount a concerted resistance shows that local villages were not closed, isolated communities. When necessary, the regional elite could make

Local political organization

unified decisions and carry them out – albeit with limited success, in this particular case.

The fighting between the Chinese militia and the British occupying force lasted two days. Soon after the militia was defeated at Tai Po, Teng informants say that British troops marched past Ha Tsuen on their way to Deep Bay. Although many women and children hid in the hills beyond the village, fearing what the British might do, the troops did not enter Ha Tsuen. As the period of active resistance came to an end, the colonial government gradually assumed control over the New Territories.

In 1899 the British created the New Territories Administration. This new administration, as we have seen, pushed ahead with an aggressive land registration program that ultimately had important consequences for local political organization. As was noted in Chapter 4, some of the agricultural land in Ha Tsuen was registered in the names of neighboring non-Teng villagers, residents of satellite villages, whose hold on the paddy fields they farmed had always been tenuous. Although the Ha Tsuen Teng did not lose as much land as some other dominant lineages, the new land tenure arrangements did have an effect on the Teng. Lands that they had considered their own now belonged to people whom the Teng had treated as dependents for at least two centuries. Largely as a consequence of colonial land policy, dominant lineages like the Ha Tsuen Teng never again had absolute control over their satellite villages. However, these dependent villages did not completely slip from the Teng's grasp. One institution, the village guard, kept the Teng in a commanding position well into the twentieth century.

Although British land policy did force changes in the leased territory, the colonial administration was not really interested in restructuring New Territories society (Freedman 1966b:8). Many of Ha Tsuen's landowners retained possession of large tracts of land, and Ha Tsuen itself remained the dominant force in the *hsiang*. However, from 1905 onward the people of the New Territories, especially the local elite, began to fight a losing battle against the intrusion of central administration.

After the colonial authorities had completed their land registration program, they remained somewhat aloof from local politics until the early 1950s. In fact, during the first decades of the twentieth century they maintained only a handful of policemen and the one district officer in the northern New Territories, which had a population of well over fifty thousand people. Given the absence of an effective police force, the village guardsmen of the dominant lineages continued their traditional role of local "protectors." The colonial judicial system did not intrude on village life, although it was available if people wanted to use it. On the whole the Teng continued to settle their own disputes. They did, of course, have to register sales of land with the new government, and they did pay taxes to colonial authorities, but for most people their direct involvement with the Hong Kong government went no further.

Inequality among brothers

After 1900 intercommunity violence may have subsided, but it by no means disappeared. Kidnapping seems to have been especially popular in the early 1900s. Members of wealthy families were the main targets of these raiders, but ordinary villagers were sometimes kidnapped as well. If captives could not be ransomed, they were sold as servants or slaves (see J. Watson 1980). Landlord-merchant families in Ha Tsuen hired private guards to protect their homes and businesses during this period.[2] Many villagers remember a bandit attack on Ha Tsuen's sugar and oil factory in the 1920s. About 20 or 30 men laid siege to the factory, but, I was told with considerable satisfaction, they were finally driven off by the Teng. Bandit gangs and pirates, who usually were based in Chinese territory, did not cease operating simply because the British had taken over southern Hsin-an. With their small police force, the colonial authorities could not hope to protect local residents.

Lineage and community leadership

Prior to the 1950s, there were no political offices in Ha Tsuen and no formal arrangements for selecting community leaders. Within the village there were, however, men who wielded great power and influence. Some Teng claim that in the past lineage elders played a leading role in community affairs, and many older men lament the passing of the elders' power and privilege. However, as one begins to collect specific accounts of how disputes were settled or decisions reached, it becomes clear that elders as a category did not play as decisive a role as some of their descendants suggest. Although elders were a source of moral authority both in the lineage and community, age was not the major criterion for leadership.

Until the 1950s, community affairs and lineage affairs were not clearly differentiated. To a large extent, political organization was embedded in lineage organization. Lineage institutions like Yu Kung T'ang had not only a religious and economic dimension but also a political one. As one of the two institutions that cut across hamlet and segment affiliations (the other was the village guard), Yu Kung T'ang played an important role in community decision making, in dispute settlement, and in local security and administration.

As noted earlier, the manager of Yu Kung T'ang had a leading role in local affairs. Although he was charged with the formal duty of administering the hall's corporate property, the manager was far more than a mere accountant. The position of manager carried with it no inherent political powers, but in the hands of a forceful individual the managership placed the incumbent in a powerful position. His job was to carry out "the will of the community," but in fact he

---

2 In fact, in the 1920s the son of one of San Wai's wealthiest landlords was kidnapped. He was returned, I was told, only after a ransom of several thousand Mexican silver dollars was paid.

Inequality among brothers

respected; he may speak out on certain moral or religious issues, but in general his role is ceremonial, not political.

Ha Tsuen's lineage elders had a number of customary rights. Only elders were entitled to participate in the Spring and Autumn Rites held in Yu Kung T'ang. As Baker points out, they were automatically invited to those marriage and birth banquets that took place in their own hamlets, and of course they were always in attendance at lineage and segment feasts. Their attendance at feasts and their extra shares of ancestral pork were rights that marked them off as a special status group. Even now these rights are assiduously guarded.

Ha Tsuen's elders also acted as guardians of lineage custom. In some adoption cases, especially if male children from outside the lineage were involved, elders publicly validated the transfer of the child (J. Watson 1975a). After they were feasted by the adopting family, the elders signed a document that verified the transfer and served as proof of the child's rights to a share in family and lineage property. According to the Teng, elders also had the right to expel (*ch'u tsu*) men from the lineage. There are no recent cases of this in Ha Tsuen, although I was told that such an expulsion was considered in 1972. The incident in question involved an intralineage marriage. The couple left the village, however, and no formal sanctions were imposed.

Aside from acting as arbiters of custom, the elders also had the responsibility for authorizing the activities of Ha Tsuen's village guard (discussed in detail later in this chapter). Every year, at the installation of the new guardsmen, elders put their seals to a document that listed the names of the guardsmen and detailed their duties. Appropriately, the installation ended with a feast given by the guard in honor of the elders. One suspects that this authorization was a pro forma recognition of decisions already taken.

In principle all elders deserve respect, and they did serve as a source of authority, especially in those affairs that touched on lineage practice and custom. Did their authority go further than this? By virtue of their position as elders, did they have the power to settle disputes and to make community decisions? There is not a great deal of evidence on this point, but it appears that the authority of some elders extended beyond purely lineage matters. In 1978 one of the community's most respected elders (a man aged 79) told me that in the past Ha Tsuen had what he described as a lineage council (this was later confirmed by other informants). According to this man there were about 100 elders in Ha Tsuen during the early twentieth century, and about 20 of these made up the lineage council. These 20 men were selected by the elders themselves. There was no voting, and the councilmen were chosen by acclamation. According to my informant, these council members were "men of reputation and wealth." It appears that the council worked with the manager of Yu Kung T'ang in settling disputes and overseeing local administration. Villagers said that if anyone disagreed with the decisions reached by the council and manager, he could, as a last resort, take his case to outside authorities. It appears, however, that this last

Local political organization
Elderhood and political decision making

The manager of Yu Kung T'ang was not, of course, the only political force in Ha Tsuen. The lineage elders also had a role to play, but as I have already noted they were not really powerful. Most writers stress the ceremonial/symbolic significance of elderhood and tend to be dismissive of elders' political power (see, e.g., Baker 1968:52; Potter 1968:29). For example, Hugh Baker writes: "Respect and feasting were the rewards of elderhood, but no overt political control was exercised by these men" (52). While this characterization is not entirely inaccurate, the role of elders cannot be so easily dismissed. Among the Teng there were, in effect, two kinds of elders. Any male Teng 61 years or over was designated an elder (*fu lao*) and as such had certain largely ceremonial rights. Some elders, however, had more influence than others, and it is this smaller, wealthier group of elders who made up the lineage council.

In some Chinese villages men did not automatically become elders upon reaching the required age. According to C. K. Yang, in the Kwangtung village of Nanching only those men who could afford to celebrate their sixty-fifth birthdays by lavish feasting were allowed to become elders (Yang 1959b:93–4). In Ha Tsuen there was no financial prerequisite for elder status, and the Teng believe that all men 61 years or older should enjoy respect. When I first moved into the village, one or two villagers suggested that I make ceremonial calls on the oldest males of the community before I began my research. The first call was made on the lineage master (*tsu chang*), the oldest man in the most senior generation of the lineage. In 1978 Ha Tsuen's lineage master was an illiterate exfarmer. He was accorded respect, but he had absolutely no power in community affairs.

Significantly, lineage masters were (and are) nearly always men from the poorest segments of the lineage. This is explained by the fact that in Chinese society there is a tendency for men from wealthy families to marry and produce children at an earlier age than men from poor families (see, e.g., Baker 1979:55–7). Among the rich, the time span between generations might be 20 or 25 years, while among the poor it might be as much as 30 or 40 years. In 1978 some of Ha Tsuen's landlord-merchant families were in their twenty-eighth generation, while Teng from poor segments were only beginning to produce sons in the twenty-sixth generation. The lineage master was a survivor of the twenty-fourth generation in 1978. Over many generations, the likelihood of producing a lineage master from a poor segment increases. Because of the pattern I have just described, it is highly unlikely that the ceremonial master of the lineage could ever compete successfully for power with Ha Tsuen's wealthy leaders. Aside from the fact that lineage masters are rarely equipped with the necessary experience for leadership, villagers do not really expect the incumbent to take part in the hurly-burly of political decision making. In fact, they would find the prospect of a politically motivated master rather unseemly. The lineage master should be

Inequality among brothers

disputants than with some abstract concept of justice, is valued by Ha Tsuen people, and this story is typical of other accounts of successful dispute settlements in the New Territories.

Villagers maintain that Cheng-ming was a "man of the world," and to emphasize this point they note that he knew important people outside Ha Tsuen. It is said that he entertained Hong Kong governors in his home, and there are a number of old photographs in the community that capture Cheng-ming's meetings with members of Hong Kong's urban elite. These contacts were an important ingredient in Cheng-ming's position of authority in the community. An effective leader must be able to speak for the village in the wider world and act as a broker for villagers in their dealings with outsiders. Judging from the way they speak of his exploits, the Teng are proud to have had Cheng-ming as a member of their lineage. In the list of Cheng-ming's qualities there is always some mention of his enormous wealth: "Of course, he was also very rich," people say. This last attribute is so evident to the Teng that it hardly needs to be stated.

Knowledge of the world outside Ha Tsuen, philanthropy, political savvy, and wealth are the qualities that the Teng themselves mention in relation to Cheng-ming. However, his position in the community did not rest simply on force of personality or on wealth. There were, after all, other rich men in Ha Tsuen. To understand Cheng-ming's role in local politics, it is necessary to examine the structural supports of that role. How did a man who held no political office become such an important force in the community?

As manager of Yu Kung T'ang, Cheng-ming was in a position to dominate many local economic activities. During his time as manager, Cheng-ming was responsible for administering Ha Tsuen's pier and market and therefore had an important voice in determining market fees and licenses. He also oversaw the maintenance of the channel that linked Deep Bay to the market pier at Lo Uk Tsuen and had overall responsibility for collecting the fees that cargo boats were charged for the use of that pier. Community projects such as the construction and care of public paths and public wells were largely the manager's responsibility. Finally, and perhaps most significantly, the manager of the central ancestral hall (along with the elders) was responsible for organizing the bidding process by which the leader of the village guard was chosen.

Cheng-ming also served as manager of a number of other large estates (for more discussion, see Chapter 4). This gave him control over a large amount of land and made him well known throughout the *hsiang* and beyond. Cheng-ming had many personal contacts with merchants in Yuen Long, Nam Tao, and urban Hong Kong. Knowing what one's neighbors were doing and what was happening in the region's market towns and governmental centers was a prerequisite of successful local leadership in 1900 (this continues to be true even now). Cheng-ming was a Teng, a Ha Tsuen man, and a member of the region's elite, and as such he was well informed about affairs both within and outside of his own community.

Local political organization

often worked to direct and interpret that will. In the past, Yu Kung T'ang's manager was chosen by lineage elders. However, because it was essential that the manager be literate, that he be a man with knowledge of business, and a man of wealth, there were only a handful of possible candidates. The openness of the "election" was further restricted by the fact that the managership was usually held for life and was often passed from father to son. Considering all these limitations, the freedom of the elders to choose a manager was more apparent than real. However, they alone had the right to legitimate the authority of Yu Kung T'ang's manager.

Because Ha Tsuen lacked formal political offices, local leaders built up their power and position by a variety of informal means. In order to understand traditional patterns of leadership, it may be helpful to examine the career of Teng Cheng-ming, the wealthy landowner and merchant discussed in Chapter 4. I have chosen to concentrate on Cheng-ming because of his obvious importance to the community and because there is more material (both anecdotal and documentary) concerning him and his career than concerning any of Ha Tsuen's other leaders who were active prior to 1950.

In conversations, villagers often compared Cheng-ming to his brother Cheng-fu; comparisons, it should be noted, that were invariably to the disadvantage of Cheng-fu and his line. Cheng-ming is said to have been a "good and rich man." In contrast, villagers insist that Cheng-fu and his descendants were concerned only with money. The miserliness of Cheng-fu and his family is the subject of many stories and jokes in Ha Tsuen. What were the qualities that made Cheng-ming into such a popular leader in contrast to his stingy brother? The Teng themselves place particular emphasis on Cheng-ming's philanthropy. As examples of his good works, people point to a picture hanging in Yu Kung T'ang and say that Cheng-ming was responsible for the local school that the photograph commemorates. He also provided a new (and very expensive) copper bell for a local temple when the original was stolen by pirates.

Teng Cheng-ming is thought to have had great ability in settling disputes. One particular story was recounted to me many times. Two *hsiang* villages had been warring for decades. Finally, their dispute was taken to Cheng-ming, who, backed by a few wealthy elders, went to each quarreling party in turn. To each disputant Cheng-ming said that he had found that the other party was in the wrong, and therefore in compensation he was handing over a sum of money. This procedure was followed with both groups, and, so the villagers report, "Everyone was satisfied, and they stopped fighting." The money used in compensation came either from Cheng-ming or from the funds of Yu Kung T'ang; villagers are unclear on this point. Invariably the storyteller ended the account by saying that at some time after the settlement, the disputants found that the money used in compensation had come from Ha Tsuen. They were so embarrassed by all the trouble they had caused that they returned the money to Cheng-ming. This style of settling disputes, which has more to do with shaming the

Local political organization

resort was rarely used. One assumes that there was considerable pressure not to break ranks and go outside the lineage.

Villagers reported that in the past the lineage council had important decision-making powers. The council, according to informants, has not been active since the 1950s, and therefore it is difficult to substantiate villagers' claims. I think it is safe to assume that the lineage council did play some role in local politics but perhaps not as important as contemporary Teng maintain. Freedman, writing of lineage councils in general, notes that these councils often included both elders and younger men of wealth and influence. He writes: "Associated with ... the hall of a lineage as a whole, there were councils, the membership of which was not regulated by any simple principle of seniority" (1966b:6). Freedman goes on to conclude, "To [the council] gravitated the men who for one reason or another were capable of exercising political leadership; they were the governors" (1966b:6). Whether this description of lineage councils fits Ha Tsuen is impossible to know for certain; however Freedman's comments do highlight the fact that age alone was not the only or even the most important criterion for local leadership.

Clearly Ha Tsuen was not ruled by a gerontocratic elite. The role of Yu Kung T'ang's manager (whose age was irrelevant to his position) shows that effective leadership fell to men of wealth who had contacts outside the village. The relationship between Yu Kung T'ang's manager and the lineage council was not highly formalized. Because the manager, and the manager alone, was involved in the day-to-day running of lineage and community affairs, a forceful manager could no doubt find ways of seeing that his wishes were acted upon.

Local administration: the bidding system

Yu Kung T'ang acted as a central clearing house for general lineage and community concerns. In a similar manner each hamlet administered its own particular affairs. As with the practice in Yu Kung T'ang, the managers of hamlet property played an important role in local administration. The residents of Sik Kong Wai, like their counterparts in other hamlets, were members of a corporation that owned a few small paddy fields, a man-made pond located just outside the hamlet wall, and a number of wells. Income from these properties was used for the repair of hamlet paths and walls and for the general upkeep of the community. The manager or committee of management (both forms appear to have been used in the past) was (like the manager of Yu Kung T'ang) responsible for collecting the income from hamlet property and for seeing that repairs were made.

To handle the mundane problems of everyday life (for example, refuse collection or the maintenance of hamlet ponds), the Teng utilized an ingenious system of bidding. This system managed to get the job done efficiently and had the added advantage of providing money for the coffers of Yu Kung T'ang and hamlet corporations. Because bidding is little discussed in the literature on rural

Inequality among brothers

China, two examples are provided: one deals with a hamlet, the other with Yu Kung T'ang.

The first step in the bidding process was the posting of a public notice that announced, for example, that on a given date the right to collect refuse in Sik Kong Wai would be put out for bids. On that day interested parties attended the bidding that was held at the gate to Sik Kong Wai. Each participant made his bid, and the manager then confirmed the amounts and notified the successful candidate. The bid in cash was then turned over to the manager, who entered it in the hamlet's accounts. At this point the manager's responsibility was at an end. For a set period the successful bidder was responsible for collecting the hamlet's refuse. The advantage to the bidder lay in his exclusive right to collect animal (and human) manure in the hamlet, which he then used to fertilize his own fields or sold to other farmers. Refuse collection in the market worked in a similar manner, except that the cash bid went into the coffers of Yu Kung T'ang.

Although Yu Kung T'ang was responsible for the overall administration of the local market and pier, the everyday management of these two facilities was in the hands of a private contractor. The bidding system for the pier and market worked much as described above. In the case of the pier, successful bidders collected fees from the boats that stopped at Ha Tsuen Market. In return they were responsible for maintaining the pier. The bidder's profit lay in the difference between the fees he collected and the amount he bid for the privilege. The bidding system did provide an important source of income for some local households, but it should be remembered that bidders had to be able to lay their hands on ready cash (in order to make the bid), which very likely precluded the participation of the poorest families.

Villagers maintain that most of the bids were sealed or made in secret. The managers who actually organized the bidding therefore had some discretion in choosing the winners. The system of bidding is still in operation in Ha Tsuen, although some tasks such as rubbish collection have been taken over by the Hong Kong government.

Security: the village guard

It is impossible to know when Ha Tsuen developed its present form of security organization. The Teng themselves cannot imagine their community without their village guard. Because of their coastal interests the Teng have in fact two guard organizations, a "water guard" (*shui hsün*) and a land-based patrol group (*hsün ting*). James Hayes, in a discussion of the Hong Kong region from 1850 to 1911, notes that dominant lineages "got a sizeable revenue from leasing fishing stations and beaches to villagers and boat people" (1977:38). Among the Ha Tsuen Teng, this sizeable revenue was protected by their special water guard.

Local political organization

The organization of Ha Tsuen's two guards is very similar, except that one watches over Teng fishing stations and oyster beds and the other over *hsiang* households. Both have their own written constitutions that set out the responsibilities of guardsmen and specify the procedures for selecting members. The term of the land (or village) guard is one year, and a new leader is chosen by an auction held at Yu Kung T'ang. The leader of the water guard is selected every three years. The bidding for both guards is organized by the hall's manager. As with other bidding, the highest bidder becomes the head of the guard, and the cash he pays goes into the coffers of Yu Kung T'ang. However, unlike in other bidding, each new leader must be formally confirmed by Yu Kung T'ang's manager and by the lineage elders. After putting their seals to a paper signifying their public acceptance of the new leader, the elders are treated to a banquet that is hosted by the newly installed guard head. The leader has the right to choose the guardsmen who will serve under him, with the understanding that each hamlet is represented by at least one member. In the past, the land guard consisted of up to 15 Teng, and the water guard had 12 members, most of whom were poor tenant farmers. No outsider has ever served in either of Ha Tsuen's security organizations.

The village guard has the sole right to collect fees from each household in Ha Tsuen *hsiang*. The guardsmen were not salaried but shared in the fees they collected – the leader, of course, receiving the largest share. As with other positions that were bid for, the leader derived his profit from the fees he collected in excess of his original bid. The income for the water guard came from their right to take 18 percent of the value of all oysters harvested along the Lau Fau Shan coast.

Prior to the 1950s, neither the imperial nor the colonial government offered any consistent protection to the villagers under their authority. The local security forces therefore served an important and useful purpose. In the past the village guard provided farmers with a kind of primitive insurance; if guardsmen could not retrieve stolen or lost goods, they were required to replace them. The guard also defended the community against bandits, pirates, and encroaching neighbors. Dominant lineages in the New Territories all had their own village guard organizations. Each guard presented a united front against the security force of the neighboring *hsiang*, and a kind of a balance of power developed.

The role of the water guard was more clearly commercial than that of the village guard. Water guardsmen kept track of the ownership of individual oyster beds. They saw to it that only those who had a right to collect oysters did so. They also, as we saw in Chapter 4, were in charge of determining who had the right to use Lau Fau Shan's fishing stations. The water guard was responsible for maintaining Teng control over the resources along the Lau Fau Shan coast.

The village guardsmen were in a position to enforce, if necessary, Teng hegemony in the *hsiang*. James L. Watson, in a forthcoming book, describes in detail how dominant lineages, through their village guards, controlled large

Inequality among brothers

territories, collected protection fees, and generally kept a careful watch over any challenges to the status quo. In 1978, Ha Tsuen villagers recalled with pride their once bellicose reputation when their guard brooked no challenges (cf. J. Watson 1977:169, 172). Only the guard was supposed to have access to weapons (both rifles and small cannon) that they kept locked in their headquarters. Guardsmen did not tolerate any signs of independence in their territory, and satellite villagers were sometimes beaten and their property destroyed if they failed to acknowledge Teng superiority.

Most of the guardsmen – perhaps, in the past, all – were trained in the martial arts. They studied under itinerant "masters" who traveled throughout southeastern China offering their services for a small fee, rice, and shelter. Some of the older villagers studied under these masters, whose training sessions were usually held in the courtyard of Yu Kung T'ang. One of the oldest residents of Ha Tsuen, now a respected elder, was famous for his fighting skill. He was especially renowned for his use of a long wooden staff that doubled as an agricultural tool. These staffs are commonly used for lifting and carrying bundles of rice straw or grass. In the past, guardsmen carried these weapon/tools when they made the rounds to collect fees in satellite villages, leaving their neighbors in no doubt of the force that lay behind Teng control. During the late nineteenth and early twentieth centuries the guard also kept rifles and small cannon (the latter for use in interlineage warfare). The Ha Tsuen Teng speak with relish of the time they ruined an important Ping Shan festival with the aid of their cannon. In 1978 an official from the Hong Kong Department of Antiquities excavated a large cannon that the Teng say they buried during the resistance to the British. It now rests just outside Yu Kung T'ang, with the muzzle pointed in the direction of Ping Shan; the Ping Shan Teng, in turn, have two small cannon aimed directly at Yu Kung T'ang. While it is not likely that either lineage will ever resort to this ancient weaponry, both sides seem to take considerable pleasure in quietly menacing each other.

Even after the colonial land registration of 1905, the Teng managed to retain their economic dominance of Ha Tsuen *hsiang*. Yu Kung T'ang continued to hold the lease to the coastline and so controlled the fishing stations and oyster beds along Deep Bay. The Teng owned many of the cargo boats that supplied Ha Tsuen Market, and Yu Kung T'ang owned the market pier over which most goods entered and left the area. Furthermore, the allocation of market stalls was controlled by Yu Kung T'ang. In Chapter 4 I noted that many satellite villagers farmed lands that belonged to Teng landlords; some sold their crops to Teng merchants and manufacturers, and others worked in Teng-owned factories. There were a variety of economic ties that bound satellite villagers to the Teng. This economic dependency was sustained and strengthened by the Teng security forces.

Who reaped the benefits that Ha Tsuen's guardsmen made possible? Obviously they offered a service to the entire *hsiang* in that their regular patrols did deter

Local political organization

criminals and greedy neighbors. This was no small matter in an area where bandit gangs laid siege to whole villages and where villagers could not count on any outside help except what they themselves could muster.

Although Ha Tsuen's security forces offered some protection to satellite villagers, there is little doubt that it was the Teng who benefited most from the guards' activities. The guardsmen themselves, all of whom came from Ha Tsuen's smallholding and tenant households, received direct rewards from their activities. Guardsmen had a vested interest in maintaining the hegemony of the Teng because their fee-taking privileges depended on their ability to maintain the local status quo. Prior to the 1950s there was no real alternative to landlord-dominated politics. Members of the landlord-merchant class held most of the economic and political power in the region. Not surprisingly, the heads of Ha Tsuen's guard organizations were usually handpicked by local landlord-merchants families. In fact, villagers report that in the past landlord-merchants often loaned potential guard leaders the money required for bidding. The bids were often substantial, amounting to as much as HK$1,000 in the 1930s. During my fieldwork in 1977–8, the leader of the water guard was a close political ally (perhaps political client is nearer the mark) of one of San Wai's landlord-merchant families.

While the guardsmen offered some advantages to ordinary villagers, clearly those who gained most from security activities were those who had the most to lose. The two guard organizations provided the force that stood behind the economic and political power of the landlords, and as such they were important factors in the maintenance of the landlord-merchant class. At the turn of the century most of the levers of local power were in the hands of a few families. Two families in particular, those of Teng Cheng-ming and Teng Cheng-fu, stood above the others in terms of power. Even today the descendants of these men carry considerable economic and political weight in Ha Tsuen, and their association with the local security forces continues.

6
Class differences in Ha Tsuen: the social and cultural dimension

In discussing social and cultural differences in China, most scholars have emphasized either the ethnic/regional dimension or have concentrated on differences between the so-called literati (the tiny elite of scholar-bureaucrats) and the masses (a term that is meant to cover the remainder of China's population, from the richest merchant to the poorest laborer). The contrast between the literati and the masses is often expressed in terms of orthodox versus heterodox culture, with the scholar-bureaucrats exemplifying the orthodox form. The present study, however, deals with social and cultural differences between classes. Although these differences exist within a small, closely knit community, they are by no means obscure or insignificant. Like land tenure and political organization, the system of education, inheritance, marriage, and affinity are very much part of the conditions under which Ha Tsuen's landlord-merchants maintained their preeminence for nearly three centuries.

The attitudes, institutions, and social patterns discussed in this chapter and the next are, I believe, broadly representative of Ha Tsuen during much of the twentieth century and perhaps earlier. These findings are based on my observations in the village (1977–8) and on interviews with middle-aged and elderly residents who told me of their own experiences in the period before the Japanese occupation. (Recent changes are discussed in Chapter 8.) While cultural and social differences among the Teng form the basis of this chapter and the next, it is important that we have some understanding of how the Teng themselves perceive this problem. As we have seen, there is a large economic gulf between Ha Tsuen's landlord-merchants and smallholder-tenants. Considering the emphasis that the Teng place on fraternal equality and cooperation, however, it is not surprising that many village men prefer not to discuss – at least directly – economic and social differences within their lineage.[1] This is particularly true of middle-aged and elderly men (as we shall see, however, women are not so reticent).

---

1 This state of affairs is changing somewhat with new forms of political organization (see Chapter 8).

Class differences in Ha Tsuen

In general, Chinese attitudes toward hierarchy and socioeconomic differences are complex and somewhat contradictory. The Confucian view holds that societies are naturally hierarchical.[2] People have different abilities or do different work, which is variously valued. Some people rule, others are ruled; some work with their hands, others with their minds. Although hierarchy is natural, the Confucians also believe that the individual's position in this hierarchy is not preordained. The individual should make of his abilities what he can. His position in society should not be a matter of inheritance but rather it should depend on his achievements. Prerevolutionary China was by no means an egalitarian society (either in thought or practice), but neither was it rigidly hierarchical.

To the Teng, and to many other Chinese, to be wealthy is to be lucky. Farmer A feels that there is no real difference between himself and landlord B except that B has more land. If he, farmer A, were lucky, then he too would become a wealthy landlord. Of course, thrift and hard work are considerations, but these qualities are insufficient in themselves to ensure wealth. In the villagers' view, it is luck that makes the difference. A Ch'ing writer, Ch'ien Yung, expresses this sentiment far more elegantly: "Wealth and high status are like flowers," he writes; "they wither in less than a day. Poverty and low status are like grass: they remain green through winter and summer. But when frost and snow ensue, flowers and grass all wither, and when spring breezes suddenly arrive, flowers and grass flourish. Wealth, high status; poverty, low status; being born and being extinguished; rising and declining; this is a principle of heaven and earth" (quoted in Kuhn 1984:25).

In Ha Tsuen I often found that a poor villager would explain another villager's wealth in terms of geomancy (*feng shui*, "wind and water"). I was told by two San Wai residents that the location of the hamlet's landlord-merchant houses gave these householders a special advantage. According to these accounts, during the late eighteenth century Tso-t'ai and his close kinsmen decided to build their houses in front of San Wai's entrance gate, thereby invading the open space between the hamlet and a nearby fish pond. By building their houses in this particular spot, Tso-t'ai and his brothers, it was believed, had managed "to steal the good geomancy of the village for themselves." Another story had it that the placement of Tso-t'ai's grandfather's grave provided this line with generations of good fortune. The grave is said to have been located in a geomantic configuration called "the eye of the elephant" in the hills behind the village. "Every time the elephant winks," an elder told me (with tongue in cheek, I have no doubt), "his descendants have 30 years of money luck."

The good fortune of whole communities is often explained by geomancy. The Teng village at Lung Yeuk Tau is said to have good geomancy for scholars, whereas Kam Tin and Ping Shan have good geomancy for wealth. Ha Tsuen's

---

2 For discussion of views on social classification in early and late imperial China, see Munro 1969 and Kuhn 1984.

Inequality among brothers

geomancy, villagers note rather unhappily, is good for producing large numbers of male descendants.

The public statements that the Teng make about themselves suggest a highly organized egalitarian group of brothers. There are, of course, personal and factional rivalries among Teng agnates, and on occasion these rivalries have led to public confrontations. However, the Teng much prefer to express their economic and political differences in more subtle ways. Present antagonisms are often discussed by reference to the past. A story told to me by San Wai's geomancer is a case in point. As he told the story, I was left in no doubt that the geomancer was speaking about the present by referring to the past. The story concerned the unfair advantage that Tso-t'ai's line had gained through the trickery and threats of his brother Tso-wen and his sons (see Chapter 2). The geomancer, it will be remembered, was a direct descendant of Teng Wei-yü, whose branch had lost out in the local economic sweepstakes. This type of story, which is similar to the geomantic stories noted above, is common in Ha Tsuen. I found that villagers often explained their dislike of or opposition to each other not in terms of present-day economic competition or domination but in terms of rivalries that had existed among their ancestors. Past antagonisms, it appears, are much safer ground for discussion than current ones.

It is very likely, I think, that economic differences were downplayed at the turn of the century even more than in the 1960s and 1970s. In the past, when Ha Tsuen was still primarily an agricultural community, the differences between rich and poor were, no doubt, more accentuated than they are today. When a tenant's livelihood depended on local landlords, caution was no doubt the better part of valor in relations with wealthy agnates.

In most Ha Tsuen hamlets, social relations were and are closely intertwined.[3] Here again the qualities of brotherliness, sharing, and cooperation are valued. Most male residents live their entire lives in these small communities. Except for the time spent in school, which in the past they may have attended irregularly, boys have little contact with children from other hamlets. The situation for Teng girls is, of course, different: "Girls," villagers say, "are born looking out." Because of surname exogamy, girls must leave Ha Tsuen when they marry, and as married women they must adjust to a new community. However, once they make this adjustment, they become closely associated with their new hamlet.

Although hamlet affiliation played (and plays) a significant part in the lives of most Teng, it is important to remember that the ties of descent serve as a counterbalance to the pull of neighborhood and locality. I have already discussed

---

3 The hamlet of Ha Tsuen Market is a special case, for obvious reasons. It is primarily a market, and although the number of residences is increasing it is not very populous. Furthermore, many of its residents are not Teng, and some have only recently moved to Ha Tsuen. Not surprisingly, Ha Tsuen Market does not have the same types of associations nor the same ritual repertoire as the other hamlets.

Class differences in Ha Tsuen

the important role that the lineage plays in unifying the Teng; the lineage is a suprahamlet organization. In Ha Tsuen, residence and segment membership tend to crosscut each other, for all of Ha Tseun's hamlets are composed of more than one major segment. Hamlets are not, therefore, undifferentiated little enclaves, but there is no doubt that they form tightly knit communities.

Like Ha Tsuen's other hamlets, Sik Kong Wai is defined by its *t'u ti* or "earth god," shrine. Such shrines embrace a specific territorial unit, and the people who live in that territory fall under the protection of their particular earth god. In most hamlets the daily care of *t'u ti* is taken in turn by the women of each household. Just as Yu Kung T'ang symbolizes the unity of the lineage, so does the earth god shrine symbolize the ritual unity of the hamlet. Throughout the year a number of rituals are organized by each hamlet, and most hamlets select one or two married male residents (called *chieh t'ou*, or "ceremonial head") to oversee these rituals. The hamlet ritual calendar is elaborate, and it is clear that people take enormous pleasure in celebrating the birth of new hamlet sons, or the dragon boat festival, or the rituals of the lunar New Year, as a hamlet community.

Women are an important force in hamlet life. To a large extent it is women who set the tone for each hamlet. This is not to suggest that women determine the pattern of hamlet social life, for women are dependent on factors well beyond their control. However, women's interaction provides excellent clues and insights into the relationships between classes in Ha Tsuen. Women of the same hamlet spend much of their working and leisure time in each other's company. In Sik Kong Wai the hamlet's older women can be found congregated near the gate to the hamlet even in cold weather. There they spend their time watching grandchildren, assembling plastic flowers, or talking. The younger women are busy with their household and gardening chores, but they too rely on each other for companionship and mutual aid. Their socializing is generally confined to their work routine, and groups of young women can be seen around the hamlet's water taps, where they spend much of their time washing clothes, cleaning vegetables, and preparing meals.

Women are particularly powerful as sanctioning agents within their hamlet enclaves. The women's society of Sik Kong Wai is fiercely egalitarian and conformist. Not surprisingly, it is often the middle-aged and older women who dominate public opinion. These women see themselves very much as the arbiters of Sik Kong Wai social life. It is no small matter for a villager to be out of favor with this group. On occasion, informal but powerful sanctions are brought to bear on Sik Kong Wai's more exceptional citizens. Conformity is exacted by gossip and withdrawal of social and economic support. Considering the pressures to conform, it is not surprising to find that some of the hamlet's most upwardly mobile and successful residents have moved out of Sik Kong Wai in recent years. Some have settled in neighboring hamlets, and others have left Ha Tsuen altogether.

The physical layout of a hamlet like Sik Kong Wai (see Chapter 1) supports

Inequality among brothers

the residents' view that it is an undifferentiated community: "We are really all the same," they say. For them, inequality is something that exists in other hamlets and villages. And yet it is important to note that Sik Kong Wai residents are not all the same. Colonial land records show that even in 1905 Sik Kong Wai was not composed entirely of tenant farmers. Although most residents were landless or land poor, some families did have private holdings, the largest being just over 5 acres (see Chapter 4). Of course, this is insignificant compared to the enormous holdings of Ha Tsuen's landlord-merchant families. But these land figures do call into question the characterization that residents make of their own hamlet.

Both men and women present a similar picture of social equality in Sik Kong Wai, but their pronouncements on other hamlets in Ha Tsuen are decidedly different. Unlike their husbands, Sik Kong Wai women are very forthright in their condemnation of San Wai's landlord families. In discussing their past lives, Sik Kong Wai women would point in the direction of San Wai and say that all of Ha Tsuen's landlords and moneylenders live there. It was these people, the women maintain, who in the past owned all the land and lent them money at high rates of interest. While Sik Kong Wai women readily point out the differences between themselves and San Wai's landlords, their husbands are more reticent. It is not that these men are blind to the fact that the landlord-merchants lived in larger houses, ate better food, and owned more land than they did. Rather, they imply that these matters are not a proper topic of conversation. These attitudes are beginning to change, however, as a new group of political leaders make economic differences between themselves and Ha Tsuen's traditional elite a point of contention (see Chapter 8).

Like their counterparts in Sik Kong Wai, San Wai women were quick to call attention to the differences between themselves and their wealthy neighbors. "They're rich, so they use a different temple from us at New Year," was a common reply to my questions regarding temple attendance. Women from San Wai's landlord-merchant families tend to remain aloof from most of their fellow villagers. In the past these women had servants, and there was no necessity for them to participate in the usual female work routines. Servants ran the errands, carried the water, and did the hundreds of tasks that brought most village women into regular contact with one another. Although they no longer have servants, these women continue to keep contacts with their poor neighbors to a minimum. Significantly, in San Wai the care of *t'u ti* and organization of hamlet rituals are not shared among resident households but are left to a hired temple keeper. Perhaps it would be thought unseemly for women from landlord-merchant families to be seen working side-by-side with the wives of tenant farmers.

Women in wealthy homes were not, of course, completely isolated. In fact, a few were directly involved in their husbands' or sons' political and business affairs. In the 1950s and 1960s, Teng Cheng-ming's daughter-in-law, I was told, sought out and made friends with the wives of her son's political allies, both

Class differences in Ha Tsuen

rich and poor. In more recent years her son's wife has become active in the management of one of the family's businesses at Lau Fau Shan. This type of involvement appears to have been unusual in the past, however. Another woman who married into a landlord-merchant household in the 1930s is probably more representative of women from this class. This particular woman has remained aloof from other village women. Until the 1950s she relied on servants to do household chores and run errands. Now she no longer has servants, but this has not forced her to have more contacts with other women in the community. She has had water piped into her house (unusual in the rural New Territories), and she does her marketing in Yuen Long, not in Ha Tsuen. For many years she devoted herself to her sons and their education. In 1977–8 she lavished her time and attention on her two grandsons, whose parents continue to live in the parental household.

Obviously, men and women take a contrasting view of economic and social differences in Ha Tsuen. Women willingly point out the differences between Ha Tsuen's rich and poor, whereas their husbands prefer to avoid the subject altogether or discuss it only obliquely (by reference to *feng shui*, or luck, or past events). Now that we have some appreciation of how the Teng themselves view the differences within their lineage and community, it is possible to examine some of those differences in more detail.

Servants and slaves

In many parts of southeastern China, the ownership of slaves and the employment of household servants were important indicators of wealth and status. Even now, long after the demise of the slave system, villagers measure their predecessors' wealth by the number of slaves (*hsi min*) they owned. While the presence of *hsi min* in Ha Tsuen is not exactly a matter of pride, it is something that can be used to clinch an argument about a particular family's past status. I was often told by wealthy villagers that their father or grandfather had once owned *hsi min*; this was considered to be proof positive of their privileged past.

Except for a row of dilapidated mud brick hovels located near the residences of San Wai's landlords, there are few reminders that slaves once lived in Ha Tsuen. Today most of these hovels are abandoned, and a few have been destroyed to provide sites for new houses. An elderly landlord whose family once kept slaves told me that there were about 20 *hsi min* living in San Wai in 1900.

Hsi min were unpaid domestic servants who had either been purchased by their masters or were descendants of slave fathers (see J. Watson 1976, 1980). The status of *hsi min* was inherited in the male line. According to Ha Tsuen people, *hsi min* served as messengers, sedan chair carriers, and domestic laborers. Two elderly men noted that *hsi min* also worked at odd jobs in their masters' business establishments in Ha Tsuen Market. *Hsi min* were acquired from families who lived outside Ha Tsuen; they were not Teng, and they were never allowed

Inequality among brothers

to become members of the lineage. Male slaves were regarded with disdain by all Teng villagers. According to local people, *hsi min* began to disappear (some ran away, others just left without opposition) about the time of the 1911 Republican Revolution in China. However, there were *hsi min* living as slaves in some parts of the New Territories well into the 1920s.

Many wealthy San Wai families kept young female servants as well as *hsi min*. The institution of indentured service for women (these girls were called *mui jai* in Cantonese) continued until the 1950s in Ha Tsuen. These servants were brought into their master's household when they were eight or nine years old. Women from landlord-merchant families said that they treated these girls much as they would a younger sister or daughter. Although there is little doubt that these girls had a higher status than male *hsi min*, they were clearly servants. Some *mui jai* retained close ties to their masters' families after their marriages, but there is no concealing the fact that these girls were purchased from their parents (the villagers use the term *mai*, "to buy," when speaking of their acquisition). *Mui jai* received no regular salary but were dependent on the largess of their master and mistress. When they reached marriageable age, their master had the responsibility of arranging a suitable match. The groom's family normally paid only a token bride price for *mui jai*; the brides in turn received very little in dowry from their masters' household. *Mui jai* marriages were therefore clearly marked off from the marriages of even the poorest farmers. It is interesting to note that some poor Teng took *mui jai* from wealthy families in San Wai as secondary wives (*hsi p'o*, lit. "minor wife") when they had no son by their principal wives (*ta p'o*, lit. "major wife"). On more than one occasion village women told me that to make a proper marriage it was essential for the basic elements of the marriage ritual to be performed and a respectable bride price to be paid. Otherwise, they said, "It would look like the marriage of a *mui jai*."

Although *hsi min* and servant girls may not have been an important source of labor in Ha Tsuen, their existence in certain households clearly marked off wealthy families from their less affluent agnates. As I have already noted, the presence of servants also made it possible for women in landlord-merchant families to carry on a leisured style of life, free of domestic toil.

Class and literacy in Ha Tsuen

In the past, China had two recognized elites, an economic elite and the literati (or scholar-official elite). Of course, these two groups were closely related; success in one sphere often led to success in the other. Nevertheless, during most of China's dynastic history, members of the literati outranked those who were merely rich. Ha Tsuen's landlord-merchant families were never members of this office-holding elite. Over the centuries a few Teng managed to attain imperial degrees, but according to the 1819 gazetteer no Ha Tsuen Teng held an official bureaucratic position (and I know of none after that date). Rather,

Class differences in Ha Tsuen

the Teng elite consisted of wealthy landlords and merchants, members of a local proprietor class.

Although Ha Tsuen was not noted for its scholars and officials, the Teng valued education. In a literate and bureaucratized society like China, literacy was of tremendous economic and social importance.[4] The ability to read and write had both status and pragmatic implications (for a general discussion of literacy in Ch'ing China, see Rawski 1979). The details of loans and property transfers were recorded, as were the adoption and sale of children. Legal ownership of land required written documentation, and of course written genealogies were used as proof of membership in landed estates. Lengthy written genealogies were kept up to date, and almanacs were regularly consulted by rich and poor alike. Literacy even played an important part in communication with the gods. Supplicants paid specialists to write out messages to a particular god, and these documents were then dispatched to the other world by burning (Ahern 1981:16–30).

Literacy was an essential ingredient of the broker or intermediary role that some of Ha Tsuen's landlords and merchants played so successfully. Education was not merely a status marker in Ha Tsuen. Control over the written word, whether it be in genealogies, land deeds, adoption contracts, or mortgages, was of obvious political importance in a society where many were illiterate (see also Goody 1968:11–12). During my fieldwork in the New Territories I was fascinated to discover the large number of important documents in the hands of wealthy villagers. In discussions with landlords it was not uncommon for one of them to disappear into a side room of his house and return with a set of temple accounts, a genealogy, or a family history to settle a point of disagreement or confusion. Three or four San Wai men kept huge wooden cupboards full of community records. They were loath, however, to let anyone examine their collections, for their stock of documents meant power. There is every reason to believe that in the past, as now, wealthy men controlled access to documents of general ritual and economic significance.

Dealing with both the imperial and colonial governments and with powerful outsiders required literate intermediaries. In the past, taxes were usually paid through these middlemen. Proof of landownership was and is an important matter to many Teng, not only to the rich. Proper documentation of ownership was a complicated affair, and ordinary villagers were forced to seek aid from their more knowledgeable kinsmen in obtaining the necessary papers. Many villagers insist that they lost land either because they lacked proper documentation or because of double-dealing on the part of their more informed kinsmen. Even

---

4 Literacy was respected not only because it allowed people to read land deeds and bills of sale but as something of value in its own right. Before the Second World War, Ha Tsuen boys were educated in the traditional manner. They studied the Chinese classics, which emphasized moral training, literature, and history.

Inequality among brothers

today misunderstandings arise over the ownership of fields or commercial lots. Villagers may think that they own one field, whereas the government's records may show that they own another. Today ordinary Teng still seek the help of educated agnates. Intermediaries are often necessary for success in acquiring government licenses and permits to build houses or establish businesses.

It is clear from local records and from informants' accounts that in the past most wealthy men were well educated by local standards; in fact, in the 1920s and 1930s the sons of Ha Tsuen's wealthiest families often attended special schools in Yuen Long, Nam Tao, and Canton. Not surprisingly, the level of education among Ha Tsuen's tenants and smallholders was low in comparison to that among their rich agnates. In a lineage community like Ha Tsuen, economic position and estate membership were important factors in determining how well one was educated.[5] Village schools were usually sponsored by lineage estates, and, because they could attract (and pay) experienced teachers, the wealthiest estates had the best schools. Not all of these schools, however, were for the exclusive use of estate members. In some cases Teng boys living anywhere in Ha Tsuen could enroll, although they were expected to pay a higher fee than boys who were members. At the turn of the twentieth century three of the five local schools were located in San Wai.

While most of Ha Tsuen's elderly men have had some formal schooling, it is not uncommon to find totally illiterate men in nearby villages. Residents of satellite villages explained to me that they were dependent on fellow villagers for their education because their parents could not afford to hire professional teachers. They attended school when someone from their home village had the time, the inclination, and the ability to teach. In Ha Tsuen, by contrast, there were always schools open throughout the year; literacy did not depend completely on the harvest cycle or on the personal whims of neighbors. Ha Tsuen was never very successful in the competition for imperial degrees, but most Teng men were trained to be minimally literate and so had some advantage in the wider society, an advantage denied to the majority of nearby satellite villagers.

Inheritance and marriage

China has often been held up as an example of a society in which the system of inheritance had the effect of diluting wealth (see, e.g., Baker 1979:133; Chang

---

5 Gender was also a major factor in determining an individual's level of literacy. In Ha Tsuen I knew of only seven literate women over the age of 45 years in 1978. Three of these women had married into landlord-merchant households, and two were the unmarried daughters of these families. In fact, four of these women belonged to one household, that of Teng Cheng-ming's grandson—the wealthiest line in Ha Tsuen. The other two women married poor Teng farmers who later emigrated to Britain (although the women remained in the village). It is interesting to note that both of these marriages were so-called "love matches," and they were considered very unusual for the 1940s and early 1950s when they took place.

Class differences in Ha Tsuen

1962:125; Fei and Chang 1948:19–20, 117; Ho 1962:162–5; Myers 1970:160–2, 288, 1975:273). The extensive property of a large landowner was divided among his male heirs upon his death. Depending on the number of heirs, a man's wealth was either concentrated or dispersed. The disposition of a family estate, it is argued, depended on the number of claimants. Of course, it was not only the rich who were affected by the system of equal inheritance among sons. The holdings of the poor were also fragmented at the death of the household head or at the time of partition. With the poor, the division was not just a matter of carving up a large estate but of making a small estate completely uneconomic. Many scholars have argued that under China's system of inheritance it was difficult for a family to retain their status and position within the class structure for very long. As a consequence, many scholars maintain, late imperial and Republican China were characterized by a high rate of social mobility (Baker 1979:131–5; Chang 1955:219, 1962:125; Elvin 1970; Hsu 1949; Myers 1970:217–40, 288–95).

In study after study, anthropologists have noted that the rule in the particular village or region they studied was equal inheritance among brothers (see, e.g., Baker 1979:9; Cohen 1976:70; Gallin 1966:145; Shiga 1978; M. Yang 1945:83; C. K. Yang 1959b:92). When the father dies, his sons inherit his property. If his wife survives, she becomes the responsibility of her husband's inheritors. Sometimes one son, usually the eldest, may be given an extra share of the patrimony; this is especially the case if he has responsibility for the care of his aged parents. By custom, daughters and wives have no rights of inheritance, although women could and often did pass on their personal valuables, especially jewelry, to their daughters and daughters-in-law. In discussing Chinese inheritance it is important to remember that property was not always divided at the father's death; sometimes it was divided before his death and sometimes long after. What is important for the purposes of this discussion is that sons are said to have equal rights to the patrimonial estate. This sketch of inheritance is one with which the Teng would agree, and it is broadly representative of inheritance patterns in Ha Tsuen.

However, some of the material I collected in Ha Tsuen does not conform to the rule of equal inheritance among sons. Equal inheritance, I found, did have its limits, particularly for those at the two economic extremes, the wealthy landlords and the landless poor.

In 1905, according to my estimate given earlier, about 55 percent of Sik Kong Wai's resident households were landless. For most peasant families, therefore, the division of land was hardly a relevant matter. The ownership and distribution of houses was, however, of great importance. Among the Teng the possession of a house implies social adulthood; to marry, a man must have access to a house, or he must be able to build one for himself and his bride. When speaking about the rigors of their past lives, villagers often told me that certain men had to leave the village because their fathers did not have houses to bequeath them

Inequality among brothers

and they could not afford to build a house for themselves. Those who had neither land nor houses were truly poor in the eyes of their fellow villagers (for a general discussion of downward mobility among China's poor, see Moise 1977).

As noted above, Ha Tsuen residents do not live in large family compounds but in terraced houses situated along narrow lanes. In recent years people have begun to build outside the boundaries of the old hamlets, but most residents continue to live in traditional-style housing. A household that eats together may inhabit two or three houses in different parts of the hamlet (cf. Hayes 1970:159; Nelson 1969:114). A newly married couple might share a house with the groom's parents, but eventually the shared house will be theirs. Usually only one married couple resides in a house. In the past, before villagers became factory workers, many younger sons were forced to leave the village. In families that had, for instance, four sons and two houses, the two youngest sons were likely to be left without any houses. Customarily sons married according to birth order, with the eldest marrying first, which means that the two oldest sons would occupy the houses. When the household divided, either on the death of the father or by mutual consent among the concerned parties, the two married sons came into full possession of the houses. Of course, if the common holdings allowed, the two younger sons might be given a portion of grain or money at the time of division, but this was by no means assured. If the family were very poor, the younger sons would receive nothing. In these circumstances younger sons sometimes, if they remained unmarried, continued to eat with their brother's family and slept in one of the lineage's branch ancestral halls. Even though they were counted as members of their brother's household, their position was ambiguous. Rather than accepting this state of affairs, many young men chose to leave the village altogether (on this point, see also Diamond 1969:64; Fei and Chang 1948:116–17). A few went to sea, some emigrated, and a handful disappeared, never to be heard from again. This process still continues today, although the situation is greatly alleviated by the higher standard of living that wage labor has made possible. In recent years younger sons have no longer been so dependent on their household's resources.

One Sik Kong Wai informant told me of a friend of his youth who was forced to leave the village in the late 1930s. He had two elder brothers who were destined eventually to acquire the family's two houses. The family was landless, and there was nothing for him to do but to try his luck outside Ha Tsuen. This man never returned; some, however, were more fortunate. In the late 1960s a few of these younger sons returned to the village after having succeeded as emigrants in Europe (see Chapter 8).

Inheritance among Ha Tsuen's landlord-merchants is very different from the patterns I have just described. Equal inheritance among sons is the stated ideal, but is it the practice? An examination of the inheritance patterns of two of San Wai's wealthiest families, those of Teng Cheng-ming and Teng Cheng-fu, over the last 100 years is instructive. During fieldwork I discovered that Ha Tsuen's

Class differences in Ha Tsuen

wealthiest family line consistently (generation after generation) had produced only one or two heirs. They had male offspring by mistresses, but these children were not recognized by their fathers. They were considered illegitimate and did not inherit a share of the family estate.

In discussing the inheritance arrangements of Cheng-ming and Cheng-fu, the question of what defines an heir becomes paramount.[6] A man can acquire an heir in different ways: males born to a man's principal wife are his heirs, or males adopted from a kinsman or purchased from a nonkinsman can be granted the status of heirs. But what of children born to a man's secondary wife or his mistress? Shiga, in an essay on inheritance in traditional China, has argued that male offspring born of the same father but different mothers are believed to share equally in the father's *ch'i* ("essence" or "breath") and therefore have equal rights in the patrimony (1978: 122–4). Many authorities argue that according to the Ch'ing legal code, male offspring born of a woman who was neither principal wife nor secondary wife still had the legal right to inherit their father's property (e.g., Evans 1973:26; Jamieson 1970:16; Meijer 1971:12; Okamatsu 1971, App. xxiii).

In Ha Tsuen there was no ambiguity about the status of children born to Teng wives resident in Ha Tsuen. Villagers were, however, less certain about the status of sons born to Teng fathers by women living outside the village. The births of male children born in the village, as we noted, are celebrated by a set of rituals that formally mark the child's acceptance into the community and the patrilineage. It is inconceivable that a male child born to a woman resident in Ha Tsuen should not go through these rituals. And yet, what of male offspring born outside the village? The decision to publicly recognize such offspring as heirs rests with the father. It is up to him to determine whether his children are to be recognized as legitimate by the people of Ha Tsuen. The data that I collected suggest that a male child whose status of heir is not validated in the eyes of the community has no rights of inheritance. He may be passed over when his father's property is divided. Because the community is not aware (in a formal sense) of the offspring's existence, the father does not run the risk of public condemnation for disinheriting "sons of his breath."

There were and are, of course, laws relating to the proper conduct of inher-

---

6 The right to be considered an heir depends in part on concepts of legitimacy, something that is extremely difficult to pin down in Chinese society. Maurice Freedman, writing about family law in British Malaya and Singapore, states that the colonial courts came to the conclusion that English and Chinese practice varied considerably in determining the legitimacy of a child. "In English law," Freedman writes, "a man's child is one born of the lawful wife ... the Chinese attitude is that any child of a man, whatever the status of its mother, is his fully legal offspring as long as he recognizes it as such. English law rests on legitimate birth, Chinese law on recognition of paternity" (1979:118). On other definitions of what constitutes a legitimate heir, see Barrett (1980:296–7) and Wolf and Huang (1980:257).

Inequality among brothers

itance in imperial China and in colonial Hong Kong.[7] Yet these laws have little effect on the village. Ha Tsuen people are either ignorant of or indifferent to these regulations. One suspects that this situation is by no means unique to Ha Tsuen. C. K. Yang noted in the study that he made in the 1940s of the Cantonese-speaking village of Nanching that local people were totally unaware of the Republican regulations dictating equal inheritance for all children, both male and female (1959b:92). Myron Cohen, in his study of a Taiwanese village, notes that membership in the community "implies a dependency upon [village] society expressed through adherence to customary usages such as those regarding marriage, residence, family organization, property and inheritance rights, and many other aspects of life" (1976:9). In at least some parts of China it is the community, not the state, that sanctions inheritance practice.

In Ha Tsuen, two rituals are crucial to the social recognition of a male as a member of his family, community, and lineage. The ritual of *k'ai teng* (lantern lighting), which marks the infant's entrance into the lineage, has already been discussed in Chapter 3. The ritual of *man yueh*, or "full month," is celebrated in the home of a male infant one month after his birth. On this occasion the father and grandfather make offerings at the household altar and at hamlet shrines. Guests (the number depending on the household's status and wealth) are invited to share a special meal with the infant's family. At *man yueh* the child is given a name (*ming*) and becomes a member of his community. After this ritual the mother is allowed to resume contact with other villagers, for, until the full month, she and the child have been isolated from all but the members of their household.

Male children whose births have been celebrated in the rituals of *man yueh* and *k'ai teng* have the status of full heirs; as far as the local community is concerned, they are entitled to their father's property and are responsible for their father when he becomes old. Doubts arise, however, concerning children born outside Ha Tsuen who have not been through *man yueh* or *k'ai teng*. Do such children have a right to their father's property? On occasions when this problem was discussed in my presence, villagers did not give a uniform response. When cases were discussed in the abstract, villagers maintained that such a "son" would have no right of inheritance. However, when specific families

---

7 Writing about the Ch'ing legal code, van der Sprenkel states that "the children of all wives [meaning both principal and secondary wives] were legitimate and no distinction was made between them in matters of inheritance" (1962:15). Male offspring, according to some interpreters of Chinese law and custom, had the right to inherit as long as they were acknowledged by the father (Jamieson 1970:16; Pegg 1981:133–4). Unfortunately the legal situation with regard to inheritance in British Hong Kong is far from clear. Although some in Hong Kong's judicial system stressed that a son cannot be legitimate (and therefore have rights to inherit) unless his parents are married, others maintained that children of illicit unions may be considered legitimate if the putative father recognizes them (Pegg 1981:133–5). Again the distinction is drawn between legitimacy defined by lawful wedlock and legitimacy defined by paternal recognition.

Class differences in Ha Tsuen

were mentioned, people were somewhat uneasy about situations in which the son or sons of nonresident mothers had been "pushed aside" during the division of their father's estate.

It appears that the status of the offspring rests to some extent upon the residence and status of the mother. With women who have undergone some form of marital ritual and reside in Ha Tsuen, the father has much less freedom in defining his heirs. There appears to be something of a continuum in this regard with offspring of principal and secondary wives living in Ha Tsuen at one extreme, and offspring of mistresses living outside the village at the other. With the children of principal wives living in their father's household, few questions of legitimacy can arise. However, with children of women living outside Ha Tsuen, the father has considerable power to define the status of the child.

At this point it may be useful to discuss the range of sexual unions in Ha Tsuen. The status of "principal wife" (*ta p'o*) is accorded to women who have gone through a specific series of marriage rites. The principal wife has been formally betrothed; her family has received a bride price; she has been formally transported to her husband's house during the marriage ritual; she has received a dowry; and her marriage has been celebrated by a formal banquet. According to local custom, she and she alone has the right to be presented to her husband's ancestors in the central ancestral hall on the first day of the marriage rites. In my informants' view, it is this combination of rituals that defines the status of principal wife. In determining what sets the principal wife off from the secondary wife, it should be noted that Ha Tsuen villagers themselves lay particular stress on two things: the formal transferral of the bride and the formal wedding banquet (for discussions of what constitutes a valid marriage in China, see Jamieson 1970:44–5; Lang 1946:38–9; Freedman 1979:99–100, 104; M. Yang 1945:113). In Ha Tsuen, "secondary wives" (*hsi p'o*, sometimes translated as "concubine") were usually taken with little ceremony. I was told by an elderly woman that the only ritual required of the secondary wife was a formal presentation of tea to the principal wife (for a discussion of the difference between principal and secondary wives, see Ch'u 1961:123–5; Kulp 1925:151).

There is little doubt that as long as a woman resides in Ha Tsuen (either as principal or secondary wife), she is defined as a member of her husband's household, and hence the male children she produces are seen as her husband's heirs. In such cases it would be inconceivable, at least in Ha Tsuen, for the father to choose not to celebrate his sons' births in the *man yueh* and *k'ai teng* rituals. However, as noted earlier, when a man's sexual partner lives outside the village the situation is different. Some Ha Tsuen men maintained a principal wife and children in Ha Tsuen and a mistress, or what the villagers call a *ch'ieh shih* (lit. "handmaiden in waiting"), in the market town of Yuen Long or in urban Hong Kong. Relationships with mistresses are characterized by a number of features. The men involved usually have male children by a principal or secondary wife. The mistress does not reside in her husband's household nor in

Inequality among brothers

Ha Tsuen, and in fact her existence is often hidden from fellow villagers. The couple have not been through any public rituals that formalize their sexual relationship. In this study, the term *mistress* is used for women whose position vis-à-vis the men who support them is unrecognized. The unions may be permanent, but the women have no legitimate status as defined by ritual or residence (for a discussion of the differences between wives and mistresses in China, see Freedman 1979:99).

In the past, having a mistress would have been beyond the means of most farmers. Although local men may have had liaisons with women in the nearby market town, most men would not have commanded the resources necessary to support a "secret family." The villagers who kept mistresses prior to the 1960s, in those cases about which I have information, were members of Ha Tsuen's leading landlord-merchant family.

The whole problem of secondary marriage, mistresses, and illegitimacy is difficult to investigate in Ha Tsuen. It was inappropriate to ask direct questions about my informants' own families, although I could in the course of a conversation ask one villager about the domestic situation of another. The matter was further complicated by the fact that people were less than forthcoming on the subject of inheritance and the division of family estates. Again one had to piece together information from many different sources.

The genealogy of Ha Tsuen's premier landlord-merchant family is given in Figure 3. It will be remembered that the men listed in this genealogy are descended from Teng Tso-t'ai, who was Ha Tsuen's leading figure in the mid–eighteenth century. Furthermore, the brothers Cheng-ming and Cheng-fu (Figure 3, generation line 2) were among the wealthiest private landowners in Ha Tsuen in 1905. Teng Cheng-ming had only one brother. This brother, Cheng-fu, had one son by his principal wife, and Cheng-ming had two sons by his principal wife. I do not know whether these men had illegitimate children by mistresses. Both of Cheng-ming's sons married, but one (*B*, generation line 3) had no children, the other (*A*) had one son and daughter by a principal wife and one son and two daughters by a mistress who lived outside Ha Tsuen. A's son by the principal wife (*C*) inherited all of A's property plus all of the property of his father's brother (*B*). A's son C had one son and two daughters by a principal wife and three sons and two daughters by a mistress living in Kowloon. At the time of C's death, *D* (his son by the principal wife) inherited all of C's property.

I was not told of the existence of A's and C's children by mistresses until I had lived in Ha Tsuen for some months. The villagers who told me about these "secret children" were both embarrassed and amused by it. The children had never visited Ha Tsuen, nor had they been through any of the legitimizing rituals described above. Villagers felt that the children, especially the sons of C's mistress, had been treated rather badly. However, they also expressed a grudging admiration for A's and C's foresight in keeping their family's property together. It should be noted that A and C did not completely reject their illegitimate

Class differences in Ha Tsuen

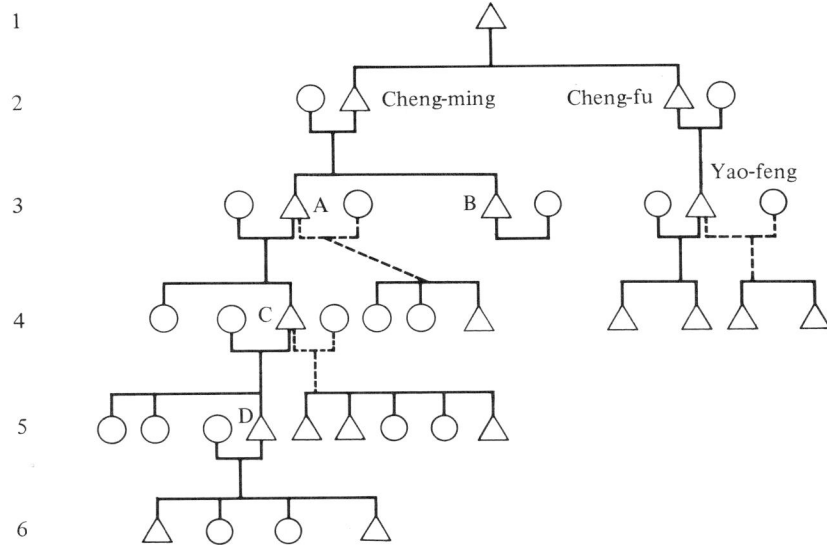

Figure 3. Descendants of Teng Cheng-ming and Teng Cheng-fu. Note: This genealogy may not include all daughters born to this line. On the diagram, C = Teng Shih-min; C inherited from both A and B. D = C's inheritor. Dotted lines show liaisons with mistresses and the children of such unions.

offspring. A's son by his mistress was, I was told, given assistance in settling in Holland. In the case of the sons born to C's mistress, one resided in Kowloon, one worked in a restaurant owned by his half-brother (*D*), and the third worked as a clerk in one of D's businesses in Yuen Long. These men do not live in Ha Tsuen. Villagers believed that D had a responsibility toward the sons of his father's mistress, and yet these men received no share of their father's patrimony.

Teng Cheng-ming's brother, Cheng-fu, had only one son. This son, Yao-feng, was reputed to be one of the wealthiest men in the New Territories and lived in Yuen Long Old Market. He had two sons by his principal wife and twin sons by a mistress with whom he lived (outside Ha Tsuen) after he was widowed. Considering the cases I have outlined above, one might expect that these twin sons would receive no share of their father's considerable property. This is not, however, the case, for these twins underwent the *man yueh* and *k'ai teng* rituals in Ha Tsuen's central ancestral hall. Their father, who was 60 years old when they were born, doted on these twins. Their marriages, which, significantly, were celebrated in Ha Tsuen, were elaborate affairs. It was the twin sons who worked most closely with their father in his many business interests. The two

Inequality among brothers

older sons by the principal wife lived in urban Hong Kong. They also worked in their father's businesses, but it is on the young twins that the father seems to have lavished his time and attention. One can only speculate on the reasons why Yao-feng chose to make his twin sons joint heirs with their older half brothers, but this case does clearly show that offspring born of a mistress living outside Ha Tsuen are not necessarily excluded from inheriting a share in the patrimony. Furthermore, it emphasizes the important point that the father has the power to make such offspring legitimate or illegitimate by the simple act of holding the rituals of *man yueh* and *k'ai teng*.

Are the cases I have just discussed aberrant, or are similar examples to be found in other parts of China? Elizabeth Johnson, who studied a Hakka community in Hong Kong, writes: "A man may take a second wife and legitimize the relationship by bringing her into the village to live." Johnson goes on to say that he "may also legitimize the union by holding a lantern-raising [*k'ai teng*] ceremony ... for sons born, even though the wife and children live elsewhere. The union may also be recognized by his bringing the wife and/or children into the village so that people can see them" (1976:174). Clearly Johnson is here defining a child's legitimacy solely in terms of the legitimacy of the parental union. Perhaps what is being legitimized by holding the lantern ceremony is the child's status, and not that of the parents as Johnson suggests.

Baker, writing about the Liao lineage in Hong Kong's New Territories, makes it clear that in the past the newly born sons of lineage members had to be formally recognized by the lineage elders and a certificate of membership issued (1968:47–8; on certificate of lineage membership, see also J. Watson 1975a). Baker also notes that "concubines ... are frequently taken with no ceremony at all, and tend to achieve full recognition only through bearing sons, who themselves only achieve recognition in many cases through the *k'ai-teng* ceremony" (1968:50). Liu, in her study of Chinese lineage rules, notes that heirs must be recognized by the lineage. She writes, "A son by a marriage unknown to the [lineage] should have neither status in the group nor the privilege to enter the ancestral hall or take part in the rites. An illegitimate son born out of wedlock is similarly rejected. However, the [lineage] after due consideration may agree to confirm such a person as a legitimate heir" (1959:72).

Unfortunately there are few detailed studies of inheritance practice or strategies in China. Johanna Meskill, in her discussion of a wealthy Taiwanese family, cites two examples of irregular inheritance. In one case a secondary wife's (or concubine's) sons (living in their father's household) were disinherited in favor of the principal wife's son (1979:221). The second case involved an adopted son who was refused a share by his father's "regular sons" (79). Norma Diamond reports that in the Taiwanese fishing village she studied often one son inherited, and the remaining sons were forced to fend for themselves (1969:64). In *Earthbound China*, Fei and Chang discuss two estate divisions in which brothers did

Class differences in Ha Tsuen

not receive equal shares,[8] although the villagers were said to subscribe to the notion of equal inheritance among brothers (1948:116–17). In the New Territories village of San Tin, there is a famous (or perhaps infamous) case in which the sons of the principal wife refused to share their considerable patrimony with the sons of the father's secondary wife (J. Watson, personal communication). Elizabeth Johnson reports that among Hakka villagers in Hong Kong "the rights of the second wife's children to inherit would not necessarily be recognized" (1976:175). There are, no doubt, many more examples of inheritance irregularities in China (see, e.g., Liu 1959:69), but unfortunately one needs more than anecdotal material to establish inheritance patterns and strategies.

The cases discussed above suggest that some members of the landlord-merchant class followed a strategy of marriage and inheritance that tended to keep property concentrated in a few hands generation after generation. When a principal wife had produced one or two heirs, the husband might establish a mistress outside Ha Tsuen. The male offspring from such unions had no standing in the lineage or the community and therefore no rights to the property of their genitor. If the father wished to recognize a son as heir he could do so, but that was a matter of personal choice.

Although there can be little doubt that equal inheritance among brothers contributed to the dissolution and fragmentation of many large estates, landlords and merchants were not completely at the mercy of the rule of inheritance. When we examine inheritance practice and the ideas regarding illegitimacy in China, we begin to appreciate that the principle of equal inheritance did not automatically lead, as many scholars have argued, to the breakup of estates nor to a high rate of social mobility. The Ha Tsuen material, coupled with case material from other studies, suggests that Chinese inheritance practice was not as uniform as has commonly been supposed. Furthermore, these and other data suggest that an individual's class position in Chinese society was not simply a matter of the rate at which a particular family produced male offspring.

Did some wealthy men limit the numbers of heirs, whereas others produced large numbers of sons? Under what circumstances did men choose to limit the number of their legitimate offspring, and what kinds of families chose to have fewer rather than many heirs? How widespread was the practice of unequal inheritance among the poor and the arrangement that we might label "discretionary inheritance" among the wealthy? These questions have yet to be fully answered. Among the Teng of Ha Tsuen, at least some landlord-merchants followed a strategy of property concentration that depended on notions of legitimacy. They could, it appears, have their cake and eat it too: by producing

---

8 In one of these cases it appears that support for elderly parents was considered a condition of inheritance (Fei and Chang 1948:116).

Inequality among brothers

a legitimate heir through the principal wife they could avoid dispersing their property, but by setting up secret families outside their home village they could have permanent sexual unions outside marriage and produce children who had no claim on the family estate.

7
Marriage, affinity, and class

In earlier chapters I argued that notions of descent express many of the values and ideals of the Teng. For most villagers the lineage encompasses the known and trusted world, but the Teng cannot remain forever in this familiar environment. Because of surname exogamy, they must find wives outside the lineage. If descent expresses many of the Teng's cherished ideals, then affinity reflects some of their deepest fears and insecurities. Lineage members are bound together by their descent from a common set of ancestors. Those beyond the circle of agnation are "outsiders" (*wai lai jen*), to be treated with suspicion and calculation. For most Teng, marriage and affinity represent the unknown and the dangerous. What role do marriage and affinity play in a community where patrilineal descent is so marked? Are affines treated as enemies? Are married women expected to sever relations with their natal families?[1]

While the economic and political world of the tenant farmer was largely circumscribed by the lineage, the world of the landlord-merchant extended well beyond the confines of Ha Tsuen. Considering the economic and social differences between Ha Tsuen's landlord-merchants and tenant farmers, it may not be surprising to learn that they also had different affinal relationships. Men from landlord-merchant families often had close ties to their affines, whereas men of tenant and small-holding families rarely had direct contact with their wives' kin. A close examination of affinal relations among Ha Tsuen's tenants and smallholders showed that women, not men, played the key role in these relationships. Marriage payments also varied according to economic standing. In fact, marriage exchanges among the wealthy of Ha Tsuen might be characterized as dowry, whereas among the poor the arrangements approached a system of bride price.

Although the ordinary villager and the landlord had two distinct systems of affinity, they shared a uniform set of marriage rites. These rites emphasized the avoidance of affines and celebrated the unity and self-sufficiency of the patrilineage. The rites of marriage downplayed economic differences among lineage

[1] I would like to thank the editor of *Man* for permission to use material in this chapter that first appeared in my article "Class Differences and Affinal Relations in South China," *Man* 16:593–615, 1981.

Inequality among brothers

mates; affinal relations, on the other hand, were firmly grounded in the world of economic differentiation. Considered together, descent and affinity serve to highlight the tensions that exist between an ideology of descent that stresses fraternal equality and an economic structure based on class difference.

In this chapter, I discuss the patterns of marriage and affinity prior to 1960. However, it is important to note that much of this discussion is still relevant to present-day Ha Tsuen. The changes in marriage and affinity that have taken place over the last 20 years are discussed in Chapter 9.

Marriage ritual and affinal relationships

During the course of my fieldwork, I learned that most Teng maintained an icy distance from their wives' kin and tended to have few dealings with their matrilateral relations. This pattern was particularly true of men over the age of 40. There is every reason, judging by my own observations and what the villagers told me, to think that this attitude towards affines was a common feature of affinity during most of the twentieth century (and probably also during the nineteenth century). Many Teng men told me that they disliked being with their affines; they felt "embarrassed," they said, in the company of a wife's father or brother. It was, in fact, not uncommon to find men in Ha Tsuen who had never visited the homes of their wife's father or brothers and who rarely or never had contact with their mother's male kin. Meaningful relationships for most Teng were circumscribed by the lineage.

This general reticence toward and avoidance of affines stands in striking contrast to much of the information we have about the role of affinity in other parts of China, especially Taiwan (on mainland China, see Freedman 1967, 1970; M. Yang 1945:107–22). In Taiwan affinal relations are institutionalized and richly elaborated in ritual (Ahern 1974; Cohen 1976:149–77; Gallin 1960; Pasternak 1972:61–4, 81–4; A. Wolf 1970). Freedman, writing about what he calls the "basic model" of Chinese marriage rites, states that affines play "crucial roles" in these rituals. For example, he notes that the bride's mother's agnates and the groom's mother's agnates have a special place in the marriage ritual. He goes on to say that the bride's younger brother "is nearly always assigned some role [in the ritual] as link between the two families" (Freedman 1967:21).

On the basis of her fieldwork in Northern Taiwan, Emily Ahern has produced a detailed discussion of the leading part that wife givers play in marriage ritual, in household division, in mortuary rites, and in rituals of birth. Ahern describes how in the village of Ch'i-nan the bride's kin (and other families who stand as wife givers to the groom's family) are invited to attend the wedding feast, where the bride's father or brother takes the place of honor (1974:291). On the last day of the marriage rituals both the bride and groom pay a ceremonial visit to the bride's natal family (286). The formal relationship between affines does not, of course, cease with the marriage rites but continues until death, when a brother

Marriage, affinity, and class

(or representative of the wife givers) attends and participates in the funeral rites for his sister and her husband (294). During household divisions, Ahern notes that "all the affinal groups that gave wives to the dividing brothers send gifts to the new household units and take part in the rituals involved in the division" (290). When the father's estate is divided, the sons call in their mother's brother or some senior male from among their mother's kin to mediate the division (291).

Data from Ha Tsuen are strikingly different from the pattern described by Ahern and others. In Ha Tsuen, ties between male affines were not an important element in domestic ritual. As I demonstrate later in this chapter, affines received little attention in the marriage rites themselves. The difference between the ritualization of affinity in Taiwan and the lack of it in Ha Tsuen can, I believe, be attributed to at least two factors. Unlike most villages in Taiwan, Ha Tsuen is composed of a highly complex, wealthy, and powerful lineage. Furthermore, class differences in Ha Tsuen were (and are) very pronounced in comparison to those that have been described for the Taiwanese villages under discussion. Among most Teng one finds a decided avoidance of affines and, not surprisingly, little ritualization of the ties of affinity in marriage rites.

The marriage ceremonies described in this chapter refer to the first marriage of an adult woman where residence was virilocal (Wolf and Huang 1980 refer to this as "major" marriage). Data derive from extensive interviews with married women (40 in all), who were asked about their own marriage rites and with whom I discussed marriage ritual in general. I also attended the complete ritual sequence for three marriages in Ha Tsuen and witnessed parts of several other marriages. Much of this analysis depends on the insights I drew from these firsthand observations. The marriage rituals that I witnessed in 1977–8 were in most respects similar to the descriptions that middle-aged and elderly Ha Tsuen women gave of their own marriage rites (see Chapter 9 for changes). Marriage ritual among the Teng is an elaborate affair, and this discussion by no means provides a complete analysis of marriage rites in Ha Tsuen. I have tended to emphasize those aspects of the ritual that deal most directly with relations between affines.

In Ha Tsuen, marriage rites were the same for both landlord and tenant. On this point villagers were in agreement; there were and still are, they said, no significant differences between the marriage ceremonies of the rich and the poor. Of course, more and better food was served at the wedding feasts of the wealthy, better clothes were worn, and more expensive gifts exchanged, but the structure of the ritual was the same (that is, all marriages followed the same basic sequence of acts over a three-day period). Both the brides of tenant farmers and those of landlord-merchants were formally transported to their husband's village, both worshiped their husband's ancestors, both paid their respects to their husband's agnatic kin, both celebrated the marriage with feasting, and both were sent back to their natal homes for a brief visit on the third and final day of the formal rites. In neither case did the male kin of the bride and the male kin of the groom have any contact with each other, and in neither case did male outsiders (non-Teng wife givers) participate in the marriage rituals held in Ha Tsuen. Many villagers went on to say that both rich and poor had the same kind of marriage payments. However, some wealthy women were adamant in insisting, at least to me, that there were important differences in marriage payments and exchanges between themselves and the poorer villagers. This point is taken up in more detail later in this chapter.

When a family made the decision to search for a spouse for their child, they usually engaged a local woman (*mei jen*, matchmaker) to find a suitable mate. Until the 1940s, some children (5 cases out of 18) were "matched" when they were eight or nine years old, whereas others were betrothed a few months or weeks before the marriage itself. Most brides married in their late teens. After a prospective spouse was found, the negotiations over marriage payments began in earnest. These negotiations were carried out by the matchmaker, who usually was personally acquainted with both families and handled the delicate discussions by meeting with each family separately. During these sometimes lengthy negotiations, members of the bride's household and members of the groom's household did not meet.

Once these important discussions were concluded, the horoscopes of the bride and groom were examined by a professional fortune-teller. If the horoscopes were found to be complementary, the groom's family presented the bride's family with some food gifts that marked the acceptance of the match. When the date of the marriage rites was decided (if the horoscopes were exchanged when the couple were very young, this might have been years later), the groom's family sent the bride's family substantial gifts of food, a cash payment (called *li chin*, or "ceremonial gold"), and a large number of betrothal cakes (*li ping*, or "ceremonial cakes"). These cakes were an important part of the marriage payment. The number of cakes that the bride's family received were specified during the negotiations over *li chin*. When I asked Ha Tsuen women about the gifts and payments their families had received at the time of their own betrothals and marriages, even women in their seventies and eighties remembered the exact number of cakes involved. These cakes, which villagers bought in the nearby market town, were distributed among the bride's kin and served, I was told, as a "betrothal announcement." There were very precise rules about the distribution of such cakes. The brothers and sisters of the bride's father, and the brothers of the bride's mother, were all given the same number of cakes. The remaining cakes were given in declining numbers to the bride's father's agnates and to hamlet neighbors. When asked who among the bride's mother's kin received cakes, village women replied that the mother's brother divided his cakes among those to whom he wished to announce the betrothal.

At the time of betrothal the bride's family hosted a feast that was attended by the bride's father's close agnates (usually descendants of the bride's paternal grandfather); by the father's married sisters (who were not accompanied by their husbands); and by neighbors of the bride's family. Some of the food consumed at this feast was provided by the groom's family (minimally they sent pork, fish, and rice). A portion of the cash payment (*li chin*), I was told, could be used to underwrite the cost of this meal. When I first attended a betrothal feast, I was surprised to learn that the brother of the bride's mother did not attend the feast, nor did he come to pick up his share of the ceremonial cakes. Long after the banquet guests had gone home, the wife of the mother's brother came to the bride's house dressed in her work clothes. After chatting briefly with the bride's mother, the brother's wife hoisted the burden of cakes onto her carry pole and left. When I asked the bride's mother why her brother had not come himself, she replied, "Men never pick up the cakes themselves." In fact, she was quite amused by my suggestion that her brother might attend the betrothal feast or show any interest in the ceremonial cakes.

In 1978 the cash payment of *li chin* was a substantial amount of money, and the total marriage expenses for the groom and his family was often as much as two years of a factory worker's salary (see Chapter 9). Unfortunately, it is far more difficult to know what proportion of income people spent on marrying their children in the past. Among the women from smallholder-tenant families who married prior to 1950, most *li chin* fell within the range of HK$60 and HK$100 (I have information on the marriage payments of 14 women; this figure excludes those married during the chaotic years of the Japanese occupation). Although their *li chin* was much smaller than present-day amounts, they did receive large numbers of betrothal cakes (often two to three thousand). J. L. Buck, in a survey of rural China during the 1930s, found that in marrying a son farm families spent a significant portion of their yearly income. For China as a whole, Buck estimates that a wedding cost a family about four months of their annual income (1937:468). However, marriage was a more expensive affair in the Southeast, where, using Buck's figures, I calculate that in marrying a male offspring families spent nearly three-fourths of their annual income (468–9).

The rites of marriage were (and continue to be) among the most expensive and elaborate of Cantonese ceremonies. The rites began on the evening prior to the bride's move to the groom's house and continued for three days. On the first night the groom's family hosted a feast to which only Teng (the groom's agnates and their dependents) were invited. On the following morning (that is, the first full day of rites) a group of young unmarried men (not including the groom or his brothers), musicians, and two old women (called *ch'ü chia*, or lit. "those who call in a marriage" or bride callers) set off with great fanfare for the bride's village. At the bride's house their entry was blocked by a group of unmarried girls, girl friends of the bride, who had to be bribed with small amounts of money before they allowed the groom's party to enter the house. Soon after the

Inequality among brothers

guests had been served tea and cakes, the bride, dressed in a red silk gown that the groom's family had provided and wearing her newly acquired gold jewelry, most of which was also provided by the groom's family, made her appearance.

A few last-minute finishing touches were added to the bride's attire, and the party was ready to leave. As the bride was escorted from her father's house, the door was slammed shut behind her – a firm reminder that she could no longer call this household her own. Until the 1960s the bride was transferred to the groom's home in a red sedan chair (*hua chiao*). Today a Mercedes Benz, decorated especially for the occasion, is used. In the past, the bride's younger brother, or failing that some other young kinsman, kicked the side of the chair as the bearers set off on their journey; today he kicks the automobile (much to the distress of the car's owner). Here the bride's younger brother plays a far different role from that described by Freedman, who saw the brother as a "link between the two families" (1967:21).

On the return journey to the groom's house the bridal party was enlarged by three new members – the bride and two old women (*sung chia*, lit. "those who send a marriage," or bride senders) from the bride's village. These women stayed with the bride until the second day of the marriage rites. It is important to note that no family members from either the groom's side or the bride's side were members of the wedding party.

It was the job of the *sung chia* (bride senders) and the *ch'ü chia* (bride callers) to assist the bride and encourage her during her three-day ordeal. They were, in effect, ritual specialists, and it was their duty to see that the marriage rites were properly conducted. They accompanied the bride everywhere and instructed her in the proper performance of her many ritual obligations. Although these women were often widows, they were supposed to have many living children, for otherwise it was believed that they would bring bad luck to the bride and groom. The bride senders and bride callers were rarely close kinswomen of the bride or groom. In Ha Tsuen each hamlet had several old women who specialized in this role.

The bride entered the groom's village to great fanfare. Long chains of firecrackers were set off, and everyone rushed to catch a glimpse of the bride. She was protected by brightly colored umbrellas both as she left her father's house and as she entered her husband's. The bride was not allowed to walk to or from the sedan chair but was carried by one of the bride senders. Upon entering the house the bride went immediately into the room that was to become the conjugal bedroom (called the "new room," or *hsin fang*). No member of the groom's family came forward to welcome the bride. Before she could be considered a member of her husband's household, she had to pay her respects to her husband's ancestors.

Soon after entering the new room the bride was led out of the groom's house to the lineage's ancestral hall, where the groom and his father awaited her. On either side the bride was supported by her two protectors (the bride senders) and

Marriage, affinity, and class

the two women from the groom's village (the bride callers), who guided her through the closely packed lanes. As the bride entered the ancestral hall she was taken through, instead of around, the interior doors that shield the ancestral altar (this was an honor that in the past was reserved for imperial officials and brides). When the wedding party arrived at the altar containing the ancestral tablets, the groom and his father worshiped while the bride looked on. Until recently, this was the first time that the bride and groom saw each other. After the groom and his father had worshiped, the bride, aided by her four ritual instructors, knelt at the ancestral altar. When the bride finished paying her respects to the ancestors, the groom and his father left the hall, while the bride and her party followed. This time the bride was led around the inner doors (which were now closed); she was no longer an honored guest. She had been transformed into the lowest of the low, the youngest daughter-in-law, if not in age at least in status, of the lineage.

The wedding party returned to the groom's house, and there the bride worshiped her husband's domestic ancestors (see Chapter 3). Again the pattern was repeated; her husband and his father worshiped first, and she followed. When the domestic worship was finished, she was ushered into the reception room of the groom's household, and here she went through two ceremonies in which she was formally introduced to the married women and unmarried girls of her husband's hamlet. During the first of these ceremonies the bride was seated with nine married women around a makeshift table. These women, usually neighbors of the groom's household, pretended to eat from ten separate bowls of rice, boiled meat, and sweet noodles. While they were eating, each in turn offered her good wishes to the bride. During this ritual the bride callers instructed the bride in the proper kin terms to use in addressing these women (in fact, throughout the three days of marriage rites the bride callers provided the bride with the appropriate kin terminology for the many people she met). The mock meal was followed by a lighthearted tug-of-war (over a tray of sweets) between the bride and young unmarried girls from the groom's hamlet. In both these ceremonies the bride met groups of women and girls who would play an important role in her adult life.

The most important marriage feast was held on the evening of the first day. Four marriage banquets, in fact, were given by the groom's family during the three days of rites. While no male outsiders (that is, non-Teng) were invited to any of these feasts, some outsider women did attend. Women from the bride's village who carried *chia chuang* (or "bridal ornaments") to the groom's house on the first day of the marriage ceremonies were invited to eat a morning banquet with the groom's other guests. This banquet preceded the main wedding feast by a few hours. The main wedding banquet was considered essential to the public recognition of the marriage. Many women who did not live in Ha Tsuen attended this feast: the groom's married sisters, and sometimes the married daughters of his father's brothers along with the sisters of the groom's father, and the wives

Inequality among brothers

of his mother's brothers. These women arrived throughout the first day of rites, and they all brought the same set of gifts for the groom: a blanket, uncooked rice, beer, and sweets. The groom's married sisters might also present the groom with a roast pig, which was then consumed at the wedding feast. A message in paper characters was pinned to the blankets, making it clear that they were presented by the husbands of these women. However, the men in whose name these gifts were given never attended any of the wedding festivities, and they certainly played no role in the marriage rites. Furthermore, no members of the bride's family (neither men nor women) participated in any of the groom's wedding banquets. In fact, until recently, the bride herself did not attend these feasts but stayed secluded in the new room.

It is important to note that those "outsider" women who did attend the banquet were not given a place of honor at the wedding feast. In fact, I discovered that the older women, especially the sisters of the groom's father and the wives of the mother's brothers, usually ate in the groom's father's house and not at the banqueting hall at all. Among all the female guests, only the wives of the mother's brothers were singled out for special attention. This did not occur at the banquet but at the entrance to the village. As the mother's brother's wife approached the entrance to the village, she was met by a kinswoman or neighbor of the groom's family, who formally escorted her to the groom's house as one would an honored guest.

All the marriage feasts, except for the last, which was an intimate family affair, were attended by the groom's close agnatic kinsmen and their wives, by all elders (males age 61 and older) resident in the groom's hamlet, and by one representative of each household in the hamlet. Banquets of the wealthy often included a representative from each household in the entire lineage, which in the case of the Teng meant upwards of a thousand people.

After the main wedding feast the bride and groom spent their first night together. But before they retired they underwent an ordeal of teasing by the groom's bachelor friends. The bride was the focus or butt of most of the joking and riddling, which went on into the late hours of the first night. This teasing sometimes continued for many nights after the marriage, and some elderly women recall this experience with distaste.

On the second day the groom's mother and father, together with his elder brothers and their wives, gathered in the main room of the groom's household. There the bride and groom served wine to each family member in turn, starting with the father and mother, then the eldest brother, and so on. The brothers of the groom's father, and their sons (if they were older than the groom) were also invited to this ceremony, and they too were formally served wine. As each person received a cup of wine, he or she presented a red envelope containing money – usually only a few dollars – to the bride. The groom's parents and his brothers might also give the bride small pieces of jewelry at this time. These gifts hereafter belonged to the bride; they were her personal property to do with

Marriage, affinity, and class

as she chose. After the last guest had been served, the bride and groom started off for the houses of the groom's closest agnatic kinsman (usually descendants of the groom's great-grandfather, or FFF). At each house the bride and groom worshiped the family's domestic ancestors. At noon there was another banquet for the groom's immediate family and the agnates at whose domestic altars the bridal couple had just worshiped.

On the third day the bride returned to her natal family, accompanied by the two bride callers and a variety of presents from the groom's family. These gifts of pork, rice, tea, and sugar signified, the villagers say, that the groom's family accepted the bride as wife and daughter-in-law. The groom did not accompany the bride but stayed in his own village. At the bride's parents' house, the bride was treated as a guest, and a special meal was prepared in her honor. However, the bride could not spend the night with her natal family; she must return to her husband's village before dark. Upon her return, the bride, still dressed in her finery, performed her last ceremonial duty. As women and children lined the narrow paths of the village to watch, the bride had to carry heavy buckets of water to her new home. Now she was truly a daughter-in-law, but until the birth of a child she had no secure position in her husband's family.

Affinity and descent: conflicting systems?

Clearly, much of this marriage ritual involves placing the bride in her new social universe. She is introduced to her husband's ancestors and shown the proper forms of respect she must pay to them. She is introduced to the female society of her husband's village and to her husband's close agnates. Not only does the bride formally meet the main actors in her new environment, but she is also instructed (by the bride callers and bride senders) in the proper demeanor she must show these people.

The marriage rites were not, however, only concerned with the social integration of an outsider; they also made important statements about the patrilineage. During the rituals of betrothal and marriage there was no direct contact whatsoever between the groom's family and the bride's family. Compared to other parts of China, in Ha Tsuen the affinal relationship did not play a significant role in marriage ritual. However, it is important to note that affinity was not completely negated. Gifts were exchanged, but, one might say, in disembodied form: male affines did not actually meet. Clearly the break that the bride made with her own family and kin was dramatized by the rites (for example, the door was firmly slammed behind her). From the point of view of the marriage ritual, we can say that a woman ceased being a daughter when she became a wife (upon her return to her family, she was treated as an honored guest). The marriage rites, taken as a whole, present a picture of agnatic solidarity undiminished by ties or loyalties outside the lineage. In the formal world of ritual, the groom and his family kept well away from entanglements with the bride's family, while

Inequality among brothers

the bride upon whom the continuation of the lineage depended was firmly incorporated into the husband's family.

Unlike in marriage rituals described for other parts of China (where, significantly, the localized lineage is relatively undeveloped), in Ha Tsuen males outside the patrilineage were conspicuously absent from the marriage festivities. Their wives, however, were present. Does this suggest that these women participated simply as representatives of their husbands? In one rather limited sense this is true, but I do not believe it is correct to see these women as functioning here simply as extensions of their husbands. In a later section of this chapter I discuss the full and active role that female affines played in domestic ritual. The fact that the more senior of these women did not really take part in the important festivities and feasts at all suggests that they were not just stand-ins for their husbands. These women, in fact, as we have seen, ate in the groom's father's house with a few elderly women of the groom's village and did not sit in the ancestral hall (where the banquets were usually held) with the guests of honor.

Only the wives of the brothers of the groom's mother were given special recognition, and this, I suggest, stemmed from the groom's relations with his mother's brother and the mother's brother's household. The mother's brother is part of the nonagnatic kin called the "outer family" (*wai chia*). The mother's brother is said to have a special relationship with his sister's son. In Ha Tsuen he was not, however, included in the marriage rites and feasts for his sister's son. In dominant lineages the relationship between mother's brother and sister's son is ambiguous. The mother's brother is the one outsider male with whom the groom has very likely had some contact throughout his childhood. As a child he accompanied his mother on her visits to her brother's household in her natal village. He is taught to think of his mother's brother as a kindly figure to whom he owes respect, but a respect tinged with warmth. In adulthood, however, the relationship between mother's brother and sister's son usually grows more distant. I discovered a few cases among older men in which relations between a mother's brother and a sister's adult son were friendly, but this was by no means common.[2] The role of the mother's brother is not ritualized except that certain gifts are expected from the mother's brother at the birth and marriage of his sister's son. As noted earlier, however, these gifts are delivered not by the mother's brother but by his wife. Ties between mother's brother and sister's son and between the more general categories of wife takers and wife givers are not elaborated in the symbolic system in Ha Tsuen as they are in other areas of China (Ahern 1974; Freedman 1967; A. Wolf 1970). It will be remembered that on the marriage day the bride came to the groom's family with only the bride senders. She was not accompanied by her natal kin.

Relations between wife givers and wife takers are nearly always unequal.

---

2 Nearly all of these cases involved middle-aged men who had become political figures in recent years.

Marriage, affinity, and class

Maurice Bloch, in his study of Merina (Madagascar) marriage rites, has argued that "except in the case of systems with direct exchange, [marriage] is an asymmetrical transaction in the short term and therefore introduces an element of hierarchy" (1978:21). He goes on to show how among the Merina this inequality is symbolically restated and reversed in the marriage ceremony. In Ha Tsuen, however, the inequality between affines is in fact highlighted. In the marriage rites the Teng appear to deny the significance of their wife givers while upholding the unity of the lineage.

Marriage payments: landlords and tenants

Marriage rites among the Teng emphasized the solidarity of agnates and deemphasized the affinal relationship. How does this ritual relate to the informal patterns of affinity? Did Teng males avoid their affines? Affinal relations were, in fact, more complex than the marriage rites would suggest. While there was one set of marriage rites in Ha Tsuen, there were, in fact, different patterns of affinity. Landlord-merchants and smallholder-tenants differed significantly in choice of marriage partners, in the payments that sealed the marriage bond, and in their informal treatment of and relationship with affines. Most villagers, however, would deny that such differences existed.

There were significant variations in the geographical origins of Teng wives. In a sample of women married into Ha Tsuen's smallholder-tenant families (consisting of 68 women over 40 years of age residing in Ha Tsuen in 1978), 76 percent (*N* 52) came from within an area that is focused on the nearby market town of Yuen Long (for a discussion of marriage distribution and marketing patterns, see Skinner 1964). Included in this figure of 52 were 16 women (or 23 percent of the total of 68) who came not only from the Yuen Long area but were born within Ha Tsuen's own *hsiang* hinterland.[3]

---

3 The geographical distribution of out-marrying Teng daughters is broadly similar to that of Teng in-marrying wives. In a sample consisting of 29 out-marrying Teng daughters over 40 years of age, 41 percent (or *N* 12) married within Ha Tsuen *hsiang*, and 86 percent (or *N* 25) married within the Yuen Long marketing area (which subsumes Ha Tsuen *hsiang*). It is difficult to know whether the higher rate of out-marriage to villages within the *hsiang* (41 percent compared to 23 percent for in-marriage from *hsiang* villages) is significant. The comparison may be affected by the fact that there is less information on out-marriage among older women (29 cases of out-marriage as opposed to 68 cases of in-marriage). Although I asked about out-marrying daughters, the figures show that villagers were likely to forget or fail to mention sisters or father's sisters who married out of Ha Tsuen decades ago. Does the finding of 41 percent of Teng daughters married into villages that were politically subordinated to the Teng suggest a trend toward hypogamy? Villagers themselves maintained that a bride should come from a family that is poorer than the groom's family. People in Ha Tsuen believed that a bride should not marry down, because, they said, "The bride will never be satisfied, and she will only cause trouble." In

Inequality among brothers

Although most wives came from a relatively small area, this does not imply that the Teng were concentrating their marriages in a few communities or kin groups. In fact, these 68 Teng wives represented many different surname groups and villages (the 68 in-marrying women were from 32 communities, 25 of which were located in the Yuen Long area). Significantly, most of these villages provided only one or two women. The neighboring settlement of Sha Kong Wai provided the largest number of wives (6 women in all). There is, however, no evidence to suggest that Teng males have attempted to "deepen" or concentrate their affinal ties in Sha Kong Wai. These 6 women came from 4 different surname groups that make up separate subsections or hamlets within Sha Kong Wai (in 1960 this village had a population of approximately 550; see Gazetteer 1969:164). The Teng families into which these women married are not closely related (they are not descendants of a common grandfather, for example). In discussing marriages with *hsiang* women, it is important to remember that relations between the Teng and residents of satellite villages like Sha Kong Wai were often hostile. This is not surprising, considering that Teng farmers were sometimes called upon to enforce in a direct and violent manner lineage hegemony in these villages (see Chapter 5). As Ha Tsuen people say, "It is not good to become involved with other communities."

In contrast to their poor kinsmen, landlords and merchants took their wives from a much larger area, mostly from urban Hong Kong or the old county capital at Nam Tao. Only 2 wives in landlord-merchant families about which I have detailed information (*N* 20) came from the marketing district of Yuen Long, and none came from Ha Tsuen's immediate hinterland. Although marriage ritual stresses the separation and avoidance of affines, I found that among the wealthy, wife givers and wife takers were without exception personally acquainted before the betrothal of their offspring. In most cases the bride's and groom's fathers or the groom and his father-in-law had had business or political dealings with each other prior to the betrothal. In effect, there was a system in Ha Tsuen whereby the rich married their friends and the poor married strangers.

Marriage payments in China have sometimes been called bride price (Wolf and Huang 1980); sometimes dowry (Fei and Chang 1948:110; McCreery 1976); and sometimes indirect dowry (Parish and Whyte 1978:182). Using Goody's framework (1973:2), it is possible to characterize most Chinese marriage exchange as indirect dowry. That is, money that passes from the groom's family to the bride's family is used to purchase a trousseau for the bride. There are, however, certain problems in applying the concept of indirect dowry to the

---

China the decisive units in negotiating marriages were not lineages or villages but rather individual families. It is therefore difficult to argue that because Teng daughters sometimes married into satellite villages this constituted a system of hypogamy. More information about the families into which these women married would be needed before an argument of this nature could be sustained.

Marriage, affinity, and class

Chinese case material. Goody subsumes indirect dowry under the more general category of dowry (1973:2, 22, 46). In his view, dowry, and by implication indirect dowry, is associated with systems of stratification and "diverging devolution" (or the "women's property complex"). Goody goes on to say that in societies that have dowry, affines and the conjugal unit usually play a central role (39, 45–6). Although there is no doubt that Chinese society is highly stratified, the other factors (the women's property complex,[4] strong affinal ties, and strong conjugal units) that Goody associates with dowry systems are not particularly salient in China, with its patrilineal bias.[5]

In the case of Ha Tsuen the use of the single category of indirect dowry obscures, I believe, important differences between classes. It is far better, I suggest, to think of Chinese marriage exchanges in terms of a continuum.[6] In some cases the exchanges tended towards a bride price system, while in others they resembled a dowry arrangement. In India a similar situation prevails; one section of a community may have a bride price system of exchange, whereas another maintains a dowry system (see Parry 1979:208–10; Tambiah 1973:68–71). Whether Indian families utilize a bride price or a dowry arrangement depends largely on the subcaste affiliation of the people involved. In China, however, the relevant variable is the class status of the intermarrying families.

If one were to ask Ha Tsuen villagers to describe their system of marriage exchange, most would reply: Cakes, food, and money are given by the groom's family to the bride's family at the time of betrothal. The bride's family returns to the groom's family a small portion of the food gifts they receive (usually only a few ounces of pork). The money (*li chin*) is used by the bride's family to defray the expenses of the betrothal feast and to buy jewelry, clothes, and small

---

4 By local custom, women in this part of China had no rights of inheritance (this is true even today in the New Territories). However, the *chia chuang* (dowry) they receive at marriage is their own personal property. They may if they choose sell their jewelry, the most valuable part of their dowry. Most women try to retain at least some of their jewelry, which in their old age they distribute among their daughters-in-law and daughters. In Ha Tsuen this pattern applies to women from both rich and poor households. Myron Cohen (1976:160–91) has written about the role that dowry and women's private property plays in a Hakka community in Taiwan. There the dowry provides the first clear recognition of the new and as yet embryonic economic unit that during the early stages of marriage (before the household divides) is focused on the bride.

5 Comaroff (1980:7–10), in his introduction to *The Meaning of Marriage Payments*, makes a similar point about dowry in patrilineal societies; Rheubottom's (1980) discussion (also in *The Meaning of Marriage Payments*) describes a society (Yugoslav Macedonia) that has patrilineal descent, corporate descent groups, and a denial of affinity. And yet in Macedonia as in China a system of dowry operates.

6 In a brief discussion of marriage payments in pre-1949 China, Parish and Whyte seem to suggest something similar to a continuum. They argue that "Chinese peasants practised a system that was part bride price and part dowry" (1978:181), but on the next page they describe the system as that of indirect dowry (1978:182).

Inequality among brothers

pieces of furniture for the bride. These items become the bride's personal property and are referred to as *chia chuang* (or "bridal ornaments"). When one asks villagers about this system, they state firmly that the bride's family should spend all the cash payment on the bridal ornaments and on the betrothal banquet. People do not admit to making a profit from the marriage payments. However, when I examined the actual sums of money involved in *li chin* and *chia chuang*, I found interesting and very revealing differences between the two classes.

The way in which the villagers speak of *li chin* and *chia chuang* suggests that they think of the two as distinct categories. *Li chin*, they say, is given to the bride's family, and their phrasing suggests that it is given free of any conditions. They speak of *chia chuang* as a completely separate transaction; *chia chuang* they say, comes from the bride's parents. The system is presented by the villagers as bride price when people are speaking of *li chin*, and dowry when they refer to *chia chuang*. Whereas some of their discussions suggest that the two transfers of wealth are separate, their actions and statements in other contexts show that they see *li chin* and *chia chuang* as being directly linked. As I noted above, it is considered morally reprehensible for a family to keep the *li chin* for themselves. They are supposed to spend it on their daughter's marriage. When the villagers emphasize the separateness of *li chin* and *chia chuang*, they are stressing, I believe, the right of the bride's family to determine the amount of their daughter's *chia chuang*. The bride's parents do not automatically turn the *li chin* into *chia chuang* or bridal ornaments. In fact, they may use some of the *li chin* to defray their own expenses in marrying off their daughter. In the remaining discussion, *li chin* is translated as "bride price" and *chia chuang* as "dowry."

Detailed data on the dowry and bride price of 21 women over 40 years of age from smallholder-tenant families were collected in Ha Tsuen. All of these women stated that their husband's family was expected to bear the costs of the marriage, even to the extent of providing the lion's share of the food that the bride's parents served to their banquet guests. For example, a 78-year-old Sik Kong Wai woman (ages refer to 1978) received HK$60 in *li chin* and 3,000 engagement cakes when she married in 1916. Her *chia chuang*, or dowry, consisted of one cupboard, one small chest, one gold necklace, one pair of silver earrings, a silver bracelet, and a few clothes. Another 73-year-old Sik Kong Wai woman, who married in the early 1920s, received HK$80 in *li chin* and 4,000 cakes. She brought one cupboard, one chest, a few clothes, a pair of gold earrings, one silver and one jade bracelet with her in dowry. She said that her family received 40 catties (about 53 pounds) of rice and 40 catties of pork at the time of her betrothal. Most women's families received a large amount of pork and rice from the groom's family at their betrothal. These food gifts were then consumed at the bride's betrothal banquets.

Judging by the information that my informants provided (especially concerning amounts of bride price, cost of banquets, and items in their dowries), most smallholder-tenant families did not spend more than the amount they received

Marriage, affinity, and class

in bride price. Some women said that a poor family might feel justified in keeping some of the bride price for themselves, even though everyone agreed that this was not the proper thing to do. It is shameful to be thought to have "sold" (*mai*) one's daughter, they said. It is important to note that among Ha Tsuen tenants and smallholders the bride's family had few expenses that were not covered by the groom's family. The groom even paid for the bride's wedding dress. Clearly these marriage exchanges approached a bride price system. That is, the *li chin* (or bride price) was used by the bride's family to pay their marriage expenses; a portion (in the form of jewelry) went to the bride herself; and her parents sometimes kept a portion of the money for themselves. The groom's family bore nearly the total burden of marriage expenses.

Most people in Ha Tsuen maintain that the system of marriage exchange I have just described applied to landlords and merchants as well as to tenant farmers. This was not, however, the case. It is true that among landlord-merchant families the wife givers used the bride price to provide dowry for their daughters. In this they did not differ; however, landlords and merchants made an effort to provide their daughters with a dowry that matched or even exceeded the cash payment given by the groom's family. Furthermore, the bride price was not used to defray their own ceremonial expenses, as was the case among tenant families. Two women from landlord families (both in their sixties) made a point of informing me that their fathers had spent considerable sums of their own money in providing a proper betrothal banquet to announce their daughters' marriages. All the adults in the brides' natal villages had been invited to these feasts, I was told. Among poor villagers, most betrothal feasts (held by the bride's family) were small affairs, rarely attended by more than 40 guests and sometimes only by members of the bride's household. The comments that the wealthy made about their own marriage payments suggest that landlord-merchant families were far more concerned than their poorer counterparts with relative status both within their village and vis-à-vis the groom's family (Freedman also makes this point, 1966a:55; see also Fei and Chang 1948:110). Goody's suggestion (1973:17, 46) that dowry is associated with a concern for status is certainly borne out by the Ha Tsuen material.

Nearly every woman I asked (both rich and poor) remembered the exact amount of her bride price and the smallest details of her dowry. However, most women from tenant families were slightly amused or even apologetic when they compared their small dowries to today's lavish displays. Women from landlord-merchant families, on the other hand, proudly enumerated their dowry items. Their splendid betrothal banquets and dowries were, in a very important sense, a public confirmation of their natal family's status. Furthermore, from the manner in which these women discussed their dowries it was clear that these displays helped determine the bride's own standing in her husband's family and community. The grand dame of one of Ha Tsuen's wealthiest families (the wife of Teng Cheng-ming's son) took great pleasure in detailing for me the complete catalogue of chairs, chests, necklaces, earrings, and other possessions that she received on her marriage. Her dowry also included a young servant girl (*mui jai*) who had been purchased by her father to act as maid and companion to her in her husband's household. In 1915 her family had received four hundred silver dollars in *li chin*.

Although informants from tenant households knew that the wealthy had more lavish dowries than they themselves could command, they did not seem to be aware of the considerable variations in marriage exchange in Ha Tsuen. Wealthy women, however, were certainly conscious of the differences. One 50-year-old woman told me that among the poor the bride's parents often kept some of the bride price back for themselves. However, among the rich, she proudly noted, the bride's family strove to make a good show by providing a handsome dowry for their daughter out of their own pocket.

The findings on bride price and dowry in Ha Tsuen support the work of Parish and Whyte, who, in a brief discussion of marriage payments in China prior to 1949, conclude: "It was only among the very poor that there was primarily a bride price with a minimal dowry, while among the rural elite dowries predominated" (1978:182). I would, however, disagree with Parish and Whyte's use of the general label "indirect dowry" for both of these arrangements. In Ha Tsuen there were in fact two systems of marriage payments that reflected important economic and political differences among the Teng.

Affinity: landlords and tenants

Anthropologists working in Taiwan have stressed the ritual role that affines play in domestic ritual. While nonagnates ("outsider" males) played no direct part in Teng marriage rites, the marriage payments themselves suggest that affinity was not altogether negated, especially among landlord-merchant men. Gift exchanges at marriage can provide important insights into the nature of affinity (see, e.g., Dumont 1957; Tambiah 1973; on more recent discussions of this, see Comaroff 1980). This is certainly true for Ha Tsuen. Among Teng farmers, marriage gifts were provided almost exclusively by the groom's family. However among landlord-merchants, both the wife givers and wife takers made substantial contributions to the dowry, and the bride's family paid for its own betrothal and third-day feast. To what extent did the Teng's relationships with their affines correspond to the formalized structures of marriage payments and rites?

Gallin's (1960) and Pasternak's (1972:61–4, 81–4) work in Taiwan clearly shows that affines are not only brought together by formal rituals but that affinal relationships are also characterized by informal economic and political collaboration. In the village of Hsin Hsing, for example, affines exchanged agricultural labor, loaned money to each other, and became political allies (Gallin 1960:637–41). In Ha Tsuen, by contrast, many women from tenant families told me that their husbands had only met the women's male kin after years of marriage, and in some cases they had never met at all. Women reported that their brothers

Marriage, affinity, and class

rarely or never visited them, and that their husbands rarely or never accompanied them on visits to the wives' families. This was confirmed by my own observation.

In contrast to their poor agnates, merchants and landlords depended on extensive interpersonal networks that included wealthy affines. For example, Teng Cheng-ming's son was married to a woman from Nam Tao whose family was, like Cheng-ming's own family, involved in coastal shipping. The only son from this union, who became a powerful political leader, married a woman whose father had been an official in Chiang Kai-shek's government prior to the revolution. In the 1940s this official and his family moved to the Yuen Long area where they became active in local politics. Another wealthy family married their son to the daughter of a large landowner from the Tuen Mun area in the 1930s, and during the same period yet another wealthy family took a wife for their son from a leading family in Yuen Long. The list continues, but these examples suggest that the wealthy in Ha Tsuen were making strategic marriages for their offspring.

Among the wealthy, affinity was an important resource open to transaction. As Emrys Peters notes in his work on a Lebanese village, affinity is, par excellence, a relationship for social maneuvering (1972:185–6). In a very real sense landlords and merchants created their affinal relationships on the basis of self-interest. It was up to each individual to define the content of his affinal relationships, but these relationships remained culturally indistinct. The Teng adhered to a common set of marriage rites irrespective of class background, but they had no uniform pattern of affinity, nor did they share a single system of marriage payments. Whereas the marriage rites emphasized the separation of male affines and the unity of agnatic kin, differences in the conduct of affinal relationships (which correlate to class differences) called into question many of the basic tenets of the patrilineal descent group. The informal links that landlord-merchants had with their affines posed a direct threat to lineage ideals of unity and self-sufficiency.

The actions of tenants and smallholders were in conformity with the model of affinity set down in the marriage rites; they kept their affines at arm's length. Landlord-merchants, on the other hand, had constantly to balance the need to build social networks through affinity with the demands of playing the game by the rules of patrilineal exclusiveness. In the ritual life of the community they managed to strike that balance. Pierre Bourdieu neatly summarizes this point when he writes, "It is practical kin who make marriages; it is official kin who celebrate them" (1977:34).

Women, class, and affinity

Thus far affinity has been discussed only as it related to men. As noted earlier, women who married into smallholder-tenant families were not simply silent bridges between males; they were (and are) active participants in affinity. Women did, of course, stand in for their men, bearing gifts back and forth between their husbands and their husbands' affines. But it would be wrong to stop here and say that what we have is simply a sub rosa form of affinity in which women served as stand-ins for their husbands in a system of silent exchange.

Women were also affines. They had close relations with their brothers' wives, their husband's brothers' wives, and their husband's sisters. Ha Tsuen women interacted in many different contexts, of course, and had ties based on friendship, kinship, locality (neighborhood), as well as on affinity. Although I only discuss affinity here, it is important to remember that women as well as men were involved in a variety of relationships. In striking contrast to the general picture of village women presented in the literature on rural China, women in Ha Tsuen appear to have been more extroverted than their husbands and fathers-in-laws, whose social relations were nearly all subsumed under agnation.

Because women from wealthy families tended to be more socially restricted than their poorer counterparts, this discussion of female affinity applies most directly to the lives of women from tenant and smallholder families. I do not suggest that wealthy women were chained to their households, but they did not, in general, have the freedom of movement that their poor neighbors enjoyed.

Among women, the affinal relationship was distinguished by the special role that female affines played in each other's life crisis rituals. Of course, others (neighbors and hamlet friends) also helped, but the important point is that affines were expected and obliged to assist. Female affines were expected to provide extra labor and food on the occasions of birth, marriage, and death. For instance, when a son married, the groom's mother's female affines gave her a great deal of support. The groom's mother's sisters-in-law (that is, the wives of her husband's brothers) provided the extra labor necessary for the wedding banquets, and, as we have seen, her husband's sisters and her own brothers' wives attended the marriage rites on the first day and brought gifts of food and, of course, gifts from their husbands for the groom.

Female affines also lent support to each other during periods of bereavement. When a family head died, for example, it was primarily his daughters-in-law and his married-out daughters who shouldered the burden of preparing for the extensive mortuary rites and feasts that were (and are) part of death observances in Ha Tsuen. There were also many less formal occasions when women visited outside their husband's village. At the lunar New Year and village festivals, women carried gifts of sweets and money to their natal households.

Women married to men who were all of the same generation formed the core of female affinity (Chinese women have no generation designations apart from those of their husbands). A woman's most important affines were her brothers' wives, husband's brothers' wives, and husband's sisters. These are the women, it will be recalled, to whom the bride was ritually introduced during the marriage rites. A woman's sisters were not, of course, affines, but then they were not exactly treated as kin either. Women seem not to have regularly visited the

Marriage, affinity, and class

homes of their married sisters, and unless they met them upon their return visits to their natal villages, contacts with sisters were rare. In adult life women were more likely to depend on those who had married into their natal village (especially their brothers' wives) than on those who had moved away.

In a society in which many families did not produce enough for their own consumption, the distribution of gifts, especially food gifts, was of crucial economic importance. The cost of rituals was and continues to be an enormous drain on most households. Food and money were not, however, the only scarce resources; labor was also in short supply. In Ha Tsuen a mother might spend weeks preparing for her son's marriage, and it was essential that she be able to call on other women for help. Contributions of food and labor were extremely important to women (and to the entire household), but, I would argue, women benefited from affinity in other less obvious ways.

Chinese women in general, and Cantonese women in particular, stand outside the patrilineal system of descent. There is even some question as to the quality of the relationship between a woman and her natal family. In Ha Tsuen, people believe firmly that a daughter does not really belong to her parents; informants stated that "a daughter is just passing through our household" – presumably on her way to her true role as wife and mother. Elizabeth Johnson reports a similar sentiment from one of her New Territories informants who said of her 25-year-old unmarried daughter, "A girl that old belongs to others" (1976:152). Most telling of all in this regard is the horror with which people react to the death of an unmarried girl or woman in her father's household. A woman who dies before she enters her proper role as wife may become a vengeful ghost, a powerful enemy of her natal family and village. In the traditional culture of the Ha Tsuen region there was no place for an unmarried woman, save that of nun or prostitute. An unmarried woman was a constant threat to her family; usually such women were forced to quit their household of birth altogether (see Topley 1975). As Margery Wolf has written, "Few women in China experience the continuity that is typical of the lives of the menfolk ... If [a woman] dies before she is married, her tablet will not appear on her father's altar; although she was a temporary member of his household, she was not a member of his family" (1972:32).

I could find no evidence in Ha Tsuen that women were incorporated into their husband's lineage when they married. Women who marry Teng men do not become lineage ancestors, although they may for a time be domestic ancestors. Women do not participate in lineage rituals, they have no rights of inheritance, they do not worship lineage ancestors,[7] and they do not even take their husband's surname at marriage. Women have no right of support from their natal families,

---

[7] The single exception to this occurs when the bride (the principal wife) worships her husband's lineage ancestors in his ancestral hall on the first day of the marriage rites. This is the only time that a woman worships her husband's lineage ancestors, as opposed to his domestic ancestors. Secondary wives do not perform this rite at all.

Inequality among brothers

and their children are never supposed to be born in their natal households. In Ha Tsuen I knew of only two cases of divorce, and the women involved remained in the village under the financial protection of their exhusbands. Widow remarriage is frowned upon and is, in fact, very rare in Ha Tsuen. I know of no cases of the remarriage of a Teng widow who was a principal wife (*ta p'o*).

In light of women's position vis-à-vis the male descent group and even their natal families, it is easy to understand the importance of affinal networks for women married into tenant and small-holding families. These networks, along with ties to consanguines and neighbors, formed a system of security and identity for women. This system was in many ways similar, at least in function, to the women's neighborhood groups that Margery Wolf describes for rural Taiwan (1972) and to Vanessa Maher's description of Moroccan women (1974). Maher emphasizes the important role that Moroccan women married to proletarian men have in maintaining and operating the kinship (or informal) system of exchange. Maher could be writing of Cantonese villagers when she remarks, "The nonconjugal roles performed by women [in informal exchange] are so vital to the survival of the population that there are substantial rewards to both men and women if they continue to carry them out" (223). For Ha Tsuen, there is little doubt that women's affinal networks benefited both men and women.

8
Economic and political changes: 1945–1978

In Chapter 2, I argued that the economic and political framework that was established in Hsin-an County during the late seventeenth and eighteenth centuries remained more or less intact until the twentieth century. Hsin-an was not of course, immune to change during this period, but the changes that occurred did not really alter the basic structural arrangements. Large lineages and their wealthy members continued to dominate the region's economic and political life. However, beginning in the early twentieth century, cracks began to appear in this structure when the new colonial land policy undercut the position of many absentee landlords.

New Territories villagers witnessed many changes in the years between 1905 and 1941, not only in landlord–tenant relations but also in commerce and industry. In 1916, for instance, a new market was formed in Yuen Long, financed by an issue of ten thousand public shares (see Young 1974:20–2). The Hop Yik Market, as it was called, quickly replaced the older market at Yuen Long (which is now little more than a residential district on the outskirts of the new market). A provision of the Hop Yik Market charter stated that no group (family, village, lineage) could hold controlling interest in the market. This provision was, of course, aimed at the old monopolistic practices of the dominant lineages, especially the Teng of Kam Tin who had controlled Yuen Long Old Market for nearly 250 years.

Coinciding with and stimulating the boom in marketing (other new markets also emerged during this period) was the development of a new transportation system in the New Territories. In 1911 the colonial government completed a railroad running along the eastern side of the New Territories that linked Kowloon to Canton, and by 1929 the main circular road that connects the marketing centers of Tai Po, Shek Wu Hui, Yuen Long, Castle Peak, and Kowloon was completed (S. G. Davis 1949:21, 129). All of these changes were something of a mixed blessing for the people of Ha Tsuen.The railroad line was far from Ha Tsuen, but the new road passed within one mile of the village. Although the road may have increased opportunities for agricultural marketing, there is no doubt Ha Tsuen's cargo boat traffic suffered as a consequence of the new transport system

Inequality among brothers

(on the competition between rail and river traffic in the delta, see S.G. Davis 1949:131). Coupled with the damage inflicted by the reclamation project that blocked Ha Tsuen's direct access to Deep Bay, the new road sealed the fate of the Teng's cargo boat business. By the 1920s, Teng-owned boats were operating on a greatly reduced basis. Considering the Teng interests in Yuen Long Old Market, Ha Tsuen's landlord-merchants could not have been pleased (at least during its early stages) to see the development of a new market on their doorstep. It did not take long, however, for these wealthy families to accommodate to Hop Yik Market. Descendants of Teng Cheng-ming now own valuable real estate and shops along Yuen Long's main thoroughfare.

Although these economic changes were important, one must not leap to the conclusion that the local society was undergoing disruption or massive dislocation. Most villagers continued to do what they had always done: work on the land. The 1911 census shows that 77 percent of the male population in the Northern District of the New Territories (which includes Ha Tsuen and Yuen Long) were employed as either agriculturalists or fishermen (cited in Brim 1970:95).

The First World War gave a boost to Hong Kong's industries (S.G. Davis 1949:151), and a few years later, in 1925, an anti-British boycott by Chinese nationalists made an increase in local agricultural production a necessity (91). The 1930s was a period of both stagnation and growth. The worldwide depression and China's protective tariffs closed down many of the colony's factories, but new markets opened up in Southeast Asia, and some industries expanded in the late 1930s (152–3).

In December 1941 the Japanese occupied Hong Kong. During the next four years the people of Hong Kong suffered great hardships (Endacott 1964:298–303). New Territories villagers are hesitant to discuss the war years; the painful memories of that era still linger in the minds of many Teng. During the Japanese war (as it is called in Hong Kong) many Chinese migrants were forced to return to their home villages. Men who had left Ha Tsuen in the 1930s, mostly to work as sailors, spent the war years living in Ha Tsuen, if they were lucky. Their ships could no longer operate, and they had no option but to fall back on their families for support. During these difficult years agriculture offered one of the few sources of livelihood and it appears that a barter economy emerged in the New Territories. Ha Tsuen villagers report that the Japanese occupiers confiscated portions of their crops and animals, but the Teng believe they were still better off than the colony's urban population. Many villagers were forced to work as laborers for the Japanese.

Anti-Japanese guerillas were active in the Canton delta during the occupation. The Sai Kung peninsula (see Map 2) was the most active pocket of resistance in the New Territories (Blake 1981:31–2). In Ha Tsuen a few villagers from landless or land poor families joined a communist-backed resistance force called the East River Brigade. Today these exguerillas count among their number some

Economic and political changes: 1945–1978

of the community's most successful entrepreneurs. These men had left or had been forced out of Ha Tsuen at a time when there seemed to be no future. During the war they acquired experience and skills that were to be useful in the coming years of rapid change and increasing opportunity. Of course, the Teng did not have to leave the village in order to be affected by the Japanese war. In the minds of the villagers the traumatic events of the Japanese occupation (1941–5) constituted a clear dividing line between what they perceive to be a stable past and an uncertain, ever-changing present.

The rural committee system: local politics since 1950

In August 1945 the Japanese surrendered to the British authorities in Hong Kong. A British military administration took over the government until May of 1946, when the colony and its leased territory were returned to civil administration (Endacott 1964:302–3). In the years immediately following the Japanese occupation, the colonial administration implemented a policy that was to have far-reaching consequences for the people of the New Territories. A system of advisory bodies, called Rural Committees, was established throughout the New Territories. Members of these committees were elected by local householders. Colonial authorities intended these committees to serve as channels of communication between the government and the villagers. The elected representatives had no decision-making powers, however; that prerogative remained firmly in the hands of colonial officials. Considering the political restraints under which the Rural Committees were forced to operate, it is surprising to find that they have evolved into a significant political force in the New Territories.

To a large extent the Rural Committee districts were based on traditional *hsiang* territories. Villagers did, however, have the right to choose the Rural Committee to which they sent their representatives. Some of Ha Tsuen's old satellite villages took advantage of this, and, no doubt in an attempt to abandon their subordinate role, chose to affiliate themselves with the neighboring Rural Committee of Ping Shan. For some satellite villagers, as we have seen, the 1905 land policy had weakened the Teng's economic hold and made it possible for them to make more independent political choices.

Unfortunately for Ha Tsuen, the largest satellite villages decided to throw in their lot with Ping Shan. Although the defection of these satellite villages marked an important turning point in the Teng's control over Ha Tsuen *hsiang*, it would be wrong to assume that these communities suddenly became independent. They still had to contend with Ha Tsuen's security forces, which continued to patrol their traditional territory. Furthermore, by opting out of the politics of their home district, satellite villagers may have operated more from motives of spite than from self-interest. As a consequence of moving their political custom to Ping Shan, they were blocked from having any say in or information about the decisions that were made regarding their own *hsiang*.

Inequality among brothers

The subservient neighbors of the Teng may have increased their self-respect in recent years, but many of the institutions and symbols of domination are still very much in evidence. The Teng's village guard continues to extract a "protection fee" from *hsiang* households. Most villages still "contribute" (often under pressure) to Ha Tsuen festivals, and there is little doubt that the Teng retain a firm grip over the lucrative development projects in the area. However, compared to the past, when the Teng were landlord, buyer of agricultural products, police, and judge to all who lived in the *hsiang*, the situation of satellite villagers has improved markedly. Not surprisingly, there is still a great deal of animosity directed against the Teng, especially among former tenants who remember the days when tough justice was administered by their economic and political masters.

Ha Tsuen's Rural Committee was formed in 1952 (Annual Report 1952–3:7). Every three years each hamlet elects a specified number of representatives (depending on population). These representatives then elect an executive committee that in turn elects a chairman and two vice-chairmen. Voter eligibility is something of an anachronism, for many New Territories residents have no vote. In practice, voting is usually restricted to heads of households who have been longstanding residents of the New Territories. Those who came to Hong Kong after the Japanese occupation (by the 1970s, emigrés constituted the majority of New Territories residents) have been effectively disenfranchised and play no role in the Rural Committee system (Chau and Lau 1982; Miners 1975). The so-called *penti* ("natives," or descendants of original inhabitants) therefore monopolize channels of communication to the government. Because the Teng are numerically dominant in Ha Tsuen *hsiang*, they have the largest number of representatives and dominate the local Rural Committee. The chairmen of the committee have always been Teng. In 1978, 15 of 21 committee members were Ha Tsuen Teng, including all the important officeholders.

Prior to the Japanese occupation, Ha Tsuen, as we saw in Chapter 5, was run by a few wealthy landlord-merchants through the framework of the central ancestral hall. With the introduction of the Rural Committee system, this situation changed. Local communities have lost much of their autonomy. The Hong Kong government now regulates dozens of activities that were left to the individual or the community in the past. House and shop construction, land use, land sales, market stalls, and personal income all come under the government's scrutiny. Identity cards have become a necessity for everyone, and, for the more affluent villagers, drivers' licences, passports, automobile registrations, and telephone service all require government forms, tests, and documentation. Disputes are no longer routinely settled by respected members of the local elite. The colonial police and courts now play a much more significant role than they did before the Japanese war.

Although the government now impinges on the lives of the Teng in ways that

Economic and political changes: 1945–1978

would have been inconceivable before the 1950s, certain political patterns and institutions remain. The village guard still plays a role, albeit somewhat subdued, in protecting or enforcing Teng interests. Also, much as in the past, there is little direct contact between the ordinary villager and government bureaucrats. Land taxes are now paid directly to the relevant government department, whereas once they were paid through wealthy agnates, but most other contacts with officialdom require, according to the villagers, a mediator or "facilitator" with knowledge of the bureaucracy and its ways. While the Rural Committee system has opened up the political arena to more broadly based groups of participants, it has also introduced a rigid hierarchy into relations between the government and the governed. The Rural Committee offers the only viable channel of communication between officials and villagers. Members of the committee have no real powers of decision making, but they have a near monopoly over important information. This is why election to the local committees and to their chairmanships is sought so assiduously. At the village level the chairman and the members of the executive committee are the central political figures, for it is they who are in closest contact with the area's colonial officials and the knowledge these officials have to dispense. The chairman, vice-chairman, and executive committee members are almost always formally aligned. In Ha Tsuen they usually belong to one political faction (see below).

Theoretically villagers should be able to approach local bureaucrats directly. However, in practice this is difficult if not impossible. A mediator is essential, and because the members of the Rural Committee are seen to have working relationships with government bureaucrats, they are invariably asked to intercede. There is also a less obvious but nonetheless important reason why elected representatives play such pivotal roles. The industrialization and urbanization of the New Territories has opened up many new financial opportunities for well-placed villagers. These opportunities are not there just for the taking, however. Inside information and contacts are essential for the negotiation of what are very often extremely lucrative business deals. In Hong Kong, big business and government are closely intertwined (see Hopkins 1971). The expression "What is good for big business is good for Hong Kong" is not just a meaningless cliché. In the New Territories the government has played a crucial role in building new industries and in the development of entire "new cities." To many villagers the government appears to be a powerful and inscrutable source of limitless wealth. Those who have the status of Rural Committee members are thought to be in an advantageous position in that they have opportunities to gather information on development projects and construction schemes. There is little doubt that the colonial government has encouraged this role for local leaders. In a study of women factory workers in Hong Kong, Janet Salaff makes the point that "the government . . . provides resources and access to colonial officials, which gives status to the local Chinese leadership" (1981:17; see also Freedman 1966b).

Inequality among brothers

Salaff goes on to say that in return Chinese leaders provide information both to the colonial authorities and to their "constituency"; it is a variation on the old system of indirect rule (17).

Today, as in the past, the political mediator is extremely important. What has changed in recent years are the people who play this role. Once only the landlord-merchants had knowledge of the world outside the village and the ability to act on that knowledge. Now the role of intermediary is just as likely to be filled by men who only 15 years ago were landless farmers. These new mediators are often wealthy men, but their wealth has been acquired in recent years, and they have no close genealogical or economic ties to the old elite.

In the past, the prerequisites for local leadership were wealth, extralineage contacts, and a prominent role in the activities of the central ancestral hall. Today the first two criteria are still important, but the manager of Yu Kung T'ang no longer plays such a prominent part in local politics. The Rural Committee has largely usurped the political functions of the central ancestral hall. Today local leaders must hold elected office; no longer can a landlord-merchant become a manager of Yu Kung T'ang and expect to dominate local politics.

Landlord-merchants make up only a fraction of Ha Tsuen's population, and this has made their election to the Rural Committee difficult. Landlord-merchants are concentrated, however, in San Wai, and they have managed to maintain control over that hamlet and its four elected representatives. Since 1952 these representatives have been either members of the old landlord-merchant elite or people closely allied to them. While some of San Wai's landlord-merchants have moved away from Ha Tsuen, preferring to base themselves in Yuen Long or more recently in urban Kowloon, those who continue to take an active role in the everyday affairs of the community have had to reach an accommodation with their former tenants and dependent agnates.

The landlord-merchants have only managed to elect the chairman of the Rural Committee for two out of nine terms. This was accomplished by putting together a coalition based upon hamlet loyalties, segmental rivalries, and paid clientage. This coalition has been led and sustained by a member of the leading landlord-merchant family, a descendant of Teng Cheng-ming. In a later section of this chapter I discuss these coalitions; however, before we can understand the contemporary political scene, it is important to know more about recent economic changes.

Economic changes: the emergence of wage labor and the new entrepreneurs

The first decade after the Japanese occupation was a difficult time in Hong Kong generally. The economy and population required time to recover from the war years. In the late 1940s and early 1950s, that recovery received a great boost. As it became clear that the communists would win the civil war in China,

Economic and political changes: 1945–1978

industries and people began to move into Hong Kong in ever-increasing numbers (see, e.g., Davis 1964:49–50; Hopkins 1971; G. Johnson 1973). In 1945, Hong Kong had a population of about 600,000, but by 1955 this had increased to nearly two million. The Korean War did present some difficulties for Hong Kong's revival, however. Ever since Hong Kong was established, in the mid–nineteenth century, Hong Kong and China have enjoyed extensive trade links with each other. The trade embargo that was imposed against China by the United Nations had a negative effect upon those links and of course on the colony itself. The effects were not uniformly unpleasant, however, for J. L. Watson has pointed out in his study of the village of San Tin that some border communities took advantage of the embargo to smuggle supplies into the People's Republic, thereby benefiting themselves and the local economy (1975b:71–2). I do not know whether the Teng were involved in this illegal traffic, but clearly the economic effects of the embargo were uneven and contradictory.

In the late 1950s and 1960s, Hong Kong's population grew by tens of thousands as migrants fled the bad harvests of rural Kwangtung. In 1931 the population of the New Territories was 98,157, in 1961 that figure had reached 409,945 (Brim 1970:109–10), and by 1971 the New Territories population stood at 665,700 (Census 1971:22). Many of the Kwangtung emigrés who settled in the New Territories set up small shops in the market towns and villages of Hong Kong. Others rented plots of land from local people to raise vegetables that were in great demand by an expanding urban population. While vegetables were becoming important to the economy of the New Territories, rice production declined (J. Watson has described this process for the village of San Tin, 1975b). Rice could be imported from Thailand at prices that New Territories farmers were unable to match. These two factors – increased migration of Kwangtung villagers into the New Territories and the decline in the local rice market – created a situation in which agriculture eventually became the domain of emigré farmers. These "outsiders" (*wai lai jen*), as they are called locally, do not own the fields they farm; the land has remained firmly in the hands of the original inhabitants.

For various reasons, few indigenous farmers made the conversion to vegetable producton (see J. Watson 1975b). By the 1970s only a small number of fields were being planted in rice. Many villagers remember when the entire plain surrounding Ha Tsuen was a sea of rice: "All you could see in every direction was rice," they said. Today many of these fields are fallow, although some women still grow small plots of rice because, they say, "Our own rice tastes better than what we can buy." Once rice cultivation was the preoccupation of nearly every Ha Tsuen farmer; now it is the concern of a few women who think of it more as an avocation than a serious economic enterprise. Many Teng who had been pushed out of agriculture took factory jobs in the new industrial centers of Tsuen Wan or Kowloon. Some villagers found work abroad, and a lucky few found salaried employment with the government as New Territories policemen, teachers, or clerks. Other exfarmers took less glamorous jobs as gardeners or

Inequality among brothers

Table 6. *Occupations of men aged 15–60 years in Sik Kong Wai and Bao Wai, March 1978*

Type of occupation	No. of men
Wage laborer	61
Emigrant (working abroad)	17
Unemployed	16
Retired	14
Policeman	11
Shopkeeper	4
Taxi driver	1
Farmer (full-time)	1
Minibus driver	1
Total	126

as street sweepers in the government's public services department. A significant proportion of local men never found regular jobs after they left agriculture, and unemployment has been a chronic problem for them (see Table 6; female employment is discussed below).

As the market towns of the New Territories became cities and industries moved to the rural areas, the value of strategically placed land increased enormously. It is a peculiarity of the local economy that agricultural rents have not kept pace with land values over the last 20 years. Rent is often calculated on the basis of the old rice system. Whereas in 1978 a plot of land planted in vegetables might have produced considerably more in income than it did in the past, the rent did not reflect this increase in production. Not surprisingly, agricultural rents are no longer a particularly important source of income. In many parts of the New Territories the value of land is no longer determined by productive capacity but rather by its potential for urban and industrial development. In the 1970s two new "industrial towns" were established in the New Territories. The one at Sha Tin has a projected population of five hundred thousand and the other at Tuen Mun (about six miles from Ha Tsuen) had a population of about one hundred fifty thousand in the late 1970s. A four-lane highway connecting Tuen Mun to urban Kowloon was completed in 1978. Aside from these dramatic developments, countless apartment complexes and "villas" have been built, and new markets and mercantile centers formed. The once quiet market town of Yuen Long had a population of less than five thousand in 1950; in 1975 this figure was nearly one hundred thousand.

In recent years a new market complex has emerged on the edge of Ha Tsuen *hsiang*, near the main Castle Peak Road. This market, known as Hung Shui Kiu, is backed by many of Ha Tsuen's new entrepreneurs, and a rival commercial center in the *hsiang*, along the coast at Lau Fau Shan, is controlled by members

Economic and political changes: 1945–1978

of the old landlord-merchant elite. These market complexes have become the foci for Ha Tsuen's two political coalitions. The group whose interests center on Lau Fau Shan is led by wealthy men from San Wai; the other coalition is composed primarily of entrepreneurs from the hamlets of Sik Kong Wai and Tung Tao Tsuen. The first group's economic interests are in real estate, trucking businesses, oyster processing, and restaurants. The rival group, some of whom began as emigrants in Europe, have built small factories and shops in and around Hung Shui Kiu.

In discussing recent trends in Ha Tsuen, it is essential to know how the landlord-merchants have fared and how a group of tenant farmers managed to challenge the old elite. As we have seen, at the turn of the century the political influence of Teng Cheng-ming was enormous (Chapter 5). His brother, Cheng-fu, however, was more heavily involved in the business side of family affairs. Upon the death of Cheng-ming, evidence from many sources indicates that Cheng-fu and his son took over the businesses in Yuen Long, and Cheng-ming's sons acquired those in Ha Tsuen Market and along Ha Tsuen's coast. Over the years, Cheng-fu and his descendants have tended to remove themselves from the everyday concerns of Ha Tsuen, although the family keeps a large but rarely used residence in San Wai. Cheng-fu's son was, however, born and raised in Ha Tsuen, and his grandsons have all celebrated their marriages in the village, even though members of the family now spend most of their time in Yuen Long and in urban Kowloon.

In recent decades it is Cheng-ming's line who have maintained a clear and consistent interest in Ha Tsuen. Until recently most of Ha Tsuen's landlord-merchants, like Cheng-ming and his descendants, continued to live in Ha Tsuen and to play an active role in local politics. Of course they too have considerable business interests outside of the village. In 1978 one of these men owned a Kowloon-based trucking business; another was a western-trained medical doctor. The eldest sons of yet another family were successful emigrants, and their father looked after the family's local property interests. In another case the eldest son of a retired landowner had taken over his family's oyster fields and shops in Lau Fau Shan market. This man also serves as the manager of some of Ha Tsuen's largest ancestral estates and is active in Rural Committee politics. The man who operates the trucking firm has been elected to the Rural Committee several times, and the father of the emigrants was vice-chairman of the committee in the 1960s.

In a number of important respects Cheng-ming and his brother Cheng-fu typify certain trends found in rural China during the nineteenth and early twentieth century. Many scholars have pointed to the fact that during this period the rural wealthy tended to become absentee landlords (see, e.g., Chen 1936:65). Increasingly, members of this class preferred to move out of their home villages and invest their rental income in money lending, in urban property, or in urban

Inequality among brothers

industries. This is very much the pattern followed by members of the Cheng-fu line. In contrast, Cheng-ming and many other Ha Tsuen landlord-merchants remained in the community and took an active part in local affairs.

Teng Cheng-ming had two sons (the genealogy and inheritance strategy of this family was discussed in Chapter 6). One of these sons had no heir, and so the family estate eventually went to Cheng-ming's only grandson. This man, Teng Shih-min, who is now dead, became an important community leader.[1] He was responsible for expanding his family's business interests in Lau Fau Shan, which included an oyster-processing factory and a large seafood restaurant. He also owned shop premises and restaurants in Yuen Long, as well as property in other urban centers.

San Wai's landlord-merchants, many of whom had substantial interests along the coast, convinced the government to build a two-lane, hard-surfaced road linking Ha Tsuen to Lau Fau Shan. In this and other matters the members of Ha Tsuen's water guard were allies of San Wai's landlords. It will be recalled that these men collected, as their fee for protecting and overseeing the oyster beds, 18 percent of the wholesale price of all oysters harvested from the Lau Fau Shan coast. The head of the water guard is usually also a member of the Rural Committee; not surprisingly, he plays a key role in the landlord-merchant coalition.

In the 1960s a group of landlord-merchants led by Teng Shih-min gained control of the Ha Tsuen Rural Committee. Their reign seems to have been punctuated by a great deal of infighting and a growing estrangement from the colonial administration. The landlord-merchants managed to control the Rural Committee by playing on a number of loyalties. They were particularly deft at using lineage segment rivalries for their own purposes, and of course they had natural allies in the shopkeepers and businessmen who had interests along the coast. Furthermore, they could count on the backing of San Wai's Rural Committee representatives. As I have already noted, San Wai's candidates are either members of landlord-merchant families or their handpicked substitutes. Elections in San Wai normally go uncontested. In 1978 the election ran true to form; there were only four candidates for San Wai's four posts. Ha Tsuen's landlord-merchants contend that San Wai's style of "quiet politics" is a model for the rest of Ha Tsuen. The people of San Wai, they claim, manage to avoid the rancor and jealousy that characterize other hamlet elections.

In 1978, to the surprise of many villagers, one of Teng Cheng-fu's grandsons became a member of the Rural Committee. This young man's entry into local affairs is certainly something of a departure from the past. Previously Cheng-fu's line had little involvement in Rural Committee politics. It is too early to determine whether this change heralds a return of the Cheng-fu branch to Ha

---

1 Teng Shih-min is a pseudonym, as are the given names of other nineteenth- and twentieth-century Teng appearing in this chapter.

Economic and political changes: 1945–1978

Tsuen. One can but speculate that the enormous development potential of the New Territories may have made it profitable to reaffirm close links to the ancestral community.

The culmination of the Chinese civil war in 1949, the influx of new migrants, and the uncertainty connected with the Korean War made for a very unsettled period in the New Territories. This instability, however, provided opportunities as well as problems for a number of poor but adventurous villagers. A brief account of the career of one such man, Teng Fu-li, highlights attitudes and experiences common to this group. During the late 1940s and early 1950s, Fu-li became something of a celebrity in Ha Tsuen while serving as the leader of the village guard. His reputation received a big boost, at least in certain quarters, when he defied Ha Tsuen's leading landlord-merchant family by abducting one of their servant girls, whom he took as a secondary wife. This open defiance of the local elite brought a great deal of prestige to Fu-li. His financial situation was very bad at this time (Fu-li owned only a small plot of land), and people in the community, I was told, joined together in a *ch'üan hui*, or "fist society," to support Fu-li and his family with donations of rice and money. Gradually Fu-li built up a restaurant business that now includes establishments in Yuen Long and in Hung Shui Kiu. He also acts as an intermediary for business deals and serves as manager of a major ancestral estate.

Of course, Fu-li's success cannot be attributed simply to his personal characteristics (which all agree are formidable). He was supported by a coalition of new entrepreneurs, most of whom had achieved their start as emigrant restaurant owners. As local rice production became more and more of an economic irrelevancy and Ha Tsuen's farmers became exfarmers, approximately 30 Teng emigrated to work in the Chinese restaurants of Britain and Holland in the 1950s. Ha Tsuen never produced the large numbers of emigrants common in other New Territories villages (see J. Watson 1975b on the "emigrant village" of San Tin), but emigrant money and experiences became important factors in local politics. In the 1950s and 1960s a handful of successful emigrants from the hamlets of Tung Tao Tsuen and Sik Kong Wai invested some of their restaurant income (earned in London and Amsterdam) into small factories and businesses in the Ha Tsuen area. These emigrant entrepreneurs were joined by other villagers who had seized upon the changing economic and political circumstances of the postoccupation period to build local businesses. These men became a powerful force in local politics; I have chosen to call them the "new entrepreneurs," thereby distinguishing them from the old elite of wealthy landlord-merchants.

Although it is difficult to prove, it is likely that colonial officials were instrumental in supporting and nurturing the new entrepreneurs. Members of this group are not necessarily sympathetic to the government, but they are willing to work with Hong Kong authorities. Certainly the government, by strategic use of its powers to grant licenses and information, can nurture a particular individual or group (see Chau and Lau 1982:146). In Ha Tsuen it appears that the authorities have tried to enhance the power and influence of the new entrepreneurs at the expense of the old landed elite. Government backing no doubt has something to do with the fact that the development plans proposed by the entrepreneurs tend to be more in line with government policies than do those of the old elite.

When discussing local politics the new entrepreneurs stress the importance of developing the Ha Tsuen area. By this they mean building new shops and factories in the area and providing Ha Tsuen with good road links to urban markets. They are forthright in their condemnation of the old elite, whom they accuse of wanting nothing more than to preserve the status quo. The new entrepreneurs tend to discuss politics in terms of common economic interest and mutual distrust of the old landlord-merchant families. I do not wish to give the impression that this group consists of a band of revolutionaries; this is far from the truth. They are, after all, wealthy businessmen who are dependent on their ties to the colonial authorities. Furthermore, they concentrate on only one set of differences, those between the old landlord-merchant class and the rest of the village. The differences between themselves (as successful entrepreneurs) and the majority of the wage laborer population are never mentioned. They stress their unity with the "ordinary villager," a unity that they base on feelings of past exploitation as much as on ties of descent. It is important to understand that the new entrepreneurs' views on economic exploitation stem in part from deep personal feelings of animosity toward San Wai landlord-merchant families. Now that they are no longer dependent on these families, it is possible for them to express and act on these feelings. The entrepreneurs tend to be less concerned with expressions of lineage unity than the landlord-merchants, although neither side can afford to ignore lineage ties altogether (see Chapter 9).

Unlike the landlord-merchant coalition, which owed much to the personal charisma of one man, Teng Cheng-ming's grandson, the new entrepreneurial coalition is much more of a common-interest group. Supporters include Teng as well as satellite villagers who are involved in the Hung Shui Kiu market complex. Many have shops and businesses there and have a vested interest in developing this section of Ha Tsuen's territory. In the 1970s they convinced the government to build a road linking Ha Tsuen with the New Territories' main ring route (Castle Peak Road). Significantly, the new extension passes through Hung Shui Kiu market and bypasses the old road that cut through the middle of Ping Shan. In 1976 the new entrepreneurial coalition opened a new Rural Committee headquarters near Hung Shui Kiu. This is an achievement of which the entrepreneurs are enormously proud, for the landlord-merchants had long pushed for Lau Fau Shan as the location of the new building.

The core of each coalition is composed of a number of leaders and their close agnates, together with long-standing clients (see Chapter 9). Combined with these core members are what might be called economic allies, men who because of a concurrence of economic interests have thrown in their lot with one side or the other. Villagers who do not have special ties to local leaders or whose

Economic and political changes: 1945–1978

Table 7. *Job location of men from Sik Kong Wai and Bao Wai, March 1978*

Type of occupation	No. in urban Hong Kong[a]	No. in New Territories
Wage laborer	27	34
Policeman	0	11
Shopkeeper	0	4
Taxi driver	0	1
Minibus driver	0	1
Farmer	0	1
Total	27	52

Note: [a] Including Kowloon, Tsuen Wan, and Hong Kong Island.

economic interests are far removed from Ha Tsuen (that is, the majority) tend to be apathetic or, in some cases, hostile to Rural Committee politics. When they do participate in local politics, usually at the time of elections, they either vote against an old enemy or for a candidate with whom they have some personal link. It is in this context that segment affiliation can play an important role. Ideology, either of the Left or the Right, does not appear to be an important factor.

Factory workers, migrants, and emigrants

In the preceding discussion the landlord-merchants and the new entrepreneurs have played the central role, but Ha Tsuen is not only a community of wealthy businessmen. In fact, Table 6 reveals that the majority of the male population are wage laborers. How do these people fit into the picture of Ha Tsuen presented above? How have the political changes and the decline of agriculture affected ordinary villagers? Once 80 percent or more of the local population was engaged in agriculture, but I knew of only two full-time farmers in 1978. Industrialization and opportunities abroad have had a profound effect upon the occupational structure of the community.

Although most Teng work outside of Ha Tsuen, the majority have found jobs in the New Territories, where modern factories are located. Many villagers prefer to avoid the hectic commuting or the long periods away from home that jobs in Kowloon demand. Table 7 shows the location of jobs for male residents of Bao Wai and Sik Kong Wai. From this table it is clear that nearly 66 percent (or 52 out of 79) of the working male population resident in Ha Tsuen work in the New Territories.

There is no doubt that the standard of living is, for most villagers, higher than in the past. In 1977–8 Teng factory workers earned from HK$1,000 to HK$1,500 per month ($200 to $300). Teng men tended to work in textile factories, furniture factories, and in toy manufacturing. Most worked 6 days per week, 8 to 10 hours per day. The top rank of Ha Tsuen's wage and salaried workers are members of the Royal Hong Kong Police Force. Most of Ha Tsuen's policemen come from the hamlet of Sik Kong Wai, which also happens to be the hamlet about which I have the most detailed occupational data. The relatively large number of policemen in this hamlet (9 in total) is not representative of the village as a whole. According to residents of Sik Kong Wai, this hamlet has long specialized in providing policemen for the Hong Kong government. The contacts that senior agnates have established make it easier for Sik Kong Wai's young men to enter the police. Unlike factory workers in Hong Kong, policemen have secure employment, relatively good pay, and opportunities for promotion. In the village a considerable amount of prestige is attached to being in the Royal Hong Kong Police Force.

Another occupational category that offers new opportunities, even the possibility of great wealth, is that of emigrant restaurant worker. The term *restaurant worker* is perhaps somewhat misleading since, as J. L. Watson has found, many ordinary emigrants are also part owners in the restaurants where they work (1975b:107–9). Because of Hong Kong's status as a British Crown Colony, people born in Hong Kong and the leased territory could, until the 1962 Commonwealth Immigrants Act, enter Britain without difficulty. In recent years, however, emigration to Britain and continental Europe has become far more difficult, and this, combined with the world recession, has made this occupational alternative less attractive. According to figures collected in Bao Wai and Sik Kong Wai, 32 percent of the households in these hamlets have one or more household members living and working abroad. Although many families are directly affected by emigration, I know of only one household in these two hamlets in which all the household members (parents and four unmarried children) live abroad. This family of emigrants does, however, maintain a house in Bao Wai to which they sometimes return for holidays.

Most Teng appear to make a reasonable living in the restaurant trade, but their work is arduous and risky. In Britain, Chinese restaurants and takeout shops open and close with great rapidity. Most dependents of emigrants living in Ha Tsuen do not have a level of consumption perceptibly higher than other villagers, although the majority of these emigrant families do live in new-style houses built during the 1960s and 1970s. Emigration is not a popular or particularly desirable method of making a living in Ha Tsuen. The Teng as a group never emigrated in large numbers and therefore did not have access to the personal networks that, at least in the formative years of the restaurant trade, were so essential for success (see J. Watson 1975b:87–102). It should be remembered, however, that emigration has one major appeal: people can make a great deal of money abroad. Everyone in the village knows of some emigrant who struck it rich. One member of the new entrepreneur coalition provides good evidence for these beliefs. The son of a landless tenant, he is now extremely rich by local standards. He owns restaurants in Britain, Belgium, and Majorca; he now spends his time building an import–export business.

Most of Ha Tsuen's younger emigrants make regular trips back to the village. However, unlike their older agnates, as they marry they take their wives with them to live abroad. If we consider emigrants in their forties and fifties, however, the story is very different. All but one of the emigrants surveyed in this age group have left members of their household in Ha Tsuen. These older emigrants plan to retire in their home village, and many of them retain a keen interest in community affairs. Some emigrants, such as the successful restaurateur discussed above, are actively involved in local politics; in fact, two have served as vice-chairmen of the Rural Committee.

Other villagers have left Ha Tsuen not to work abroad but to be closer to jobs in the factories and businesses of Kowloon or Tsuen Wan. Many of these internal migrants (that is, those who migrate within the colony) maintain houses in Ha Tsuen that they use during holidays. It is difficult to judge the precise number of migrants in this category; according to my survey of Bao Wai and Sik Kong Wai, 16 Teng men born and brought up in Ha Tsuen have moved with their families to another location in the New Territories. The true figure is probably higher. Many of these migrant families return to Ha Tsuen for family celebrations, but few take an active part in lineage and community affairs. Like international emigrants who are registered as heads of household, internal migrants may vote in local elections. However, in 1978 I discovered that many migrants were less than enthusiastic about exercising their voting rights. Some managed to escape the pressure of even the most determined local politicians by simply staying away during the election period. Many migrants told me that "you only make enemies in these elections." Having witnessed the pressures that some candidates bring to bear on their kinsmen and neighbors, I find the migrants' reactions understandable.

According to my household census, 12 percent of the male working-age population (ages 15 to 60 years) in Bao Wai and Sik Kong Wai were unemployed. It is important to note that this category includes men who are intermittently employed and men who may have been between jobs. In the late 1970s there was no doubt that jobs were readily available in the colony as a whole. In fact, the government and many manufacturers periodically complain of a labor shortage in the colony (Brown 1971:3). However, these unfilled jobs are not always close enough to Ha Tsuen or lucrative enough to make the long hours of commuting worthwhile. A bus or minibus journey to Tsuen Wan or Kowloon may involve two or three hours of commuting per day. Furthermore, many young men told me that they were not qualified for the better-paying factory jobs, and they disliked unskilled or semiskilled factory work. How do Ha Tsuen's unemployed manage? Some of the men in this category are unmarried (however, 7 of the 16 unemployed were heads of households). Some unemployed men manage to work occasionally, and others are involved in illegal activities. Many of these jobless men belong to large households and are supported by their children or siblings.

Women's labor is extremely important in Ha Tsuen. Married women often tend large gardens that supply the family with fresh vegetables and with cash. Surplus vegetables are sold to a marketing cooperative or to peddlers in Ha Tsuen's daily market. A handful of married women have factory jobs, but this is uncommon. Most local women spend their afternoons doing "putting out" work for Hong Kong factories.[2] The situation for unmarried women is very different. These Teng daughters are employed in large numbers. The majority work in the small textile factories that dot the countryside. Out of a total of 37 unmarried Teng women between the ages of 15 and 25 years (1978 sample), 33 were employed outside the home.[3] Many village women make a substantial contribution to their households' finances. In one Sik Kong Wai household consisting of parents, two adult daughters, and four sons (ranging in age from 13 to 32), only one male, a youth of 19 years, was regularly employed in 1978, whereas the mother and two daughters provided the major source of the family's income. The working son in fact earned very little because he was enrolled in a training course. The mother is a hard-working gardener who supplies much of her family's food and sells the surplus vegetables in Ha Tsuen Market. The two daughters both work in a New Territories textile factory.

The wages of women factory workers are less than those of their male counterparts. Most unmarried Teng daughters earned HK$800 to HK$1,000 per month, which was about HK$500 less per month than their brothers received for the same type of factory job. Unmarried daughters hand over a large part of their wages to their mothers, who use the money to supplement the general household budget. The mother may set aside a portion of this income for her daughter's own personal use; in the final analysis, however, mothers control most or all of their unmarried daughters' wages. In one family a woman of 21 years gave nearly all of her HK$800 monthly wage to her mother, keeping only a small amount of pocket money for herself. When I asked this woman if her mother were saving the money for her, she replied that her mother used the wages to run the household. She said that if she needed to make a large purchase her

---

2 This may involve packaging finished products, assembling plastic flowers, or putting the finishing touches on garments. Although the wages for this work are usually very small, it is popular among women as a way of earning some extra money without leaving their homes.

3 Two of these 37 unmarried women were incapable of working; therefore the ratio of employed was in fact 33 employed out of a total of 35 women. Janet Salaff reports in her study of women factory workers in urban Hong Kong that in 1971, 88 percent of the single women (age 20 to 24 years) were in full-time employment (1981:294–5).

Economic and political changes: 1945–1978

mother would provide her with money. From this and other conversations with unmarried women, I gathered that mothers did not keep any strict accounting of their daughters' wages, nor were they viewed as personal bankers from whom their daughters might collect at some future time. Rather it was felt that the daughter had a duty to provide financial aid to her mother and her household; in turn she could expect to receive money for her personal use and help with her marriage expenses.

What is particularly interesting about these cases is the striking difference in the treatment of employed, unmarried sons and employed, unmarried daughters. Whereas unmarried women were supporting their households, their unmarried brothers were not expected to make the same level of contribution to general household expenses. Bachelor sons managed their own wages; they were saving, I was told, for their marriage expenses. Janet Salaff, in a study of unmarried women factory workers in urban Hong Kong, has found similar patterns of income disposal: she notes that in the 1970s "working women" were giving their family "control of their wages," keeping only a small portion of their earnings for themselves (Salaff 1981:9). The earnings of working daughters, Salaff reports, are used to achieve family goals that may involve educating sons, improving the parent's business, paying for ritual expenses, or simply keeping the family afloat (259, 262–6). In practice we may say that unmarried daughters in Ha Tsuen play an important role in keeping the household solvent, while unmarried sons save their income for their eventual marriages.

Class in Ha Tsuen: 1945–1978

Since the Japanese occupation, Ha Tsuen's class structure has changed significantly. Prior to that time, land formed the basis of economic life, and villagers were divided over their control of this scarce resource. A privileged few managed to live off land rents and invest their profits in manufacturing, money lending, and cargo boats. Most villagers owned little or no land (see Chapter 4). In the 1950s and 1960s the economic and political life of the New Territories was substantially changed. Urbanization, industrialization, and the decline of agriculture all contributed to the movement to wage labor and entrepreneurial activity.

Does the success of the new entrepreneurs, who themselves were tenant farmers only 15 to 20 years ago, suggest that a radical reordering has taken place in local society? Are the landlord-merchants now a demoralized and defeated class? The simple answer to both of these questions is no: extenants have not taken over the village, nor is the landlord-merchant class retreating in disarray. Whereas once there were two classes based on the ownership of land, there are now three distinct economic groups. The descendants of the old elite still retain their land and their interests in the coast, and they are involved in local development schemes. They remain very much a distinct propertied class. Like their predecessors, members of this class are employers, not employees. They own their

Inequality among brothers

businesses and control large amounts of capital. Although the descendants of Ha Tsuen's original landlord-merchants are no longer seen to be the rightful and inevitable leaders of the community, they are still very much involved in local politics. Landlord-merchant politicians tend to use descent and hamlet loyalties in attracting allies. For them descent continues to be a powerful force binding the people of Ha Tsuen together. Without descent they might become an isolated and powerless group of leisured landlords.

Participation in local politics (which now means the Rural Committee) is essential for success in the new world of industrial development and government monopoly. One has but to look at the fallow fields that surround Ha Tsuen to know that land alone can no longer provide a foundation for economic preeminence. Of course, large amounts of money can be made by owning the right piece of land at the right time, but the mere possession of land does not assure the owner financial returns. Being privy to government policy and the plans of developers is of increasing importance, as is sophistication in dealing with colonial authorities. The ties of descent (and locality) are of particular importance to the members of Ha Tsuen's landlord-merchant class as they come more and more to depend upon the votes of their wage-earning agnates (for more discussion of descent and politics, see Chapter 9). Whereas land no longer binds Teng landlord to Teng tenant, descent and locality continue to draw their modern counterparts together.

The new entrepreneurs are an independent, individualistic group of villagers. They number less than 20 men who own shops, factories, import–export businesses, and apartment complexes. Since 1952 they have controlled the Rural Committee for seven of its nine terms. The entrepreneurs are strident in their denunciation of the old elite. They tend to discuss community affairs in terms of economic interests and do not rely on descent as the center point of their political rhetoric. Whether colonial officials have followed a concerted policy of favoring the new entrepreneurs is difficult to judge. It is clear, nonetheless, that the long-term effect of government decisions has made it possible for the entrepreneurs to thrive.

The third group of Teng is by far the largest. Most of these "ordinary villagers" are wage laborers, although a few work as policemen and shopkeepers. Their standard of living is high by Asian standards. How do they relate to the new entrepreneurs and to the old landed elite? First, from a strictly economic point of view, the majority of ordinary villagers work outside their home community. They no longer have to depend on their wealthy kinsmen in order to make a living. A few villagers work in shops and factories owned by their agnates, but these numbers are not high. Some emigrants, especially during the early phases of their migration to Europe, utilized ties to successful Teng kinsmen who themselves are important members of the new entrepreneurial group. Furthermore, a few families are tied to landlord-merchant agnates by long association, in what amounts to a kind of patron–client relationship. As clients, they have

Economic and political changes: 1945–1978

been loaned or given money by their patrons to build new houses or to educate sons. Wealthy patrons also recommend members of their client families for jobs or recruit them into new business ventures. These clients can be counted upon to serve as loyal supporters of local political leaders. However, wealthy villagers have far fewer economic strings to pull than they did in the past. By the 1970s it had become much more difficult for a successful villager to convert his economic dominance into political power.

Some ordinary villagers support the landlord-merchant coalition, and others support the new entrepreneurs. The majority, however, prefer to avoid politics altogether. Although the entrepreneurs make appeals to these villagers based on claims of economic solidarity in opposition to the old elite, most Teng tend to vote according to personal, hamlet, or segment loyalties – not according to a dawning sense of past injustices. "What does it matter?", they say; "All politicians are the same." Most male villagers seem hesitant to use or endorse the rhetoric of economic difference. They still find it embarrassing or unmannerly to talk about their lineage brothers in the strident language of the new entrepreneurs.

The Rural Committee as an institution does not have much significance for ordinary workers. In the past, as we have seen, the tenant farmer was politically and economically dependent upon the landlord-merchant. The ordinary villager of today has considerably more choice than his predecessor. Of course, the Rural Committee is not totally irrelevant to these men, for a committee member may help to place one's son in a police academy or assist in obtaining a passport. The factory worker is linked to the local politician by a host of bureaucratic necessities; building permits, passports, land registration, and drivers' licenses all require intervention. There is little doubt that the important community decisions that determine the future development of the Ha Tsuen region are still beyond the ordinary villager. The major break with the past, however, is that instead of having one clearly defined ruling group at the village level, there are now two, and neither of these has total control of local politics.

9
Social and cultural transformations

The dramatic economic and political changes of the last two decades have had a profound effect on village life-styles. New two-story houses can be seen in every hamlet. Villagers own private cars, refrigerators, and television sets. Traditional schools, where village boys once learned the Confucian classics, have given way to modern forms of education. Ha Tsuen boasts a new school that caters to both boys and girls. Young people wear the latest Hong Kong fashions, and a number of Teng families send their teenage children to Kowloon for secondary education and technical training.

All of these innovations are important, but a less obvious and more significant change is the extent to which ordinary Teng have become involved in the world outside their lineage. No longer are villagers confined to Ha Tsuen, with an occasional visit to Yuen Long. Most now work outside the village; young people make regular visits to the teahouses and cinemas of Yuen Long and Tuen Mun; and they have non-Teng friends whom they meet at school or work. Not surprisingly, there have been similar changes in relationships with affines. Affinity was once the concern of wealthy men and the wives of Ha Tsuen's tenants and smallholders; affinal relations are now important to many Teng males, including laborers and entrepreneurs. Several Teng work with their wives' fathers or brothers in restaurants abroad. Other villagers have moved into urban flats with the help of their affines. Obviously the social distance between male affines is beginning to give way to closer contacts, especially among the recently married.

Marriage choices also reflect the changing life-styles of Ha Tsuen's exfarmers. In the past, 76 percent of Teng wives came from the Yuen Long marketing area (based on a 1978 sample of 68 women over 40 years of age). However, a sample of 34 young Teng wives (those under the age of 40 in 1978) shows that only 44 percent were from the Yuen Long area, whereas 14 women, or 41 percent, came from urban Kowloon. Among the older women (those over 40 years) the number of Kowloon-born wives was 6, or 9 percent. Ordinary villagers are now going well outside the confines of their *hsiang* and the Yuen Long marketing

Social and cultural transformations

district for their brides.[1] Brides from the cities are popular not only because they are knowledgeable about urban life (a good thing in itself) but also because they provide contacts with their male kin. These men can help with urban jobs or housing in ways that even wealthy lineage mates cannot.

In the last 10 years exfarmers who are active in local politics have contracted politically advantageous marriages for their sons and daughters. The Man of San Tin are particularly sought after by Ha Tsuen politicians. The chairman of the Rural Committee has a Man daughter-in-law and an ex–vice-chairman married two of his children to San Tin Man. The Man are valued affines because their success abroad is legendary in the New Territories. A number of Man entrepreneurs have become extremely wealthy, and perhaps of even more importance in the local marriage sweepstakes is the fact that some of these men are beginning to convert their emigrant earnings into New Territories business ventures and political office.

Age is an important factor in determining affinal relationships among the Teng. Older men may seek out good matches for their children, and young people expect to have at least some contact with their affines. However, the older men themselves often have little to do with their own affines (that is, their wives' kin or sisters' husbands). This is especially true if their wives' brothers or their sisters' husbands are poor or politically insignificant. Politicians may be an exception to this pattern, but most of the changes in affinity have been taking place with recent marriages.

Marriage expenses are very high among the Teng. In 1978 the cash payment, or *li chin*, was a substantial amount of money, and the total marriage expenses for the groom and his family was often as much as two years of an average factory worker's salary. For the marriages that took place during my stay in the village, the *li chin* varied from HK$6,000 to HK$10,000. Most young men calculated that they needed about HK$30,000 (approximately $7,000 in 1978) to marry. This figure includes *li chin*, the cost of the marriage feasts and food gifts to the bride's family, and the purchase of betrothal cakes. The cakes usually cost about HK$2,500 to HK$3,500. In the case of a Teng daughter who married out of Ha Tsuen in 1978, 3,000 cakes costing HK$3,200 were distributed.

In the 1970s the groom bore most – perhaps all – of the costs of his marriage, whereas in the past it was his parents' responsibility to make the financial arrangements. However, the change is not as great as one might at first suppose. The groom may handle his own marriage expenses, but he is able to do this by being part of a household that provides for his necessities, often subsidized by his unmarried sisters' and his mother's wages. In recent years bride price has

---

1 In the past, 23 percent of Teng wives came from within the *hsiang*. However, out of the 34 more recently married Teng wives, only 3 (or 9 percent) came from villages within the *hsiang*.

Inequality among brothers

risen but dowry has also escalated, so there is no significant change in the relation between the two. In the last decade banquet costs have risen steeply.

As in the past, expensive dowries are still associated with Ha Tsuen's wealthy families (now these families include both landlord-merchants and the successful entrepreneurs). Among the wealthy, both the groom (and his family) and the bride's family continue to contribute to the dowry, whereas among ordinary villagers the groom still bears most of the marriage expenses, including the cost of the dowry (or *chia chuang*).

Some of the changes that Ha Tsuen people have experienced in recent years are reflected in the rites of marriage. Not surprisingly, it is in the area of affinal relations that the ritual has changed most dramatically, although even these changes are as yet somewhat tentative. Some families tend to follow the "old way," whereas others have adopted new conventions. There was, in fact, much discussion among villagers about the new ritual treatment of affines. Most people were uncertain about what should be considered the proper form.

As noted earlier, until the 1960s wife takers had no formal contact with wife givers during the marriage negotiations or during the rites themselves. Marriage negotiations are still handled through an intermediary (*mei jen*), but, in striking contrast to earlier arrangements, the groom now takes an active part in the betrothal celebrations at the bride's house. In all the cases about which I have information (including the five betrothal banquets I attended), the groom took part in the procession that carried the betrothal gifts (betrothal cakes, food, and bride price) to the bride's family. After the gifts had been presented, the groom and his party joined the bride's family's betrothal feast. Until the late 1960s the groom would never have participated in these betrothal celebrations.

In recent years the groom has also begun to accompany his bride when she returns to her natal home on the third and last day of the marriage rites (an innovation many older Teng consider to be scandalous). Prior to 1970 the bride was accompanied only by the bride callers; today, however, the groom himself presents food gifts to the bride's parents and joins them in a meal that is sometimes quite elaborate. Thus the groom and the bride celebrate their change in status together with the bride's family.

The contacts that young men now have with their future affines vary a great deal. In some cases a Teng groom and his bride's father or brother were fellow workers; in one of the marriages that I witnessed, the groom was an employee of the bride's father. In another marriage, which took place just before I moved to Ha Tsuen, the groom and the bride's brother worked together in the same small factory. However, in two of the marriages that occurred during my stay in the village the relations between the groom and his bride's kin were formal and by no means intimate. In one case the groom was a returned emigrant who had only met his bride two weeks before the actual marriage. The young couple were introduced by the groom's married sister, who had been instructed by her brother to help him find a wife during his two-month holiday in Hong Kong.

Social and cultural transformations

Before the marriage the groom had a meal with the bride's family, but there was no evidence of intimacy between the groom and the bride's family, nor, it appeared, was there any intention of maintaining close ties in the future. The bride's family was poor, but, as one of the groom's friends told me, "The bride is very pretty." Another groom had even less contact with his bride's male kin; he met them for the first time at the betrothal feast.

Like the changes at the time of betrothal, the most dramatic innovations in the marriage rites themselves all involve the groom's formal contacts with the bride's family. In all three of the marriages that I witnessed, the groom accompanied the bridal party to the bride's house on the marriage day, whereas in the past the groom dispatched a party to fetch the bride while he waited at home. Significantly, there has been no change in the bride's party; none of her relatives accompanies the bride to the groom's home.

One of the most striking changes in the marriage celebrations, and the one about which the Teng themselves are least comfortable, is the presence of the bride's kin at the groom's principal marriage feast. This feast is held on the second night of the marriage rites, and until recently, as was noted earlier, the guests were restricted to the groom's kin and neighbors. However, in all three marriage feasts that I attended, some of the bride's kin were present. In one case a full table (seating 12 people) was set aside for the bride's family and friends. In the second case the bride's party had two tables, and in the third only the bride's household attended.

The Teng were as yet uncertain about the propriety of these new joint banquets. Some villagers told me that they felt embarrassed when they were invited to a wedding feast as the bride's guests. The bride's kin are always outnumbered by the groom's guests, and many men said that they felt uncomfortable accepting the hospitality of a virtual stranger. One villager confessed that he did not know how to act when he came as the guest of the bride, and he admitted that he avoided these formal affairs whenever possible. The bride's guests, he said, were in an inferior position at these banquets. Although there is some unease about joint banquets, there is every likelihood they they will continue. In the last few years more and more people (acting as wife givers) have been making joint banquets a condition of the marriage payments. The bride's family demands a certain number of betrothal cakes and food gifts as well as a specific amount of bride price; to this they now add the number of tables that they require for their guests at the principal marriage feast. The groom and his family, of course, pay for the entire feast. The bride's family contributes nothing to its cost.

These joint banquets mark an important juncture in the changing ritual relations between wife givers and wife takers. For the first time the two families are formally brought together. Clearly the Teng are making some ritual accommodation to their newly acquired affines, even though the process seems to be characterized by a certain amount of hesitation and awkwardness.

Considering the ritual rapprochement between the groom and the bride's fam-

Inequality among brothers

ily, can we now expect other changes in the marriage rites? For instance, does the groom's mother's brother now take an active part in his sister's son's marriage festivities? My Ha Tsuen research suggests that there is little change in this relationship. The groom's mother's brother still does not participate in any of the marriage rites; his wife continues to act for him. The bride's kin are the only "outsiders" involved in the marriage rites. Whether the relationship between mother's brother and sister's son will become closer remains to be seen. Perhaps as the Teng have more contact with their wives' families, their male offspring may develop longer-lasting relationships with their mother's fathers and brothers. It will be interesting to watch the development of affinity in Ha Tsuen, especially to see what effect it will have on lineage solidarity. As the Teng are absorbed into Hong Kong's industrialized, urbanized sector, these extralineage contacts will no doubt become even more important. Whatever happens, affinity will certainly play an increasingly significant role in widening the personal networks of individual Teng.

Thus far I have discussed affinity only as it relates to men. What of women's affinity? As male affines establish closer contacts, will women's affinity cease to be important? If women were simply standing in for their husbands, this might indeed be the case. But, as we saw in Chapter 7, women establish and maintain affinal relations in their own right. There is, I would argue, every likelihood that affinal relationships among women will continue to be socially significant and perhaps become even stronger. Affines remain an important source of support among women, and there is no evidence that this has changed.

In 1977–8 there was a decided trend toward closer relations between recently married women and their natal families. This reflects the fact that young women now have more opportunities to visit their parents. In general, their mothers-in-law exert less control over their actions than in the past; young daughters-in-law have more free time and more money to spend as they please. An interesting example of the closer contacts that young wives now have with their natal families is the case of a Teng wife who gave birth to her first child in 1978. Because the woman's mother-in-law was living abroad and her husband's grandmother was unwell, it was decided that the mother and her baby daughter should spend the first two weeks after leaving the hospital with the mother's parents. The old grandmother was not happy with this state of affairs, but she was forced to accept it. She did, however, make sure that she did her part in protecting the infant, and presumably the family, from this highly irregular action. Upon their return from the mother's natal family and before the baby entered the main hall of her father's house, the infant was passed over an open fire by the grandmother. This purified the baby, I was told, of the noxious influences or "airs" of the outsiders. Only after this precaution was the grandmother satisfied to let the infant enter her father's house, where, after all, as far as she was concerned, it should have been all along. In the past it would have been unthinkable for a

Social and cultural transformations

woman to have spent the first weeks after delivering her baby with her own family.

A less dramatic but more common example of the increase in contacts between women and their families is the extent to which Teng wives have been asked to contribute to fund-raising drives in their natal communities. Usually these drives, which proliferated in postwar Hong Kong, involve funds for building and furnishing community halls (or *kung so*). In the late 1960s and 1970s, women who had long since been married were asked to send money back to their natal villages. In 1978 I accompanied two Teng wives to the opening ceremony of a community hall in their home village of Mong Jeng (in Ha Tsuen *hsiang*). These women were extremely proud of the small part they had played in helping their natal village. After the ceremony that they both attended, the day was spent with their brothers' families, enjoying a good meal and catching up on village affairs. I think it unlikely that in the past the wives of poor farmers could have afforded (or would have been asked) to contribute to community projects like this. Although Ha Tsuen women took pleasure in making these contributions, their husbands could be heard grumbling darkly about "outsiders begging for money." While conveniently disregarding the fact that Teng married-out daughters provided some of the furnishings for the public hall at Sik Kong Wai, Teng men take a dim view of their one-time dependent neighbors soliciting funds from their wives.

No doubt closer contacts between women and their natal families are also likely to further cement the bonds among women affines (especially among married women and their brothers' wives). Furthermore, these contacts may serve to strengthen the links among male affines.

Significantly, the one aspect of marriage ritual that has undergone little or no change is that part that is concerned with the alienation of the bride from her natal family and her incorporation into her husband's household. The lowly and subservient status of the bride vis-à-vis her mother-in-law and her husband's family continues to be emphasized in the rites. This may seem surprising, considering that young wives now have closer contacts with their natal families and are no longer so thoroughly dominated by their mothers-in-law as was the case 10 to 15 years ago. However, as long as the patrilineal system remains strong and postmarital residence continues to be virilocal, it is not really surprising that marriage rites continue to highlight the bride's withdrawal from her natal family and her incorporation into her husband's family.

Changes in the system of descent

A casual visitor to Ha Tsuen in the 1970s might conclude that the lineage continues to play an important role among the Teng. The central ancestral hall is well kept and is obviously a source of great pride to villagers. On most days

Inequality among brothers

men can be seen relaxing and talking at the entrance gate to Yu Kung T'ang. Old and middle-aged men continue to devote considerable time to the hall's ritual activities, and young men celebrate their marriages and sons' births there. The ancestral rites are well attended and choreographed with a precision that makes Ha Tsuen known throughout the New Territories as a place where the "old rituals" are still performed. But what about the less obvious indicators of lineage activity? Have recent economic and political changes affected lineage solidarity?

Villagers are proud to be "Ha Tsuen Teng"; of this there is little doubt. Membership in a dominant lineage with a documented history of nearly 900 years allows ordinary factory workers to feel a special sense of identity. The New Territories is rapidly becoming an emigré society. The Teng themselves are surrounded by outsiders from China, and to the east and west are the booming urban centers of Yuen Long and Tuen Mun. The residents of these new towns have no collective past, and until recently they had no representation in local politics.[2] In a society where most people are cut off from their past, those who have links to one of the indigenous lineages often find themselves in a unique and privileged position.

In Ha Tsuen the past has a very real significance. When I first came to live in Ha Tsuen I was told story after story of the lineage's great and colorful history. Young and old alike took pains to impress upon me that the Teng (in this they included Kam Tin and Ping Shan) were the oldest, the richest, and the most populous lineage in the New Territories. During my year-long stay in the village, nothing that I did excited more interest than the kinship diagram I produced, graphically linking the various settlements of New Territories Teng according to their genealogical relationship. This was carefully examined, arguments ensued, corrections were made, and in the process I was found to be acceptable. If I were interested in what the Teng themselves deemed to be important (namely their own local history), my work must have some value, they decided.

The past has a nearly sacred quality in Ha Tsuen; it reassures the Teng that they are people of consequence. One must perhaps live in Hong Kong with its political and social instability, its competitiveness, and its high rate of immigration to understand this point. The past provides an identity, but the past is also a commodity to be traded upon. Over the years colonial authorities have given the indigenous peoples of the New Territories (the so-called natives or *pen-ti jen*) a special status (see Chau and Lau 1982). The "natives," of course, own the land that the recent emigrés farm and that the developers seek. They also monopolize local politics. When one's standing as a *pen-ti* is coupled with

---

2 In 1982 a system of District Boards was established to represent everyone in the New Territories. But the old Rural Committees have been preserved to handle the special problems of indigenous villagers (such as the Teng).

Social and cultural transformations

membership in a dominate lineage, it is easy to see why it is still important to be a Teng.

The political importance of the lineage presents something of a problem for Ha Tsuen's "new entrepreneurs," who on the one hand are attempting to distance themselves from many aspects of the past but on the other hand are dependent upon their kinsmen for political support. The rhetoric that the entrepreneurs use to marshal support is based on a combination of antilandlord feelings and lineage solidarity, with a heavy emphasis on the former. On close examination, appeals for support on the grounds of agnatic loyalties and economic differentiation are not as contradictory as they might at first appear. In openly opposing the landlords, the new entrepreneurs are making use of the past to remind their fellow lineage mates of the injustices and indignities that they all suffered at the hands of Ha Tsuen's landlords. In a sense they are defining the landlords out of the lineage: "We lineage brothers," they say, "are united against the landlords." For the entrepreneurs the past is much safer ground for political discussion than the present, with its embarrassing economic gap between themselves and their fellow villagers. Of course, playing on antilandlord feelings does not imply that the idea of a unified lineage must be abandoned. The entrepreneurs are unwilling – perhaps unable – to relinquish the rhetoric of lineage loyalty that still has a great appeal to ordinary villagers.

The survival of the lineage as a viable institution makes it possible for the Teng, especially politicians, to exert an influence and power beyond their numerical strength. Without the lineage, Ha Tsuen would be 11 discrete hamlets, each with its own requirements and loyalties. Even though its members may be politically split, the Teng as a group continue to extract special privileges from the colonial administration, and they continue to dominate the development of Ha Tsuen *hsiang*. The leaders of the local coalitions can call upon the apparatus of the lineage, its village guard, its organizational framework, its reputation in the New Territories, and its ties to other Teng communities, and so bolster their position in local society.

Ha Tsuen's security forces continue to enforce Teng interests. Of course, these interests are more complex than they were in the past. Teng and landlord-merchant interests were once seen as the same thing, but this is no longer the case. Today there is a conflict between the interests of the new entrepreneurs centered on the market of Hung Shui Kiu and those of the old elite focused on the coastal development of Lau Fau Shan. Because the political climate allows more freedom of action in the Lau Fau Shan area, both guard organizations have tended to support the landlord-merchant camp. In spite of their obvious sympathies, guardsmen have tried to avoid becoming a wedge between groups of Teng. Their activities continue to be directed primarily against non-Teng residents of the *hsiang*. In recent years they have been particularly useful in keeping a firm hold over the area's new emigré settlements.

For many Teng, clinging to the past is closely related to their attempts to

Inequality among brothers

retain special status with the Hong Kong government. This is especially true of the landlord-merchant elite, whose position depends heavily (and perhaps tenuously) upon the votes, if not the loyalites, of fellow agnates. For some Teng the lineage has become important in terms of personal identity, for others it provides a reservoir of loyal political supporters, and for yet others it is useful for keeping the recent emigrés from China "in their place."

Among the Ha Tsuen Teng, estate membership plays an important role in local politics. The manipulation of intralineage rivalries is central to the political strategy of the landlord-merchant group. Because segments tend to proliferate in those lines where property is concentrated, it is only reasonable to expect that wealthy members will belong to more estates than poor members (see Baker 1979:55). This logic is certainly borne out by the Ha Tsuen evidence. The leaders of the landlord-merchant coalition belong not only to the wealthiest estates in the lineage but also to the most populous. In 1978, Szu-le tsu (see Figure 2) had 510 members. If, by appealing to agnatic solidarity, the landlord-merchant coalition could galvanize the support of Szu-le members, they would have a solid foundation upon which to dominate local opinion. They have, in fact, managed to do this in the hamlet of Sik Kong Wai, which has a large percentage of the Szu-le membership. The core members of the new entrepreneurial coalition, on the other hand, belong to only a few estates that are not as well endowed (or as populous) as those that unite their rivals.

Although it is true that the old elite play on segment loyalties, they also stress the lineage ideals that unite the Teng as a whole. Lineage ideology is employed both to emphasize the fact that all Teng, even the wealthy, are bound together into a unified group and to encourage segment members to be loyal followers. As in the past, the two principles of the lineage, one emphasizing unity and the other differentiation, are utilized for the benefit of the landlord-merchants. However, unlike in the past, the old elite is being openly challenged by a group of nouveau riche entrepreneurs.

Politics is not a new field for Teng estates. I noted in Chapter 3, for instance, how groups of Teng banded together to form ancestral estates that were designed to counteract the organized influence of other estates. With the advent of electoral politics, however, the political role of the estates has become more overt; many have become the focus of political cliques. This is certainly a change from the past, when Teng leaders, while guarding the interests of their own estates, were careful to underplay the divisive potential of segment rivalries.

Clearly it is the local leaders – the entrepreneurs and the old elite – who have most to gain from the survival of the lineage. To many factory workers who work outside Ha Tsuen, the lineage as a political institution is largely irrelevant. These men are not involved in land deals (most own no land); they do not intend to establish small factories or shops; and they have few political aspirations. To them Ha Tsuen is primarily a cheap place to live and raise their families. Their world has become that of the urban factory and the household. Although they

Social and cultural transformations

retain an interest in lineage rituals, their 10- to 12-hour days and 6-day workweeks give them little time to dabble in lineage politics. Nevertheless, as noted earlier, many ordinary Teng do feel a sense of pride in their lineage heritage, something that is denied to the vast majority of their fellow workers. On this score the lineage is important to them. At a more practical level, we should also remember that the lineage provides factory workers with a valuable source of contacts with powerful leaders. Agnatic kinship still gives ordinary villagers an extra advantage vis-à-vis their less well-connected neighbors and fellow workers.

In 1978 the Spring Rites were attended by over 80 elders, and the *k'ai teng* (lantern lighting) ceremony for newly born sons was an elaborate affair. I was told that every new male born in Ha Tsuen in the previous year was represented in the ceremony and had his name added to the lineage's membership list, the "Record of New Males." In the autumn of 1977 (during the *chung yang* festival in the ninth lunar month) there were dozens of Teng grave sacrifices, many of which cost a great deal of money. These ceremonies are much enjoyed by the participants, who include Teng males of all ages. During the *chung yang* festival the weather is usually warm and sunny, and the sacrifices involve long walks to the graves in the hills, followed by leisurely picnics. As long as an ancestral estate has funds, its members are obliged to celebrate the annual sacrifices. Judging by the large number of these rituals and the atmosphere they create, the lineage, as an ancestor-worshiping group, still constitutes an important religious community. However, ancestral sacrifices are expensive and can only take place when the estate's coffers allow. What is the financial condition of Teng estates?

Now that many fields are fallow, some estates have little or no income. When this happens, the focal ancestor of a bankrupt estate is usually forgotten, and the group whose focus was the estate eventually dissolves. This has happened to estates in Ha Tsuen, although some elders have tried to keep penniless estates "alive" by member subscriptions. It is very unlikely, however, that these voluntary rescue attempts can continue for long. Some form of income-producing corporate property is necessary if an estate is to survive indefinitely. Although many Teng estates have only small amounts of property (in 1905, out of 82 estates, 50 had less than 1 acre), thus far the majority have managed to maintain some form of ritual activity. In fact, a few small estates have refurbished old ancestral tombs; two such renovations occurred in 1978 and cost thousands of Hong Kong dollars.

While most Teng estates are struggling to survive, a handful have found themselves in possession of extremely valuable properties. In 1977 the government compulsorily purchased the lands of a small and relatively insignificant ancestral estate in Ha Tsuen (insignificant in the sense that its members were not well off and the land no longer produced much rental income). The village was awash with rumors concerning the amount of money received by the members of this estate. The actual figure was a closely guarded secret, but most estimates clustered around the figure of eight hundred thousand Hong Kong dollars. Since

Inequality among brothers

there were only 30 surviving members of this estate, each was said to have received approximately twenty-six thousand Hong Kong dollars (about $5,000). This was a considerable windfall, but it cannot compare with the sale of ancestral lands by an estate in the Teng settlement of Kam Tin. This sale, which took place in 1978, was widely reported in the Hong Kong press to involve over twelve million Hong Kong dollars. In order to realize such profits, however, the estate lands must be sold. Unless provision is made for maintaining the ancestral sacrifices by some other corporate means, the sale of estate land eventually leads to the dissolution of the group. Ultimately the ancestor around whom the group is focused also "disappears." What at first glance may appear to be an economic renaissance of estates is often their death knell.

There is, however, at least one aspect of the property boom that operates to keep valuable land tied up in ancestral estates. Estate members sometimes cannot agree on the sale price of the property or on the division of the proceeds. There are many examples of this in the New Territories. Jack Potter discusses a case in Ping Shan involving estate members who could not agree whether to distribute their profits according to a per capita or a *per stirpes* division (1968:108–11). Thus far the estate in question has remained intact while the legal argument about division proceeds through the court (the case had not been resolved in 1978). In Ha Tsuen a similar situation prevails. Members of one of San Wai's wealthy estates cannot agree on what to do with the money they received for the sale of a valuable piece of property. Everyone concerned believes that some of the money should be used to rebuild the estate's ancestral hall. One faction, however, wants to keep surplus money in the estate, while their opponents argue that the remaining funds should be divided among the surviving members. It is unlikely, considering the personalities and the large amount of money involved, that this argument will be quickly settled.

Although the estate system remains more or less intact, one might expect increasing change in the management and disposition of estate holdings. As land fails to produce regular income due to the decline in agriculture (or because plots are sold off to land developers), the property base of the lineage will decline. How will these changes affect the Teng lineage? Research in other parts of the New Territories has shown that a lineage can prosper even after its land base has dwindled. J. L. Watson (1975b) demonstrates that as landholdings in San Tin deteriorated the lineage as a corporate institution continued to flourish. In the 1950s and 1960s the Man lineage at San Tin became heavily involved in emigration to Europe. Lineage ties became crucial for obtaining passports and work permits, for finding jobs and accommodations, and for gaining access to the specialized information necessary to succeed abroad. Obviously the Chinese lineage can continue to operate even when it is based on resources other than land. In the case of the Man, these resources were largely intangible (personal contacts, information, and technical assistance), but nonetheless they were essential to the success of individual lineage members.

Social and cultural transformations

Like the Man lineage of San Tin, the Teng continue to enjoy some special advantages because of their lineage membership. For Ha Tsuen's wage earners the lineage provides access to influential agnates. It gives ordinary Teng a sense of privilege and identity in the uncertain environment of present-day Hong Kong. The Teng lineage is still a valuable resource, but, much as in the past, it is more valuable to some lineage members than to others. Now, as in the eighteenth and nineteenth centuries, the lineage provides special advantages to Ha Tsuen's landlord-merchants. The lineage constitutes a useful structure for the protection of traditional privileges, including commercial and manufacturing monopolies. The local village guard continues to protect landlord-merchant properties just as it did in the past. Furthermore, the general lineage membershp still provides a ready source of political followers for the old elite. The landlord-merchants may now be more dependent on their lineage mates, but thus far they have been successful enough in their dealings with fellow agnates to retain some control over local affairs.

The lineage once constituted a structure of closure for its ordinary members. Their political lives were dominated by Yu Kung T'ang and the handful of landlord-merchants who controlled it. And, as demonstrated in Chapter 4, their economic lives were largely restricted by the boundaries of the lineage. The survival of the ancestral rites means that the membership of the lineage still constitutes an active ritual community, and the traditions of the Teng lineage remain important to ordinary members. Most Teng would still agree that they are not only neighbors but they are also kinsmen and lineage mates. Nevertheless, there is no doubt that the lineage's economic and political role is becoming increasingly irrelevant to the majority of Ha Tsuen's residents. The politicians appear to be fighting a difficult, if not a losing, battle in their attempts to take the lineage into the 1980s and beyond.

10
Class and kinship

In previous chapters I have argued that although all of the Ha Tsuen Teng may have been equal "in the eyes of the ancestors," they were by no means equal in the everyday world of landowning and political power. The Chinese lineage was not an institution dedicated to the pursuit of mutual advantage with all members sharing equally in the benefits or profits. Nor was it simply a tool devised by the landlord-merchants and manipulated by them at will. The relationship between the system of descent and the system of class relations is not so simple. This relationship is best understood not at the level of personal manipulation but as part of a complex of interlocking structures that create the conditions by which one class dominates another.

The concept of class has played a central role throughout this study. Before turning to a detailed discussion of the relation between class and kinship in Ha Tsuen, I would like to briefly explain how I have used the term *class* and why it seems to me to be useful for this analysis.

Class and class analyses in Chinese society

Control over important resources is crucial to any discussion of class difference and class structure. The ownership of land has always been central to discussions of class relations in rural China.[1] Using a conceptual scheme based largely on landownership figures, many analysts have divided China's prerevolutionary rural society into five classes: landlords, rich peasants, middle peasants, poor peasants, and landless laborers (for discussions of this system of classification,

---

1 Philip Huang discusses the importance of landownership and a number of other criteria for defining classes in the Chinese countryside. Huang reports that during the Land Reform of the 1950s the Chinese communists themselves took a number of factors into account in their analysis of rural China. Huang writes: "Exploitation remained the central yardstick for class differentiation, but no longer merely on the basis of a simplified dichotomy between landlord and tenants. The final analysis took into account ... the intricate intermingling of exploitation through rent and exploitation through wage labor, as well as usury and the subletting of land" (1975:148).

Class and kinship

see Chao 1960; Huang 1975; Kraus 1977; Mao 1965; C. K. Yang 1959b:40–53). However, the multiplicity of classes belies what many see as fundamentally a dual class structure.

The most widely accepted view tends to regard rural China as a society dominated by class antagonism between the propertied and exploiting, on the one hand, and the propertyless and exploited on the other (see Huang 1975:150). According to this scheme, landlords and rich peasants were easily categorized as exploiting classes because of their extraction of land rent. Similarly, poor peasants and laborers were defined as exploited classes because of their alienation from the means of production. Middle peasants often presented a problem. Some in this class owned enough land to support themselves, while others owned small amounts of land and rented additional fields. Yet another category of middle peasants rented out their land because it was too far away to work themselves or because they did not command sufficient labor. Middle peasants were thus assigned class labels depending upon their exploitation of other peasants. In the case of China, those who acquired the bulk of their income through the extraction of rent from tenants were defined as exploiters.

On the basis of the landownership data for Ha Tsuen that were analyzed in Chapter 4, it is possible to differentiate a class of landlord-merchants and a class of smallholder-tenants. According to these data, 36 percent of Teng-owned land in Ha Tsuen *hsiang* belonged to a few large landholders, and 50 percent was owned by ancestral estates. Among those villagers who worked the land, a majority of farm households (55 percent) were landless, and nearly all households (97 percent, by one count) were forced to rent some land. At the risk of oversimplifying, one might say that Teng landlord-merchants collected rents, whereas Teng smallholder-tenants paid rents. Of course, neither of these classes was entirely homogeneous. Some tenants owned land, others did not, and no doubt some smallholder-tenant households rented out land to others. Furthermore, neither smallholder-tenants nor landlord-merchants form a neat occupational category. Many tenants engaged in part-time fishing, oyster cultivation, or petty trading. Some worked as casual laborers, and a few were sailors. Similarly landlord-merchants owned shops and factories, they were moneylenders and cargo-boat owners.

There is no doubt that studies that focus on differential landownership provide useful and compelling analyses of rural China. However, although landownership was extremely important in Ha Tsuen, it is not the only criterion for dividing the Teng into two classes. I have already noted that control over local decision making and marketing arrangements were important factors in differentiating Ha Tsuen's landlord-merchants from its smallholder-tenants. There were also important social and cultural differences that marked the two classes. Some years ago the anthropologist Fei Hsiao-t'ung noted that classes in rural China were divided not only with respect to control over resources but also by a "social gulf" (1946). In Ha Tsuen, landlord-merchants and smallholder-tenants had

Inequality among brothers

different patterns of marriage, affinity, and inheritance (see Chapters 6 and 7). Their world views and the life-styles of their wives and daughters varied enormously. Men from smallholder-tenant households had few contacts outside the lineage; landlord-merchants had many.

Landlord-merchants were extremely successful in monopolizing links to the world beyond the lineage. Their contacts in the region's administrative centers and in the nearby market towns greatly strengthened their position vis-à-vis their poorer kinsmen. As we saw in Chapter 7, marriage and affinity played an important role in establishing and sustaining these all-important contacts. In contrast, the world of Ha Tsuen tenants and small-holding farmers was closely circumscribed by the lineage. Outside the bonds of the lineage, all were enemies to be treated with suspicion and calculation; inside the lineage agnates shared a special relationship, and cooperation was said to be the ideal, if it was not always the practice. When this ideology was coupled with the fact that Teng smallholder-tenants were economically and politically dependent on their wealthy kinsmen, it is not surprising to find that most Teng rarely ventured beyond their lineage world.

It is, therefore, on the basis of economic, political, and sociocultural criteria that I have divided Ha Tsuen's pre-1960s population into two distinct classes. To understand the relationship between landlord-merchants and smallholder-tenants one must begin by analyzing economic and political data. But in order to appreciate how the relations between these two classes have been reproduced generation after generation, one must also consider patterns of marriage, affinity, inheritance, and the related issues of lineage ideology and organization. In this study the cultural and social dimensions of class have been emphasized because it is my contention that one cannot appreciate the dynamics of class relations in rural China without looking beyond landholding and politics.

Before returning to the discussion of descent it is perhaps necessary to consider one more aspect of class in Ha Tsuen. Marx, in an often quoted passage from his "Eighteenth Brumaire of Louis Bonaparte," summarizes the analytical difficulties of dealing with the French peasantry. These difficulties, in my view, also apply to the rural society of China, and of course to Ha Tsuen. Marx wrote:

> In so far as millions of families live under economic conditions of existence that separate their mode of life, their interests, and their culture from those of the other classes and put them in hostile opposition to the latter, they form a class. In so far as there is merely a local interconnection among these small-holding peasants and the identity of their interests begets no community, no national bond, and no political organization among them, they do not form a class. (1959 [1869]:338–9)

There is little doubt that Ha Tsuen's landlord-merchants constituted a class "for itself"; that is, the members of this group were conscious of their mutual interests and acted accordingly. They had ties to landlord-merchants well beyond the boundaries of Ha Tsuen. It is possible to argue that they were part of a regional, perhaps even a national, class of landlord-merchants. In fact, as we have seen,

Class and kinship

their position rested at least in part on their extralineage contacts. The smallholder-tenants, on the other hand, remained very much a class "in itself," in that the individuals involved were not always aware of their collective interests. According to Marx, during the first half of the nineteenth century the French peasantry did not yet constitute a class "for itself"; however, when contrasted with other groups, they could be said to have formed a class. It is in this latter sense that the usefulness of applying the concept of class to Ha Tsuen is most apparent. In discussing agnatic relations it is easy to fall into the trap of thinking only about the unity of lineage members. The use of the term *class* sharpens the distinction between two contrasting socioeconomic groups and provides important insights into the analysis of what are usually considered to be intralineage, intravillage relations.

Descent and class

In the introduction to this study I suggested that prerevolutionary China was a complex, class-based society in which descent and lineage organization played an important role (particularly in the Southeast). Like many other Chinese, the Teng are united by common descent and residence, and yet they are divided by differential control over resources, by differing marital and affinal patterns, and by variations in life-style. Earlier in this study I argued that the Africanist model that has been applied to the Chinese system of descent has obscured the relationship between lineage organization and class structure. Although the descent model does "make sense" of some aspects of the Chinese kinship system, it can also lead to misunderstanding and confusion. In those areas of southeastern China where the model has been applied most thoroughly, the preoccupation with descent has led many fieldworkers to overlook important relationships and social forms.

In what ways, if any, does the Teng lineage fit the descent paradigm described in Chapter 1? First, according to this paradigm, membership in a lineage is defined by a clear principle of descent. Because members are recruited by birth or adoption, one would expect little confusion over who does and who does not belong to a lineage. Descent is not, however, the only criterion of membership among the Teng; in this case descent from a specific ancestor is a necessary but not a sufficient condition of membership. Only those whose predecessors made a financial contribution toward the lineage's estate at the time of its formation (in 1751) can now claim to be members of the Teng lineage. However, after the initial period of lineage formation, recruitment operated as the descent paradigm would suggest (that is, men became members by right of birth). In China it appears that descent is sometimes combined with other principles of organization to create a lineage.

The second characteristic of the descent paradigm is corporation. A lineage is said to have a single, legal personality, and its members share in an estate

Inequality among brothers

that may be land or territory or rights to office or occupation. In other words, a lineage has continuity beyond the lifetime of its individual members. The Chinese lineage is, of course, a corporation. The lineage and its segments are focused on common property, usually land. What is interesting about the Chinese case is how this landed property is managed and how class differences become intertwined with lineage estates and segmentation. Estates do not just "appear" in every generation; they have to be organized and managed, often by a literate elite who have gained their skills in the competitive world of commerce and industry. If an estate is not managed properly, it may disappear in only two or three generations. The corporate estates of Chinese lineages are not, therefore, built into the natural fabric of the society; they must be defended and nurtured by each generation.

Last, the descent paradigm implies a particular system of segmentation. Fortes notes that lineages are internally differentiated and that segmentation takes place according to a "model laid down in the parental family" (1970 [1953]:86). The group supposedly divides according to "natural" cleavages found in the family – between men with wives and those without, between sons of the same father but different mothers, between siblings. As the model predicts, Chinese lineages are internally differentiated or segmented. The system of segmentation in Ha Tsuen, however, is significantly different from that outlined by Fortes. Among the Teng, segmentation is asymmetrical: there is no expectation that two brothers will necessarily form two segments. The segments of Chinese lineages are property-holding groups, and they are set up with the express purpose of managing this property for the benefit of living and dead members. As noted in Chapter 3, private wealth is celebrated in the Chinese lineage, and differential access to property is built into the very structure of the segmentary system. In China, the most successful lineages (in terms of long-term survival) are precisely those that foster the widest possible segmentary divisions, based on vast differences in wealth and status. The segmentary system of the Chinese lineage does not mitigate or neutralize class differences; it is, in fact, an expression of class cleavages in the wider society.

Obviously there are significant differences between the Chinese lineage and the kind of lineages the descent model seeks to represent. While sinological anthropologists have sometimes pointed out these differences, they have tended to ignore the dynamic relationship that exists between the system of descent and the wider system of social and economic inequality.

Because of the outward similarities between Chinese lineages and lineages found in many parts of Africa, it is often assumed that lineages have a similar social significance in both places. China is not a "descent society" (or a "segmentary society") like the Nuer or the Tallensi. Nor was it governed by what some scholars refer to as the "lineage mode of production" (see, e.g., Terray 1975; for general discussion, see Kahn 1981). Emmanuel Terray writes of the lineage mode of production, "In contrast to the capitalist mode of production,

Class and kinship

where a whole series of functions is divided among different units, here they are concentrated in the same groups and institutions at their respective levels. Thus in the lineage mode of production, the lineage and the segment in their respective concerns are simultaneously units of production, consumption, political organization, and religion'' (1975:94).

Once we have appreciated that Chinese society was not structured by a framework of unilineal descent groups but by a state apparatus and a complex market economy, we are in a position to better understand the role that patrilineages played in China. In a study of kinship in two Malagasy societies, Maurice Bloch (1975) found that the same kinship system had a different social significance in each society. Among the Zafimaniry, the kinship system was embedded in the relations of production, whereas among the Merina, kinship was part of the ideological system or the superstructure. A similar argument could be made for patrilineal descent groups; in other words, patrilineages do not have the same social "place," or significance, in all the societies where they are to be found (for general discussion of this problem, see Godelier 1977; Kahn 1981). Although this may seem obvious, it is perhaps still necessary to reiterate Leach's warning that many of our anthropological categories (such as lineage) may have little or no general sociological significance (1961:4). There are lineages and there are lineages, and to confuse Chinese lineages with Tallensi lineages causes only misunderstanding and distortion.[2]

In many societies where descent groups are found, the principles of descent tend to structure or even dominate the economic and political order. We might say that in these societies descent is part of the infrastructure. Although the Chinese lineage may seem to dominate political organization, religion, and perhaps even production and consumption, it does not in fact do so. This is why perspective is so important. If we take the lineage as our object of analysis, we may well find that it is all-pervading, all-powerful. However, if we remember that the Chinese lineage existed in a class-based society with a complex state and religious system, we begin to see that the lineage did not dominate but was dominated by these wider social forms. The important question becomes not how the lineage operates but how it relates to this wider system.

In China, descent is not the foundation upon which society is constructed, nor is it strictly part of the relations of production. Nevertheless, I would stress that where descent groups are present, they do play an important economic and political role. What, then, are we to make of the role of patrilineages in China? China's corporate lineages were not passive reflections of China's economic order. Rather, the Chinese lineage should be considered as part of the conditions under which that order was reproduced. Class differences and lineage organization are by no means incompatible phenomena. In fact, the patrilineage, along

---

2 For a recent attempt to tighten the concept of descent group, see Verdon 1980, 1982.

with affinity, played an important role in maintaining a system of class privilege in the Chinese countryside.

Class in a Chinese lineage

The descent model assumes an ahistorical bias that, in the case of China, tends to obscure the relationship between class and lineage. Once it is understood that lineages were formed and developed in response to specific economic and political conditions, it is possible to see that lineages were part of a wider social system. No longer can the lineage be studied on its own terms. In China, lineage formation is a problem to be explained, not something to be taken for granted. Chinese lineages are not the inevitable outgrowths of a system of descent. Lineages like that of the Ha Tsuen Teng are, in fact, relatively rare in China. Why should we find such uneven development? The answer must be sought in a close analysis of economic and political conditions and not, I would submit, by looking at the internal dynamics of descent.

During the late seventeenth and eighteenth centuries a favorable economic climate, coupled with increasing competition, encouraged the formation of a lineage at Ha Tsuen. Lineages like that of the Teng thrived in the absence of effective state control and soon came to dominate political life in many parts of southeastern China. Lineages controlled markets, temple committees, and of course local defense corps. Those lineages that were able to organize effectively grew and developed at the expense of the less well organized.

The formation and development of the Teng lineage and the growth of Ha Tsuen's landlord-merchant elite are closely related phenomena. Unification under the administrative umbrella of the main ancestral hall, Yu Kung T'ang, gave rich and poor Teng many economic advantages, but there is little doubt that it was the wealthy who benefited most. Fei Hsiao-t'ung argues that the lineage (or "clan," as he calls it) served elite interests (1946). He regards such kin groups as "gentry," or elite, organizations and remarks that lineage organization "among the landless or even petty owners is superfluous" (5). Although Fei is correct in stressing the importance of the link between the wealthy and large-scale lineage organization, he misses an important point in excluding the poor from the Chinese lineage. For hundreds of years Chinese lineages have incorporated men from diverse class backgrounds. The lineage provided the rich with a steady supply of loyal tenants and defenders of their interests. In fact, I would argue that one of the great strengths of the Chinese lineage was that it united the loyal tenant and the wealthy landlord, the poor guardsman and the successful merchant.

The recent past provides clues to the forces that both affect and were affected by lineage organization. As we have seen, in the 1950s and 1960s Ha Tsuen underwent a number of profound changes. Soon after the Japanese occupation, Hong Kong's colonial authorities introduced a new system of local government in the New Territories. Local politicians were henceforth to be elected, and these elected representatives were given a near monopoly over contacts with government officials. The older system of political organization, with its landlord-merchant intermediation, was swept away. As these political changes were making themselves felt, villagers were also coping with the effects of massive industrialization. In the 1950s and 1960s hundreds of new factories were built, land values skyrocketed, and the population of the colony rose from an estimated two million in 1950 to nearly four million in 1967(Hong Kong Statistics 1969:14). Many farmers in the New Territories abandoned the land and took jobs in factories or emigrated to Europe, where they worked in Chinese restaurants. In a period of 15 years the rural landscape of the New Territories was completely transformed. What do these changes tell us about the general problem of descent in a class-based society?

One consequence of the industrial boom was that the economic and political ties that once bound Teng tenants to their landlord kinsmen were broken. The process of fragmentation was mitigated, however, by the fact that the villagers of Ha Tsuen are both neighbors and agnates. Members of the old elite, in particular, have continued to emphasize the virtues of agnation. Their electoral prospects largely depend on lineage loyalties; hence they have a vested interest in downplaying class differences. Class relations in Ha Tsuen have changed in important ways since the mid-1950s. With the appearance of a group of nouveau riche entrepreneurs, the traditional class dichotomy of landlord-merchants and smallholder-tenants no longer applies. The new entrepreneurs have openly attacked the traditional elite, and for the first time in lineage history the exploitative activities of the landlord-merchants have become an issue in local politics. New forms of local government have made the lineage's old political functions redundant. New ways of earning a livelihood have allowed ordinary villagers to throw off the economic bonds that once tied them to their lineage mates.

Although members of the old elite have been forced to change their strategies, descent continues to be an important political resource among the Teng. In the past, descent provided an ideological foundation for the suppression of class differences. The lineage played a central role in perpetuating an economic and political system in which the landlord-merchant class was dominant. Today the descendants of the landlord-merchants continue to call upon the rhetoric of descent in their attempts to maintain the status quo ante. It is hardly surprising that members of this privileged elite should cling so tenaciously to an institution that has served them so well in the past.

References

Key: *JBRAS (HK)*: *Journal of the Hong Kong Branch of the Royal Asiatic Society*.

Ahern, Emily Martin. 1973. *The Cult of the Dead in a Chinese Village*. Stanford: Stanford University Press.
    1974. "Affines and the Rituals of Kinship." In *Religion and Ritual in a Chinese Society*, ed. Arthur P. Wolf. Stanford: Stanford University Press.
    1976. "Segmentation in Chinese Lineages: A View through Written Genealogies." *American Ethnologist* 3:1–16.
    1981. *Chinese Ritual and Politics*. Cambridge, England: Cambridge University Press.
Anderson, Eugene N., Jr. 1972. *Essays on South China's Boat People*. Asian Folklore and Social Life Monographs, No. 29. Taipei: Orient Cultural Service.
Annual Report. 1952–3. *Annual Report of the District Office, New Territories*. Hong Kong: Government Press.
Atwell, William S. 1977. "Notes on Silver, Foreign Trade, and the Late Ming Economy." *Ch'ing-shih wen-ti* (Journal of the Society for Ch'ing Studies) 3(8):1–33.
Baker, Hugh D. R. 1966. "The Five Great Clans of the New Territories." *JBRAS (HK)* 6:25–48.
    1968. *A Chinese Lineage Village: Sheung Shui*. Stanford: Stanford University Press.
    1977. "Extended Kinship in the Traditional City." In *The City in Late Imperial China*, ed. G. William Skinner. Stanford: Stanford University Press.
    1979. *Chinese Family and Kinship*. London: Macmillan.
Barnes, J. A. 1962. "African Models in the New Guinea Highlands." *Man* 62:5–9.
Barrett, Richard E. 1980. "Short Term Trends in Bastardy in Taiwan." *Journal of Family History* 5:293–312.
Beattie, Hilary. 1979. *Land and Lineage in China: A Study of T'ung-Ch'eng County, Anhwei, in the Ming and Ch'ing Dynasties*. Cambridge, England: Cambridge University Press.
Blake, C. Fred. 1981. *Ethnic Groups and Social Change in a Chinese Market Town*. Asian Studies at Hawaii, No. 27. Honolulu: University Press of Hawaii.
Bloch, Maurice. 1975. "Property and the End of Affinity." In *Marxist Analyses and Social Anthropology*, ed. Maurice Bloch. London: Malaby Press.
    1978. "Marriage amongst Equals: An Analysis of the Marriage Ceremony of the Merina of Madagascar." *Man* 13:21–33.
Bourdieu, Pierre. 1977. *Outline of a Theory of Practice*, trans. Richard Nice. Cambridge, England: Cambridge University Press.
Brim, John A. 1970. "Local Systems and Modernizing Change in the New Territories." Ph.D. thesis, anthropology, Stanford University. Ann Arbor: University Microfilms No. 71-12, 862.

References

Brown, E. H. Phelps. 1971. "The Hong Kong Economy: Achievements and Prospects." In *Hong Kong: The Industrial Colony*, ed. Keith Hopkins. Hong Kong: Oxford University Press.

Buck, John L. 1937. *Land Utilization in China*. Nanking: University of Nanking Press.

Census. 1971. *Hong Kong Population and Housing Census: Main Report*. Hong Kong: Census and Statistics Department.

Chang, Chung-li. 1955. *The Chinese Gentry: Studies on Their Role in Nineteenth Century Chinese Society*. Seattle: University of Washington Press.

1962. *The Income of the Chinese Gentry*. Seattle: University of Washington Press.

Chao, Kuo-chun. 1960. *Agrarian Policy of the Chinese Communist Party, 1921–1959*. Bombay: Asia Publishing.

Chau, Lam-yan and Lau Siu-kai. 1982. "Development, Colonial Rule, and Intergroup Conflict in a Chinese Village in Hong Kong." *Human Organization* 41:139–46.

Chen, Han-seng. 1936. *Landlord and Peasant in China: A Study of the Agrarian Crisis in South China*. New York: International Publishers.

Chesneaux, Jean. 1973. *Peasant Revolts in China, 1840–1949*, trans. C. A. Curwen. London: Thames & Hudson.

Ch'u, T'ung-tsu. 1961. *Law and Society in Traditional China*. Paris: Mouton.

Cohen, Myron L. 1969. "Agnatic Kinship in South Taiwan." *Ethnology* 8:167–82.

1976. *House United, House Divided: The Chinese Family in Taiwan*. New York: Columbia University Press.

Comaroff, John L., ed.. 1980. *The Meaning of Marriage Payments*. London: Academic Press.

Davis, Fei-ling. 1971. *Primitive Revolutionaries in China*. London: Routledge & Kegan Paul.

Davis, Richard L. 1980. "The Shih Lineage at the Southern Sung Court." Ph.D. thesis, history, Princeton University. Ann Arbor: University Microfilm No. 80–18,654.

Davis, S. G. 1949. *Hong Kong in Its Geographical Setting*. London: Collins.

1964. "Rural–Urban Migration in Hong Kong and the New Territories." In *Land Use Problems in Hong Kong*, ed. S. G. Davis. Hong Kong: Hong Kong University Press.

De Lepervanche, Marie. 1967–8. "Descent, Residence and Leadership in the New Guinea Highlands." *Oceania* 38:134–58, 163–89.

Dennerline, Jerry. 1979–80. "The New Hua Charitable Estate and Local-level Leadership in Wuxi County at the End of the Qing." In *Select Papers from the Center for Far Eastern Studies* (University of Chicago), ed. Tang Tsou, 4:19–70.

1981. *The Chia-ting Loyalists: Confucian Leadership and Social Change in Seventeenth-century China*. New Haven: Yale University Press.

Diamond, Norma. 1969. *K'un Shen: A Taiwanese Village*. New York: Holt, Rinehart and Winston.

Dumont, Louis. 1957. *Hierarchy and Marriage Alliance in South Indian Kinship*. Royal Anthropological Institute Occasional Paper, No. 22. London: Royal Anthropological Institute.

Ebrey, Patricia, B. 1978. *The Aristocratic Families of Early Imperial China: A Case Study of the Po-ling Ts'ui Family*. Cambridge, England: Cambridge University Press.

1983. "Conceptions of the Family in the Sung Dynasty." Paper prepared for The American Council of Learned Societies conference on Family and Kinship in Chinese History, Jan. 2–7, 1983.

Elvin, Mark. 1970. "Early Communist Land Reform and the Kiangsi Rural Economy." *Modern Asian Studies* 4:165–69.

Endacott, G. B. 1964. *A History of Hong Kong*. Hong Kong: Oxford University Press.

Esherick, Joseph. 1981. "Number Games: A Note on Land Distribution in Prerevolutionary China." *Modern China* 7(4):387–411.

References

Evans, D. M. Emrys. 1973. "The New Law of Succession in Hong Kong." *Hong Kong Law Review* 3:7–50.
Fairbank, John K. 1953. *Trade and Diplomacy on the China Coast*. Stanford: Stanford University Press.
Faure, David. 1981. "Hong Kong and China in the Village World." *JBRAS (HK)* 21:75–90.
Fei, Hsiao-t'ung. 1946. "Peasantry and Gentry: An Interpretation of Chinese Social Structure and Its Changes." *American Journal of Sociology* 52:1–17.
Fei, Hsiao-t'ung and Chang Chih-i. 1948. *Earthbound China: A Study of Rural Economy in Yunnan*. London: Routledge & Kegan Paul.
Festival. 1964. *Ha Tsuen Hsiang-yüeh shih-nien t'ai-p'ing ch'ing-chiao* (Ha Tsuen Hsiang Decennial Chiao Festival). Hong Kong New Territories: published locally.
   1974. Ibid., 1974 edition.
Feuchtwang, Stephan. 1974. *An Anthropological Analysis of Chinese Geomancy*. Vientian: Editions Vithagna.
Fitzgerald, C. P. 1965. *China: A Short Cultural History*. New York: Praeger.
Fortes, Meyer. 1945. *The Dynamics of Clanship among the Tallensi*. London: Oxford University Press.
   1969. *Kinship and the Social Order*. London: Routledge & Kegan Paul.
   1970. "The Structure of Unilineal Descent Groups." In Meyer Fortes, *Time and Social Structure*. London: Athlone. (First published in 1953, *American Anthropologist*, 55 (1):17–41.)
Fox, Richard G. 1971. *Kin, Clan, Raja, and Rule: State–Hinterland Relations in Preindustrial India*. Berkeley: University of California Press.
Freedman, Maurice. 1958. *Lineage Organization in Southeastern China*. London: Athlone.
   1966a. *Chinese Lineage and Society: Fukien and Kwangtung*. London: Athlone Press.
   1966b. "Shifts of Power in the Hong Kong New Territories." *Journal of Asian and African Studies* 1:3–12.
   1967. *Rites and Duties, or Chinese Marriage*. London: G. Bell & Sons.
   1970. "Ritual Aspects of Chinese Kinship and Marriage." In *Family and Kinship in Chinese Society*, ed. Maurice Freedman. Stanford: Stanford University Press.
   1974. "The Politics of an Old State: A View from the Chinese Lineage." In *Choice and Change: Essays in Honour of Lucy Mair*, ed. John Davis. London: Athlone.
   1979. "Colonial Law and Chinese Society." In *The Study of Chinese Society: Essays by Maurice Freedman*, ed. G. William Skinner. Stanford: Stanford University Press. (First published in 1950, *Journal of the Royal Anthropological Institute* 80:97–126.)
Fried, Morton. 1953. *Fabric of Chinese Society*. New York: Praeger.
   1957. "The Classification of Corporate Unilineal Descent Groups." *Journal of the Royal Anthropological Institute* 87:1–29.
   1966. "Some Political Aspects of Clanship in a Modern Chinese City." In *Political Anthropology*, ed. M. Swartz, V. Turner, and A. Tuden. Chicago: Aldine.
Gallin, Bernard. 1960. "Matrilateral and Affinal Relationships of a Taiwanese Village." *American Anthropologist* 62:632–42.
   1966. *Hsin Hsing, Taiwan: A Chinese Village in Change*. Berkeley: University of California Press.
Gazetteer. 1819. *Hsin-an hsien-chih* (Hsin-an County gazetteer). Taipei: Ch'eng-wen Reprint Series. (Originally published in Canton, 1819.)
Gazetteer of Place Names. 1969. *A Gazetteer of Place Names in Hong Kong, Kowloon, and the New Territories*. Hong Kong: Government Press.
Godelier, Maurice. 1977. "Politics as 'Infrastructure': An Anthropologist's Thoughts on the Example of Classical Greece and the Notions of Relations of Production and

References

Economic Determinism." In *The Evolution of Social Systems*, ed. J. Friedman and M. J. Rowlands. London: Duckworth.
Goody, Jack. 1962. *Death, Property and the Ancestors*. Stanford: Stanford University Press.
——— 1968. Introduction. In *Literacy in Traditional Societies*, ed. Jack Goody. Cambridge, England: Cambridge University Press.
——— 1973. "Bridewealth and Dowry in Africa and Eurasia." In Jack Goody and S. J. Tambiah, *Bridewealth and Dowry*. Cambridge, England: Cambridge University Press.
Grant, Charles J. 1964. "The Extension of the Arable Area in Hong Kong." In *Land Use Problems in Hong Kong*, ed. S. G. Davis. Hong Kong: Hong Kong University Press.
Groves, Robert G. 1964. "The Origins of Two Market Towns in the New Territories." In *Aspects of Social Organization in the New Territories*, ed. Marjorie Topley. Hong Kong: Royal Asiatic Society, Hong Kong Branch.
——— 1969. "Militia, Market and Lineage: Chinese Resistance to the Occupation of Hong Kong's New Territories in 1899." *JBRAS (HK)* 9:31–64.
Hayes, James. 1970. "Old Ways of Life in Kowloon: The Cheung Sha Wan Villages." *Journal of Oriental Studies* (Hong Kong) 8:154–88.
——— 1974. "The Hong Kong Region: Its Place in Traditional Chinese Historiography and Principal Events Since the Establishment of Hsin-an County in 1573." *JBRAS (HK)* 14:108–35.
——— 1977. *The Hong Kong Region, 1850–1911*. Hamden, Conn.: Shoestring Press.
Hinton, William. 1966. *Fanshen: A Documentary of Revolution in a Chinese Village*. New York: Monthly Review Press.
Ho, Ping-ti. 1959. *Studies on the Population of China, 1368–1953*. Cambridge, Mass.: Harvard University Press.
——— 1962. *The Ladder of Success in Imperial China*. New York: John Wiley & Sons.
Hong Kong Statistics. 1969. *Hong Kong Statistics, 1947–1967*. Hong Kong: Census and Statistics Department.
Hopkins, Keith, ed. 1971. *Hong Kong: The Industrial Colony*. Hong Kong: Oxford University Press.
Hsiao, Kung-chuan. 1960. *Rural China: Imperial Control in the Nineteenth Century*. Seattle: University of Washington Press.
Hsieh, Kuo-ching. 1932. "Removal of Coastal Population in Early Tsing Period." *Chinese Social and Political Science Review* 15:559–96.
Hsieh, Winston. 1974. "Peasant Insurrection and the Marketing Hierarchy in the Canton Delta, 1911." In *The Chinese City Between Two Worlds*, ed. Mark Elvin and G. William Skinner. Stanford: Stanford University Press.
Hsu, Francis L. K. 1949. "Social Mobility in China." *American Sociological Review* 14:764–71.
——— 1963. *Clan, Caste and Club*. Princeton: Van Nostrand.
Hu, Hsien-chin. 1948. *The Common Descent Group in China and Its Functions*. Viking Fund Publications in Anthropology, No. 10. New York: Viking Fund.
Huang, Philip C. C. 1975. "Analyzing the Twentieth-century Chinese Countryside: Revolutionaries versus Western Scholarship." *Modern China* 1:132–60.
Jamieson, G. 1970. *Chinese Family and Commercial Law*. Hong Kong: Vetch & Lee. (First published in 1921.)
Johnson, David G. 1977. *The Medieval Chinese Oligarchy*. Boulder: Westview Press.
——— 1983. "Comment on J. L. Watson's 'Chinese Kinship Reconsidered.' " *China Quarterly* 94:362–65.
Johnson, Elizabeth L. 1976. "Households and Lineages in a Chinese Urban Village."

References

Ph.D. thesis, anthropology, Cornell University. Ann Arbor: University Microfilm No. 77–18, 170.
Johnson, Graham E. 1973. "In-Migration and Community Expansion in Hong Kong: The Case of Tsuen Wan." *Journal of Oriental Studies* (Hong Kong) 11:107–14.
Jordan, David K. 1972. *Gods, Ghosts, and Ancestors: The Folk Religion of a Taiwanese Village*. Berkeley: University of California Press.
Kahn, Joel S. 1981. "Marxist Anthropology and Segmentary Societies: A Review of the Literature." In *The Anthropology of Pre-Capitalist Societies*, ed. Joel Kahn and Josep Llobera. London: Macmillan.
Kam Tin Teng Chia-p'u. n.d. *Kam Tin Teng Chia-p'u* (Kam Tin Teng family genealogy). Vol. 2. Hong Kong University Library Genealogy Collection.
Kamm, John T. 1977. "Two Essays on the Ch'ing Economy of Hsin-an, Kwangtung." *JBRAS (HK)* 17:55–84.
Kraus, Richard. 1977. "Class Conflict and the Vocabulary of Social Analysis in China." *China Quarterly* 69:54–74.
Krone, Rev. 1967. "A Notice of the Sanon District." *JBRAS (HK)* 7:104–37. (Essay originally published in 1859, *Transactions of the China Branch of The Royal Asiatic Society* 6:71–105.)
Kuhn, Philip A. 1970. *Rebellion and Its Enemies in Late Imperial China*. Cambridge, Mass.: Harvard University Press.
 1984. "Chinese Views of Social Classification." In *Class and Social Stratification in Post-Revolution China*, ed. James L. Watson. Cambridge, England: Cambridge University Press.
Kulp, Daniel H. 1925. *Country Life in South China*. New York: Columbia University Press.
Kuper, Adam. 1983. "Lineage Theory: A Critical Review." *Annual Review of Anthropology for 1982*, Vol. 11.
La Fontaine, Jean. 1973. "Descent in New Guinea: An Africanist View." In *The Character of Kinship*, ed. Jack Goody. Cambridge, England: Cambridge University Press.
Lamley, Harry. 1977. "Hsieh-tou: The Pathology of Violence in South-Eastern China." *Ch'ing-shih wen-ti* (Journal of the Society for Ch'ing Studies) 3(7):1–39.
Lang, Olga. 1946. *Chinese Family and Society*. New Haven: Yale University Press.
Leach, Edmund R. 1961. *Rethinking Anthropology*. London: Athlone.
Lin, S. Y. 1967. "Salt Manufacture in Hong Kong." *JBRAS (HK)* 7:138–51.
Liu, Hui-chen Wang. 1959. *The Traditional Chinese Clan Rules*. Monographs of the Association for Asian Studies, No. 7. Locust Valley, N.Y.: J. J. Augustin.
Lo, Hsiang-lin. 1963. *Hong Kong and Its External Communications before 1842*. Hong Kong: Institute of Chinese Culture.
Lockhart, Stewart. 1899. "Extracts from a Report by Mr. Stewart Lockhart on the Extension of the Colony of Hong Kong, Oct. 8, 1899." *Hong Kong Government Gazette*, 45.
 1900. "Memorandum on Land." Report on the New Territory at Hong Kong, 1900: Appendix 3. In *Hong Kong Sessional Papers*.
 1901. "Report on the New Territory for the Year 1900." In *Hong Kong Sessional Papers, 1909–1912*. Hong Kong: Government Press.
McCreery, John L. 1976. "Women's Property Rights and Dowry in China and South Asia." *Ethnology* 15:163–74.
Maher, Vanessa. 1974. *Women and Property in Morocco*. Cambridge, England: Cambridge University Press.
Mao, Tse-tung. 1965. "Analysis of the Classes in Chinese Society." In *Selected Works of Mao Tse-tung*, Vol. 1 (originally published 1926). Beijing: Foreign Languages Press.

References

Marx, Karl. 1959. "The Eighteenth Brumaire of Louis Bonaparte." In *Marx and Engels: Basic Writings on Politics and Philosophy*, ed. Lewis Feuer. Garden City, N.Y.: Doubleday (Anchor Books). (Originally published in 1869.)

Mathias, John. 1977. "A Study of the Jiao, A Taoist Ritual, in Kam Tin, in the Hong Kong New Territories." D. Phil. thesis, anthropology, University of Oxford.

Meijer, M. J. 1971. *Marriage Law and Policy in the Chinese Peoples' Republic*. Hong Kong: Hong Kong University Press.

Meskill, Johanna M. 1979. *A Chinese Pioneer Family: The Lins of Wu-feng, Taiwan, 1729–1895*. Princeton: Princeton University Press.

Miners, Norman. 1975. *The Government and Politics of Hong Kong*. Hong Kong: Hong Kong University Press.

Moise, Edwin E. 1977. "Downward Social Mobility in Pre-Revolutionary China." *Modern China* 3:3–31.

Munro, Donald. 1969. *The Concept of Man in Early China*. Stanford: Stanford University Press.

Murray, Dian H. 1979. "Sea Bandits: A Study of Piracy in Early Nineteenth-century China." Ph.D. thesis, history, Cornell University.

Myers, Ramon H. 1970. *The Chinese Peasant Economy: Agricultural Development in Hopei and Shantung, 1890–1949*. Cambridge, Mass.: Harvard University Press.

— 1975. "Cooperation in Traditional Agriculture and Its Implications for Team Farming in the People's Republic of China." In *China's Modern Economy in Historical Perspective*, ed. Dwight H. Perkins. Stanford: Stanford University Press.

Nelson, Howard G. H. 1969. "The Chinese Descent System and the Occupancy Level of Village Houses." *JBRAS (HK)* 9:113–23.

Ng, Peter Y. L., and Hugh Baker. 1983. *New Peace County: A Chinese Gazetteer of the Hong Kong Region*. Hong Kong: Hong Kong University Press.

Okamatsu, Antaro. 1971. *Provisional Report on Investigation of Laws and Customs in the Island of Formosa*. Taipei: Ch'eng-wen Reprints. (First published in English in 1902.)

Orme, G. N. 1912. "Report on the New Territories, 1899–1912." In *Hong Kong Sessional Papers, 1909–1912*. Hong Kong: Government Press.

Parish, William L. and Martin K. Whyte. 1978. *Village and Family in Contemporary China*. Chicago: University of Chicago Press.

Parkin, David. 1978. *The Cultural Definition of Political Response: Lineal Destiny among the Luo*. London: Academic Press.

Parry, Jonathan. 1979. *Caste and Kinship in Kangra*. London: Routledge & Kegan Paul.

Pasternak, Burton. 1969. "The Role of the Frontier in Chinese Lineage Development." *Journal of Asian Studies* 28:551–61.

— 1972. *Kinship and Community in Two Chinese Villages*. Stanford: Stanford University Press.

— 1973. "Chinese Tale-telling Tombs." *Ethnology* 12:259–73.

Pegg, Leonard. 1981. *Family Law in Hong Kong*. London: Butterworth.

Peters, Emrys L. 1972. "Shifts in Power in a Lebanese Village." In *Rural Politics and Social Change in the Middle East*, ed. Richard Antoun and Illiya Harik. Bloomington: Indiana University Press.

Potter, Jack M. 1968. *Capitalism and the Chinese Peasant: Social and Economic Change in a Hong Kong Village*. Berkeley: University of California Press.

— 1969. "The Structure of Rural Chinese Society in the New Territories." In *Hong Kong: A Society in Transition*, ed. I. C. Jarvie and Joseph Agassi. New York: Praeger.

— 1970. "Land and Lineage in Traditional China." In *Family and Kinship in Chinese Society*, ed. Maurice Freedman. Stanford: Stanford University Press.

References

Pritchard, Earl. 1936. "The Crucial Years of Early Anglo-Chinese Relations, 1750–1800." *Research Studies of the State College of Washington*, No. 4.
Rawski, Evelyn S. 1972. *Agricultural Change and the Peasant Economy of South China*. Cambridge, Mass.: Harvard University Press.
　1979. *Education and Popular Literacy in Ch'ing China*. Ann Arbor: University of Michigan Press.
Rheubottom, David B. 1980. "Dowry and Wedding Celebrations in Yugoslav Macedonia." In *The Meaning of Marriage Payments*, ed. John L. Comaroff. London: Academic Press.
Rhoads, Edward J. M. 1974. "Merchant Associations in Canton, 1895–1911." In *The Chinese City between Two Worlds*, ed. Mark Elvin and G. William Skinner. Stanford: Stanford University Press.
Sahlins, Marshall. 1965. "On the Ideology and Composition of Descent Groups." *Man* 65:104–7.
Salaff, Janet. 1981. *Working Daughters of Hong Kong: Filial Piety or Power in the Family?* Cambridge, England: Cambridge University Press.
Scheffler, H. W. 1964. "Descent Concepts and Descent Groups: The Maori Case." *Journal of the Polynesian Society* 73:126–33.
　1966. "Ancestor Worship in Anthropology: Or, Observations on Descent and Descent Groups." *Current Anthropology* 7:541–51.
Schneider, David. 1967. "Kinship and Culture: Descent and Filiation as Cultural Constructs." *Southwestern Journal of Anthropology* 23:65–73.
Shepherd, Bruce. 1900. "Memorandum of Work Done in the Land Office in Hong Kong." In "Report on the New Territory at Hong Kong, 1900," Appendix 8. In *Hong Kong Sessional Papers, 1909–1912*. Hong Kong: Government Press.
Shiga, Shuzo. 1978. "Family Property and the Law of Inheritance in Traditional China." In *Chinese Family Law and Social Change*, ed. David Buxbaum. Seattle: University of Washington Press.
Skinner, G. William. 1964–5. "Marketing and Social Structure in Rural China." *Journal of Asian Studies* 24:3–43, 195–228.
Smith, M. G. 1956. "On Segmentary Lineage Systems." *Journal of the Royal Anthropological Institute* 86:39–79.
Strathern, Andrew. 1972. *One Father, One Blood: Descent and Group Structure among the Melpa People*. London: Tavistock.
Sung, Hok-p'ang. 1973. "Legends and Stories of the New Territories: Kam T'in." *JBRAS (HK)* 13:111–32.
　1974. "Legends and Stories of the New Territories, Kam T'in (continued)." *JBRAS (HK)* 14:160–85.
Tambiah, S. J. 1973. "Dowry and Bridewealth and the Property Rights of Women in South Asia." In Jack Goody and S. J. Tambiah, *Bridewealth and Dowry*. Cambridge, England: Cambridge University Press.
Teng Shih Tsu P'u. n.d. "Teng-shih tsu-p'u" (Teng lineage genealogy). Manuscript, privately owned. Ha Tsuen, Hong Kong New Territories.
Terray, Emmanuel. 1975. "Classes and Class Consciousness in the Abron Kingdom of Gyaman." In *Marxist Analyses and Social Anthropology*, ed. Maurice Bloch. London: Malaby Press.
Topley, Marjorie. 1958. "The Organization and Social Function of Chinese Women's *Chai T'ang* in Singapore." Ph.D. thesis, anthropology, University of London.
　1975. "Marriage Resistance in Rural Kwangtung." In *Women in Chinese Society*, ed. Margery Wolf and Roxane Witke. Stanford: Stanford University Press.
Twitchett, Denis. 1959. "The Fan Clan's Charitable Estate, 1050–1760." In *Confucianism in Action*, ed. David Nivison and Arthur Wright. Stanford: Stanford University Press.

References

1961. "Documents of Clan Administration: I, The Rules of Administration of the Charitable Estate of the Fan Clan." *Asia Major* 8:1–35.
1965. "A Critique of Some Recent Studies of Modern Chinese Socio-Economic History." *Transactions of the International Conference of Orientalists in Japan* 10:28–41.
1982. "Comment on J. L. Watson, 'Chinese Kinship Reconsidered.'" *China Quarterly* 92:623–27.
Van der Sprenkel, Sybille. 1962. *Legal Institutions in Manchu China*. London: Athlone.
Verdon, Michel. 1980. "Descent: An Operational View." *Man* 15:129–50.
1982. "Where Have All Their Lineages Gone? Cattle and Descent among the Nuer." *American Anthropologist* 84:566–79.
Wakeman, Frederic, Jr. 1966. *Strangers at the Gate: Social Disorder in South China, 1839–1861*. Berkeley: University of California Press.
Ward, Barbara E. 1959. "Floating Villages: Chinese Fishermen in Hong Kong." *Man* 59:44–45.
Watson, James L. 1975a. "Agnates and Outsiders: Adoption in a Chinese Lineage." *Man* 10:293–306.
1975b. *Emigration and the Chinese Lineage: The Mans in Hong Kong and London*. Berkeley: University of California Press.
1976. "Chattel Slavery in Chinese Peasant Society: A Comparative Analysis." *Ethnology* 15:361–75.
1977. "Hereditary Tenancy and Corporate Landlordism in Traditional China: A Case Study." *Modern Asian Studies* 11:161–82.
1980. "Transactions in People: The Chinese Market in Slaves, Servants, and Heirs." In *Asian and African Systems of Slavery*, ed. J. L. Watson. Oxford: Blackwell Publisher.
1982a. "Chinese Kinship Reconsidered: Anthropological Perspectives on Historical Research." *China Quarterly* 92:589–622.
1982b. "Of Flesh and Bones: The Management of Death Pollution in Cantonese Society." In *Death and the Regeneration of Life*, ed. Maurice Bloch and Jonathan Parry. Cambridge, England: Cambridge University Press.
Watson, Rubie S. 1981. "Class Differences and Affinal Relations in South China." *Man* 16:593–615.
1982. "The Creation of a Chinese Lineage: The Teng of Ha Tsuen, 1669–1751." *Modern Asian Studies* 16:69–100.
Wesley-Smith, Peter. 1980. *Unequal Treaty, 1898–1997: China, Great Britain and Hong Kong's New Territories*. Hong Kong: Oxford University Press.
Wickberg, Edgar. 1981a. "Another Look at Land and Lineage in the New Territories, ca. 1900." *JBRAS (HK)* 21:25–42.
1981b. "Continuities in Land Tenure, 1900–1940." In *The Anthropology of Taiwanese Society*, ed. Emily Martin Ahern and Hill Gates. Stanford: Stanford University Press.
Wiens, Harold J. 1967. *Han Chinese Expansion in South China*, 2nd ed. Hamden, Conn.: Shoestring Press.
Wolf, Arthur P. 1970. "Chinese Kinship and Mourning Dress." In *Family and Kinship in Chinese Society*, ed. Maurice Freedman. Stanford: Stanford University Press.
1974. "Gods, Ghosts, and Ancestors." In *Religion and Ritual in Chinese Society*, ed. Arthur P. Wolf. Stanford: Stanford University Press.
Wolf, Arthur P. and Huang Chieh-shan. 1980. *Marriage and Adoption in China, 1845–1945*. Stanford: Stanford University Press.
Wolf, Margery. 1972. *Women and the Family in Rural Taiwan*. Stanford: Stanford University Press.

References

Wood, A. E. 1916. "Report on the New Territories for the Year 1915: Northern District." In *Hong Kong Annual Reports*. Hong Kong: Government Press.

Woon, Yuen-fong. 1979. "The Non-localized Descent Group in Traditional China." *Ethnology* 18:17–29.

Yang, C. K. 1959a. *The Chinese Family in the Communist Revolution*. Cambridge, Mass.: MIT Press.

——— 1959b. *A Chinese Village in Early Communist Transition*. Cambridge, Mass.: MIT Press.

Yang, Martin. 1945. *A Chinese Village: Taitou, Shantung Province*. New York: Columbia University Press.

Young, John A. 1974. *Business and Sentiment in a Chinese Market Town*. Asian Folklore and Social Life Monographs, No. 60. Taipei: Orient Cultural Service.

Yuen Long History. 1962. "Historical and Genealogical Notes, New Territories." Yuen Long District Office, File No. 204/6/01.

Zurndorfer, Harriet. 1981. "The *Hsin-an ta-tsu chih* and the Development of Chinese Gentry Society, 800–1600." *T'oung Pao* 67:154–215.

Glossary of Chinese terms and personal names

Chinese characters for the Hong Kong village names used in this book can be found in *A Gazetteer of Place Names in Hong Kong, Kowloon, and the New Territories* (Hong Kong: Government Press, 1969). Personal names listed in the following glossary are those of Teng founding ancestors or historical figures; all other names used in the text are pseudonyms. Terms followed by (C) are in colloquial Cantonese, Yale romanization system. All other terms are in Mandarin, standard Wade-Giles romanization.

Chang Pao-tzu 張保仔
Cheng Ch'eng-kung 鄭成功
ch'i 氣
chi wen 祭文
chia chuang 嫁妝
chieh t'ou 節頭
ch'ieh shih 妾侍
chin shih 進士
chin t'a 金塔
ch'ü chia 娶嫁
ch'u tsu 出族
ch'üan hui 拳會
chung yang 重陽
fang 房
feng shui 風水
feng shui hsien-sheng 風水先生
fu lao 父老
Ha Tsuen (C) 廈村
Ha Tsuen Shi (C) 廈村市
hsi min 細民
hsi p'o 細婆
hsiang 鄉
hsien 縣
hsien chih 縣志
Hsin-an 新安
hsin fang 新房
hsin ting 新丁
hsin ting shu 新丁書
hsün ting 巡丁
hua chiao 花轎
hung ch'i 紅契
k'ai teng 開燈
Kou-yüeh tsu 鈎月祖
Kuan Ti 關帝
kung so 公所
li chin 禮金
li ping 禮餅
liang 兩
Liao 廖
Ling Tu Szu 靈渡寺
mai 賣
Man (C) 文
man yueh 滿月
mei jen 媒人
ming 名
mui jai (C) 妹仔

Glossary

Nam Tao (C)　南頭
Neih yauh mouh fan a? (C)　你有冇份呀？
Niao-chang tsu　鳥章祖
p'ei hsiang chu　配享主
Pei Ti　北帝
pen-ti　本地
pen-ti jen　本地人
Sham Chun (C)　深圳
shen chu wei　神主位
shen t'ai　神臺
shui hsün　水巡
sung chia　送嫁
Szu-le tsu　思樂祖
szu-li　司理
ta p'o　大婆
T'ai-shan　台山
t'ang　堂
T'ao　陶
Teng　鄧
Teng Chien-wu　鄧儉吳
Teng Fei-wu　__非吾
Teng Fu-hsieh　__符協
Teng Hung-chih　鄧洪贄
Teng Hung-hui　__洪惠
Teng Hung-sheng　__洪生
Teng Pao-sheng　__豹生
Teng Shou-tsu　__壽祖
Teng Tso-t'ai　__作泰
Teng Tso-wen　__作文
Teng Wei-yü　__爲玉
ti ku　地骨
ti p'i　地皮
T'ien Hou　天后
tou　斗
Tou Ch'ing T'ang　都慶堂
tou chung　斗種
tsu (ancestor, estate)　祖
tsu (lineage)　族
tsu chang　族長
Tsu-le tsu　醉樂祖
Tu　杜
t'u ti　土地
T'ung-ch'eng　桐城
Tung-kuan　東莞
tz'u yü　祠宇
wai (C)　圍
wai chia　外家
wai lai jen　外來人
wei　位
Yang Hou　楊侯
yü　宇
Yu Kung T'ang　友恭堂

Index

affines, 118–20, 127, 128, 156; and ritual, 132–36
affinity, 6–7, 125–26, 132–36, 156, 157, 160, 170; differences in, 127, 128, 132–33; and men, 118–19, 125–16; and women, 126, 133–36, 160
agriculture, 77–78, 80, 143, 144; rice production, 77, 143
ancestor, 49; domestic, 123; founder, 3, 18; worship, 17; *see also* ancestral tablets
ancestral hall, 2, 3, 12–13, 26, 34, 40, 108, 111, 113, 126, 142, 161–62; as community center, 43; construction of, 26, 31–33; description of, 40; and marriage rites, 122–23; political role of, 88, 142, 167; rites in, 42–43; as school, 44
ancestral tablets, 40–41, 41–42, 50

benefactors, 32–33, 39–40
betrothal, 120–21, 158; feast, 120–21, 131
bidding, 93–95
bride price, 120, 121, 128–32, 157–58
bride callers, 121, 122, 123, 158
bride senders, 122
British takeover of New Territories, 86
burial, 50, 52

Canton, 18, 19, 24
cash crops, 80
census, Ha Tsuen, 10
ch'i (breath), 17, 109
chia chuang, see dowry
ch'ieh shih, see mistress
chin-shih (imperial degree), 23
ch'ü chia, see bride callers
class, 7, 15; changes in, 153–55; and descent, 4–6, 14, 36, 171–75; differences, 98, 102–16, 168–71; and women, 101; *see also* landlord-merchant, smallholder-tenant
concubine, 111; *see also* secondary wife
corporate land, 15, 61, 68, 69
corporation, 6, 12, 171–72

descent: and class, 4–6, 14, 36, 171–75; ideology, 16, 17, 37, 38, 175; group, 4; model, 5–6, 171–72; politics, 148, 154; principles, 173
diet, 76
dowry, 123, 128–29, 130, 131–32, 158

economic difference: expression of, 100; perception of, 99; *see also* class difference
education, 104–106
elders, 43, 90, 91; duties of, 92; political role of, 91, 92; rights of, 92
elder council, 92–93
employment, 143–44
entrepreneurs, 144, 145, 147–48, 153, 154, 175; and politics, 142, 148–49, 163–64
estate: ancestral, 31, 33, 34, 37, 44, 48, 51, 61, 68–72, 165–66, 169; charitable, 34; formation of, 48–49; politics of, 164; rental land, 69; size of holdings, 70
evacuation, 21–23

factories, 75, 76, 147, 149, 151, 152
fang, 32
feng-shui, see geomancy
fishing, 79
fu lao, see elders
funerals, 49–50, 134

gazetteer, 15
genealogies, 7, 15, 17, 105
geomancy, 49, 52, 53, 99–100, 103
graves, 52; rites, 52, 165
guerillas, anti-Japanese, 138–39

hamlets, 2–3, 100; and lineage, 100–101; property of, 93; ritual, 101, 102; and women, 101–102
heirs, 109, 110–14, 116
household, 78, 108, 119, 150
hsi min, see slaves
hsi p'o, see secondary wife

187

Index

hsiang (district), 13
hsien chih (county gazetteer), 9
Hsin-an County, 18
hsün ting, see village guard

inheritance, 17, 44, 106–16, 170; discretionary, 115; irregular, 114–15; among poor, 107–108; among wealthy, 108–16; by women, 129n4

Japanese occupation, 138–39

k'ai teng, 42–43, 110, 113, 114
Kam Tin, 18, 19, 31

labor: agricultural, 77, 78; wage labor, 143, 149–50, 152–153; and women, 77–78, 152–53
land: development, 144; fallow, 165; British policy regarding, 59–60, 87; records, 8; rent, 144; types of, 61; see also corporate land
landless, 7, 65–66
landownership, 7, 55–72, 105–106, 168–69, 169
land tenure, 55–72, 143–44
landlord-merchant, 2, 22, 60, 61–62, 63, 64, 76–77, 145–47, 153–54, 170, 171, 175; and inheritance, 108–16; and marriage, 119–20, 131–32; and politics, 142, 146, 154, 163–64, 167; and rent, 64; size of holdings, 62
leadership, 88, 89–90, 93, 139, 140, 141–42, 146, 147, 148
li chin, see bride price
lineage, 3–6, 16–17, 18, 162, 174; ideology, 170; differentiation, 6, 36–37; dominant, 4, 13, 19, 22–23, 25; formation and development, 13, 14, 15–16, 24, 30–31, 32–34, 35, 174; higher order, 27; leadership, 53–54; master, 39, 91; membership, 6, 33, 34, 35, 42, 171; mode of production, 172–73; models, 13 (see also descent model); and politics 83, 88, 91–93, 163–64, 175; and pork division, 42, 43; rites, 39, 43, 52, 162, 165
literacy, 104–106; see also education

Macao, 19, 20
man yueh (full month ceremony), 110, 111, 113, 114
manager, 70–72, 88–89, 90, 93, 142
markets, 25, 26, 80–81; Ha Tsuen, 29, 72–74, 75–76, 81, 90, 94; Hung Shui Kiu, 144–45, 163; Yuen Long, 74, 137, 138, 144
marriage, 6, 104, 108, 111–12, 113, 114, 115–16, 119, 153, 170; cost of, 157; gifts, 124–25; distribution of Teng wives, 127–28, 156–57; feast, 118, 119, 123, 124, 125, 126, 158, 159; negotiations, 158; outmarriage, 27n3; payments, 120–21, 129, 130–32; residence, 119; rites, 118–20, 121–25, 127, 133, 159–60, 161
matrilateral kin, 118
men (gender distinctions): and affinity, 118–19, 125–26; and economic difference, 98, 99–100, 103; and factory work, 149–50; and hamlet 100–101, 102; occupations, 143–44
mei jen (matchmaker), 120
migration, 108, 147, 150–51
mistress, 111–12, 113, 114, 115
mother's brother, 121, 124, 126, 160
mui jai (servant girl), 104

oyster industry, 29, 79–80

patrilineal principles, 16–17, 38
pawnshop, 76
p'ei hsiang chu, see benefactors
pen-ti jen (natives), 162–63
Ping Shan, 22, 63, 64, 65, 66; conflicts with Ha Tsuen, 19
piracy, 20
principal wife, 111–16
population, 20, 21, 28, 143
pork division, see lineage

rural committee, 139, 140, 141, 142, 146, 149, 151, 154, 155

sailors, 80
San Tin, 41, 63–64
satellite villages, 20, 28–29, 56, 58–59, 60, 75, 87, 95–96, 97, 139–40
schools, 106
secondary wife, 104, 111–12, 114, 115
segmentation, 33, 37, 44, 45, 45–48, 172
self-defense corps, see village guard
shui hsün, see water guard
slaves, 103–104
smallholder-tenant, 77–82, 170, 171; and marriage payments, 130–31; marriage rites, 119–20
sung chia, see bride senders
szu li, see manager

ta p'o, see principal wife
t'ang, see ancestral hall, estate
temple, 1, 25, 26, 28
tenancy, 56–59, 61, 65, 66–70
Tou Ch'ing T'ang, 27
transportation, 13, 73, 137–38, 148
tsu, see estate (ancestral)
tsu (patrilineage), 3
tsu chang, see lineage master
t'u ti (earth god shrine), 101, 102

Index

Tuen Mun, 19
Tung-kuan, 22

village guard, 25, 83, 88, 90, 94, 95, 97, 139, 141, 147, 163; leader of, 95; training of, 96
violence, 85–86, 88, 95–96

wage laborers: and lineage, 167; and politics, 154–55, 164–65
water guard, 94–95
wives, *see* principal wife, secondary wife

women (gender distinctions): and affinity 126, 133–36, 160; contacts with natal family, 135–36, 161; education, 106n5; economic difference, 98, 101–103; and hamlet social life, 100–103; inheritance, 107, 129, 129n4; labor and gift exchange, 134–35, 136; work by, 77–78, 152–53, 157
unemployment, 151–52

Yu Kung T'ang, *see* ancestral hall

CAMBRIDGE STUDIES IN SOCIAL ANTHROPOLOGY

General Editor: Jack Goody

1. The Political Organisation of Unyamwezi
   R. G. ABRAHAMS
2. Buddhism and the Spirit Cults in North-East Thailand*
   S. J. TAMBIAH
3. Kalahari Village Politics: An African Democracy
   ADAM KUPER
4. The Rope of Moka: Big-Men and Ceremonial Exchange in Mount Hagen, New Guinea*
   ANDREW STRATHERN
5. The Majangir: Ecology and Society of a Southwest Ethiopian People
   JACK STAUDER
6. Buddhist Monk, Buddhist Layman: A Study of Urban Monastic Organisation in Central Thailand
   JANE BUNNAG
7. Contexts of Kinship: An Essay in the Family Sociology of the Gonja of Northern Ghana
   ESTHER N. GOODY
8. Marriage among a Matrilineal Elite: A Family Study of Ghanian Senior Civil Servants
   CHRISTINE OPPONG
9. Elite Politics in Rural India: Political Stratification and Political Alliances in Western Maharashtra
   ANTHONY T. CARTER
10. Women and Property in Morocco: Their Changing Relations to the Process of Social Stratification in the Middle Atlas
    VANESSA MAHER
11. Rethinking Symbolism*
    DAN SPERBER, *translated by Alice L. Morton*
12. Resources and Population: A Study of the Gurungs of Nepal
    ALAN MACFARLANE

13. Mediterranean Family Structures
    Edited by J. G. PERISTIANY
14. Spirits of Protest: Spirit Mediums and the Articulation of Consensus among the Zezuru of Southern Rhodesia (Zimbabwe)
    PETER FRY
15. World Conqueror and World Renouncer: A Study of Buddhism and Polity in Thailand against a Historical Background*
    S. J. TAMBIAH
16. Outline of a Theory of Practice*
    PIERRE BOURDIEU, *translated by Richard Nice*
17. Production and Reproduction: A Comparative Study of the Domestic Domain*
    JACK GOODY
18. Perspectives in Marxist Anthropology*
    MAURICE GODELIER, *translated by Robert Brain*
19. The Fate of Shechem, or the Politics of Sex: Essays in the Anthropology of the Mediterranean
    JULIAN PITT-RIVERS
20. People of the Zongo: The Transformation of Ethnic Identities in Ghana
    ENID SCHILDKROUT
21. Casting out Anger: Religion among the Taita of Kenya
    GRACE HARRIS
22. Rituals of the Kandyan State
    H. L. SENEVIRATNE
23. Australian Kin Classification
    HAROLD W. SCHEFFLER
24. The Palm and the Pleiades: Initiation and Cosmology in Northwest Amazonia
    STEPHEN HUGH-JONES
25. Nomads of South Siberia: the Pastoral Economies of Tuva
    S. I. VAINSHTEIN, *translated by Michael Colenso*
26. From the Milk River: Spatial and Temporal Processes in Northwest Amazonia
    CHRISTINE HUGH-JONES
27. Day of Shining Red: An Essay on Understanding Ritual
    GILBERT LEWIS
28. Hunters, Pastoralists and Ranchers: Reindeer Economies and their Transformations
    TIM INGOLD
29. The Wood-Carvers of Hong Kong: Craft Production in the World Capitalist Periphery
    EUGENE COOPER
30. Minangkabau Social Formations: Indonesian Peasants and the World Economy
    JOEL S. KAHN
31. Patrons and Partisans: A Study of Politics in Two Southern Italian *Comuni*
    CAROLINE WHITE
32. Muslim Society*
    ERNEST GELLNER
33. Why Marry Her? Society and Symbolic Structures
    LUC DE HEUSCH, *translated by Janet Lloyd*

34. Chinese Ritual and Politics
    EMILY MARTIN AHERN
35. Parenthood and Social Reproduction: Fostering and Occupational Roles in West Africa
    ESTHER N. GOODY
36. Dravidian Kinship
    THOMAS R. TRAUTMANN
37. The Anthropological Circle: Symbol, Function, History*
    MARC AUGE, *translated by Martin Thom*
38. Rural Society in Southeast India
    KATHLEEN GOUGH
39. The Fish People: Linguistic Exogamy and Tukanoan Identity in Northwest Amazonia
    JEAN E. JACKSON
40. Karl Marx Collective: Economy, Society and Religion in a Siberian Collective Farm*
    CAROLINE HUMPHREY
41. Ecology and Exchange in the Andes
    Edited by DAVID LEHMANN
42. Trades without Trade: Responses to Trade in two Dyula Communities
    ROBERT LAUNAY
43. The Political Economy of West African Agriculture*
    KEITH HART
44. Nomads and the Outside World
    A. M. KHAZANOV, *translated by Julia Crookenden*
45. Actions, Norms and Representations: Foundations of Anthropological Inquiry*
    LADISLAV HOLY *and* MILAN STUCHLIK
46. Structural Models in Anthropology*
    PER HAGE *and* FRANK HARARY
47. Servants of the Goddess: The Priests of a South Indian Temple
    C. J. FULLER
48. Oedipus and Job in West African Religion*
    MEYER FORTES *with an essay by* ROBIN HORTON
49. The Buddhist Saints of the Forest and the Cult of Amulets: A Study in Charisma, Hagiography, Sectarianism, and Millennial Buddhism*
    S. J. TAMBIAH
50. Kinship and Marriage: An Anthropological Perspective
    ROBIN FOX
    (paperback available in U.S. only)
51. Individual and Society in Guiana: A Comparative Study of Amerindian Social Organization*
    PETER RIVIERE
52. People and the State: An Anthropology of Planned Development*
    A. F. ROBERTSON
53. Inequality Among Brothers: Class and Kinship in South China
    RUBIE S. WATSON

*Also available as a paperback.